Getting Started with Amazon SageMaker Studio

Learn to build end-to-end machine learning projects in the SageMaker machine learning IDE

Michael Hsieh

BIRMINGHAM—MUMBAI

Getting Started with Amazon SageMaker Studio

Publishing Product Manager: Dhruv Jagdish Kataria
Senior Editor: David Sugarman
Content Development Editor: Priyanka Soam
Technical Editor: Devanshi Ayare
Copy Editor: Safis Editing
Project Coordinator: Aparna Ravikumar Nair
Proofreader: Safis Editing
Indexer: Pratik Shirodkar
Production Designer: Roshan Kawale
Marketing Coordinators: Abeer Riyaz Dawe, Shifa Ansari

First published: March 2022
Production reference: 1240222

Published by Packt Publishing Ltd.

Livery Place
35 Livery Street
Birmingham
B3 2PB, UK.

ISBN 978-1-80107-015-7

www.packt.com

This is for my wife, and my parents.
Thank you for unconditionally supporting me
and being there for me.

Contributors

About the author

Michael Hsieh is a senior AI/**machine learning** (**ML**) solutions architect at Amazon Web Services. He creates and evangelizes for ML solutions centered around Amazon SageMaker. He also works with enterprise customers to advance their ML journeys.

Prior to working at AWS, Michael was an advanced analytic consultant creating ML solutions and enterprise-level ML strategies at Slalom Consulting in Philadelphia, PA. Prior to consulting, he was a data scientist at the University of Pennsylvania Health System, focusing on personalized medicine and ML research.

Michael has two master's degrees, one in applied physics and one in robotics.

Originally from Taipei, Taiwan, Michael currently lives in Sammamish, WA, but still roots for the Philadelphia Eagles.

About the reviewers

Brent Rabowsky is a principal data science consultant at AWS with over 10 years' experience in the field of ML. At AWS, he leverages his expertise to help AWS customers with their data science projects. Prior to AWS, he joined Amazon.com on an ML and algorithms team, and he has previously worked on conversational AI agents for a government contractor and a research institute. He also served as a technical reviewer of the books *Data Science on AWS* by Chris Fregly and Antje Barth, published by O'Reilly, and *SageMaker Best Practices and Learn Amazon SageMaker*, published by Packt.

Ankit Sirmorya is an ML lead/senior ML engineer at Amazon and has led several machine-learning initiatives across the Amazon ecosystem. Ankit works on applying ML to solve ambiguous business problems and improve customer experience. For instance, he created a platform for experimenting with different hypotheses on Amazon product pages using reinforcement learning techniques. Currently, he works in the Alexa Shopping organization, where he is developing ML-based solutions to send personalized reorder hints to customers for improving their experience.

Table of Contents

Part 2 – End-to-End Machine Learning Life Cycle with SageMaker Studio

3

Data Preparation with SageMaker Data Wrangler

4

Building a Feature Repository with SageMaker Feature Store

5

Building and Training ML Models with SageMaker Studio IDE

6

Detecting ML Bias and Explaining Models with SageMaker Clarify

7

Hosting ML Models in the Cloud: Best Practices

8
Jumpstarting ML with SageMaker JumpStart and Autopilot

Part 3 – The Production and Operation of Machine Learning with SageMaker Studio

9
Training ML Models at Scale in SageMaker Studio

10

Monitoring ML Models in Production with SageMaker Model Monitor

11

Operationalize ML Projects with SageMaker Projects, Pipelines, and Model Registry

Index

Other Books You May Enjoy

Preface

Amazon SageMaker Studio is the first **integrated development environment (IDE) for machine learning (ML)** and is designed to integrate ML workflows: data preparation, feature engineering, statistical bias detection, **Automated Machine Learning (AutoML)**, training, hosting, ML explainability, monitoring, and MLOps in one environment.

In this book, you'll start by exploring the features available in Amazon SageMaker Studio to analyze data, develop ML models, and productionize models to meet your goals. As you progress, you will learn how these features work together to address common challenges when building ML models in production. After that, you'll understand how to effectively scale and operationalize the ML life cycle using SageMaker Studio.

By the end of this book, you'll have learned ML best practices regarding Amazon SageMaker Studio, as well as being able to improve productivity in the ML development life cycle and build and deploy models easily for your ML use cases.

Who this book is for

This book is for data scientists and ML engineers who are looking to become well versed in Amazon SageMaker Studio and gain hands-on ML experience to handle every step in the ML life cycle, including building data as well as training and hosting models. Although basic knowledge of ML and data science is necessary, no previous knowledge of SageMaker Studio or cloud experience is required.

What this book covers

Chapter 1, *Machine Learning and Its Life Cycle in the Cloud*, describes how cloud technology has democratized the field of ML and how ML is being deployed in the cloud. It introduces the fundamentals of the AWS services that are used in the book.

Chapter 2, *Introducing Amazon SageMaker Studio*, covers an overview of Amazon SageMaker Studio, including its features and functionalities and user interface components. You will set up a SageMaker Studio domain and get familiar with basic operations.

Chapter 3, Data Preparation with SageMaker Data Wrangler, looks at how, with SageMaker Data Wrangler, you can perform exploratory data analysis and data preprocessing for ML modeling with a point-and-click experience (that is, without any coding). You will be able to quickly iterate through data transformation and modeling to see whether your transform recipe helps increase model performance, learn whether there is implicit bias in the data against sensitive groups, and have a clear record of what transformation has been done for the processed data.

Chapter 4, Building a Feature Repository with SageMaker Feature Store, looks at SageMaker Feature Store, which allows storing features for ML training and inferencing. Feature Store serves as a central repository for teams collaborating on ML use cases to avoid duplicating and confusing efforts in creating features. SageMaker Feature Store makes storing and accessing training and inferencing data easier and faster.

Chapter 5, Building and Training ML Models with SageMaker Studio IDE, looks at how building and training an ML model can be made easy. No more frustration in provisioning and managing compute infrastructure. SageMaker Studio is an IDE designed for ML developers. In this chapter, you will learn how to use the SageMaker Studio IDE, notebooks, and SageMaker-managed training infrastructure.

Chapter 6, Detecting ML Bias and Explaining Models with SageMaker Clarify, covers the ability to detect and remediate bias in data and models during the ML life cycle, which is critical in creating an ML model with social fairness. You will learn how to apply SageMaker Clarify to detect bias in your data and how to read the metrics in SageMaker Clarify.

Chapter 7, Hosting ML Models in the Cloud: Best Practices, looks at how, after successfully training a model, if you want to make the model available for inference, SageMaker has several options depending on your use case. You will learn how to host models for batch inference, do online real-time inference, and use multimodel endpoints for cost savings, as well as a resource optimization strategy for your inference needs.

Chapter 8, Jumpstarting ML with SageMaker JumpStart and Autopilot, looks at SageMaker JumpStart, which offers complete solutions for select use cases as a starter kit to the world of ML with Amazon SageMaker without any code development. SageMaker JumpStart also catalogs popular pretrained **computer vision (CV)** and **natural language processing (NLP)** models for you to easily deploy or fine-tune to your dataset. SageMaker Autopilot is an AutoML solution that explores your data, engineers features on your behalf, and trains an optimal model from various algorithms and hyperparameters. You don't have to write any code as Autopilot does it for you and returns notebooks to show how it does it.

Chapter 9, Training ML Models at Scale in SageMaker Studio, discusses how a typical ML life cycle starts with prototyping and then transitions to production scale, where the data is going to be much larger, models are much more complicated, and the number of experiments grows exponentially. SageMaker Studio makes this transition easier than before. You will learn how to run distributed training, how to monitor the compute resources and modeling status of a training job, and how to manage training experiments with SageMaker Studio.

Chapter 10, Monitoring ML Models in Production with SageMaker Model Monitor, looks at how data scientists used to spend too much time and effort maintaining and manually managing ML pipelines, a process that starts with data processing, training, and evaluation and ends with model hosting with ongoing maintenance. SageMaker Studio provides features that aim to streamline this operation with **continuous integration and continuous delivery (CI/CD)** best practices. You will learn how to implement SageMaker Projects, Pipelines, and the model registry, which will help operationalize the ML life cycle with CI/CD.

Chapter 11, Operationalize ML Projects with SageMaker Projects, Pipelines, and Model Registry, discusses how having a model put into production for inferencing isn't the end of the life cycle. It is just the beginning of an important topic: how do we make sure the model is performing as it is designed and as expected in real life? Monitoring how the model performs in production, especially on data that the model has never seen before, is made easy with SageMaker Studio. You will learn how to set up model monitoring for models deployed in SageMaker, detect data drift and performance drift, and visualize feature importance and bias in the inferred data in real time.

Download the example code files

You can download the example code files for this book from GitHub at `https://github.com/PacktPublishing/Getting-Started-with-Amazon-SageMaker-Studio`. If there's an update to the code, it will be updated in the GitHub repository.

We also have other code bundles from our rich catalog of books and videos available at

https://github.com/PacktPublishing/. Check them out!

Download the color images

We also provide a PDF file that has color images of the screenshots/diagrams used in this book. You can download it here: `https://static.packt-cdn.com/downloads/9781801070157_ColorImages.pdf`.

Conventions used

Bold: Indicates a new term, an important word, or words that you see onscreen. For instance, words in menus or dialog boxes appear in **bold**. Here is an example: "The two types of metadata that need to be cataloged include **Functional** and **Technical**."

> **Tips or Important Notes**
> Appear like this.

Get in touch

Feedback from our readers is always welcome.

General feedback: If you have questions about any aspect of this book, mention the book title in the subject of your message and email us at customercare@packtpub.com.

Errata: Although we have taken every care to ensure the accuracy of our content, mistakes do happen. If you have found a mistake in this book, we would be grateful if you would report this to us. Please visit www.packtpub.com/support/errata, selecting your book, clicking on the Errata Submission Form link, and entering the details.

Piracy: If you come across any illegal copies of our works in any form on the Internet, we would be grateful if you would provide us with the location address or website name. Please contact us at copyright@packt.com with a link to the material.

If you are interested in becoming an author: If there is a topic that you have expertise in and you are interested in either writing or contributing to a book, please visit authors.packtpub.com.

Reviews

Please leave a review. Once you have read and used this book, why not leave a review on the site that you purchased it from? Potential readers can then see and use your unbiased opinion to make purchase decisions, we at Packt can understand what you think about our products, and our authors can see your feedback on their book. Thank you!

For more information about Packt, please visit packt.com.

Share Your Thoughts

Once you've read *Getting Started with Amazon SageMaker Studio*, we'd love to hear your thoughts! Scan the QR code below to go straight to the Amazon review page for this book and share your feedback.

https://packt.link/r/1-801-07015-6

Your review is important to us and the tech community and will help us make sure we're delivering excellent quality content.

Part 1 – Introduction to Machine Learning on Amazon SageMaker Studio

In this section, we will cover an introduction to **machine learning** (**ML**), the ML life cycle in the cloud, and Amazon SageMaker Studio. This section also includes a level set on the domain terminology in ML with example use cases.

This section comprises the following chapters:

- *Chapter 1, Machine Learning and Its Life Cycle in the Cloud*
- *Chapter 2, Introducing Amazon SageMaker Studio*

1
Machine Learning and Its Life Cycle in the Cloud

Machine Learning (**ML**) is a technique that has been around for decades. It is hard to believe how ubiquitous ML is now in our daily life. It has also been a rocky road for the field of ML to become mainstream, until the recent major leap in computer technology. Today's computer hardware is faster, smaller, and smarter. Internet speeds are faster and more convenient. Storage is cheaper and smaller. Now, it is rather easy to collect, store, and process massive amounts of data with the technology we have now. We are able to create sizeable datasets that we were not able to before, train ML models using compute resources that were not available before, and make use of ML models in every corner of our lives.

For example, media streaming companies can now build ML recommendation engines at a global scale using their title collections and customer activity data on their websites to provide the most relevant content in real time in order to optimize the customer experience. The size of the data for both the titles and customer preferences and activity is on a scale that wasn't possible 20 years ago, considering how many of us are currently using a streaming service.

Training an ML model at this scale, using ML algorithms that are becoming increasingly more complex, requires a robust and scalable solution. After a model is trained, companies are able to serve the model at a global scale where millions of users visit the application from web and mobile devices at the same time.

Companies are also creating more and more models for each segment of customers or even one model for one customer. There is another dimension to this – companies are rolling out new models at a pace that would not have been possible to manage without a pipeline that trains, evaluates, tests, and deploys a new model automatically. Cloud computing has provided a perfect foundation for the streaming service provider to perform these ML activities to increase customer satisfaction.

If ML is something that interests you, or if you are already working in the field of ML in any capacity, this book is the right place for you. You will be learning all things ML, and how to build, train, host, and manage ML models in the cloud with actual use cases and datasets along with me throughout the book. I assume you come to this book with a good understanding of ML and cloud computing. The purpose of this first chapter is to set the level of the concepts and terminology of the two technologies, to define the ML life cycle that is going to be the core of this book, and to provide a crash course on Amazon Web Services and its core services, which will be mentioned throughout the book.

In this chapter, we will cover the following:

- Understanding ML and its life cycle
- Building ML in the cloud
- Exploring AWS essentials for ML
- Setting up AWS environment

Technical requirements

For this chapter, you will need a computer with an internet connection and a browser to perform the basic AWS account setup in order to run Amazon SageMaker setup and code samples in the following chapters.

Understanding ML and its life cycle

At its core, ML is a process that uses computer algorithms to automatically discover the underlying patterns and trends in a **dataset** (which is a collection of **observations** with **features**, also known as **variables**), make a prediction, obtain the error measure against a **ground truth** (if provided), and "learn" from the error with an **optimization** process in order to make a prediction next time. At the end of the process, an **ML model** is fitted or trained so that it can be used to apply the knowledge it learned to apply a decision based on the features of a new observation. The first part, generating a model, is called **training**, while the second part is called **prediction** or **inference**.

There are three basic types of ML algorithms based on the way the training process takes place – supervised learning, unsupervised learning, and reinforcement learning. A **supervised learning** algorithm is given a set of observations with a ground truth from the past. A ground truth is a key ingredient to train a supervised learning algorithm, as it drives how the model learns and makes future predictions – hence the "supervised" in the name, as the learning is supervised by the ground truth. **Unsupervised learning**, on the other hand, does not require a ground truth for the observations to learn how to apply the prediction. It finds patterns and relationships solely based on the features of the observations. However, a ground truth, if it exists, would still help us validate and understand the accuracy of the model in the case of unsupervised learning. **Reinforcement learning**, often abbreviated as **RL**, has quite a different learning paradigm compared to the previous two. RL consists of an **agent** interacting with an **environment** with a set of **actions**, and corresponding **rewards** and **states**. The learning is not guided by a ground truth, rather by optimizing cumulative rewards with actions. The trained model in the end would be able to perform actions autonomously in an environment that would achieve the best rewards.

An ML life cycle

Now we have a basic understanding of what ML is, we can go broader to see what a typical ML life cycle looks like, as illustrated in the following figure:

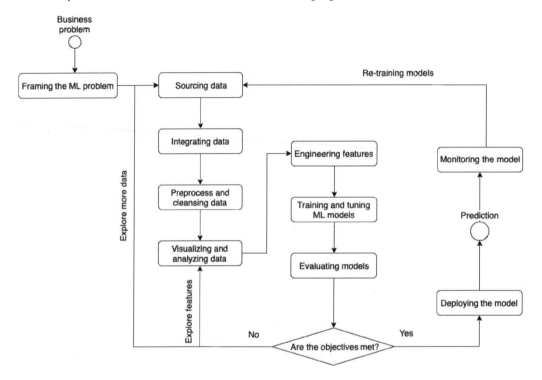

Figure 1.1 – The ML life cycle

Problem framing

The first step in a successful ML life cycle is framing the business problem into an ML problem. Business problems come in all shapes and forms. For example, *"How do we increase sales of a newly released product?"* and *"How do we improve the QA Quality Assessment (QA) throughput on the assembly line?"* Business problems such as these, usually qualitative, are not something ML can be directly applied to. But looking at the business problem statement, we should think about how it can be translated into an ML problem. We should ask questions like the following:

- *"What are the key factors to the success of product sales?"*
- *"Who are the people that are most likely to purchase the product?"*

- *"What is the bottleneck in throughput in the assembly line?"*
- *"How do we know whether an item is defective? What differentiates a defective one from a normal one?"*

By asking questions like these, we start to dig into the realm of **pattern recognition**, a process of recognizing patterns from the data at hand. Having the right questions that can be formulated into pattern recognition, we are a step closer to framing an ML problem. Then, we also need to understand what the key metric is to gauge the success of an approach, regardless of whether we use ML or other approaches. It is quite straightforward to measure, for example, daily product sales. We can also improve sales by targeting advertisements to the people that are mostly like to convert. Then, we get questions like the following:

- *"How do we measure the conversion?"*
- *"What are the common characteristics of the consumers who have bought this product?"*

More importantly, we need to find out whether there is even a target metric for us to predict! If there are targets, we can frame the problem as an ML problem, such as predicting future sales (supervised learning and regression), predicting whether a customer is going to buy a certain product or not (supervised learning and classification), or identifying defective items (supervised learning and classification). Questions that do not have a clear target to predict would fall into an unsupervised learning task in order to apply the pattern discovered in the data to future data points. Use cases where the target is dynamic and of high uncertainty, such as autonomous driving, robotic control, and stock price prediction, are good candidates for RL.

Data exploration and engineering

Sourcing data is the first step of a successful ML modeling journey. Once we have clearly defined both our business problem and ML problem with a basic understanding of the scope of the problem – meaning, what are the metrics and what are the factors – we can start gathering the data needed for ML. Data scientists explore the data sources to find out relevant information that could support the modeling. Sometimes, the data being captured and collected within the organization is easily accessible. Sometimes, the data is available outside your organization and would require you to reach out and ask for data sharing permission.

Sometimes, datasets can be sourced from the public internet and institutions that focus on creating and sharing standardized datasets for ML purposes, which is especially true for computer vision and natural language understanding use cases. Furthermore, data can arrive through streaming from websites and applications. Connections to a database, data lake, data warehouse, and streaming source need to be set up. Data needs to be integrated into the ML platform for processing and engineering before an ML model can be trained.

Managing data irregularity and heterogeneity is the second step in the ML life cycle. Data needs to be processed to remove irregularities such as missing values, incorrect data entry, and outliers because many ML algorithms have statistical assumptions that these irregularities would violate and render the modeling ineffective (if not invalid). For example, the linear regression model assumes that an error or residual is normally distributed, therefore it is important to check whether there are outliers that could contribute to such a violation. If so, we must perform the necessary preprocessing tasks to remedy it. Common preprocessing approaches include, but are not limited to, removal of invalid entries, removal of extreme data points (also known as outliers), and filling in missing values. Data also need to be processed to remove heterogeneity across features and normalize them into the same scale, as some ML algorithms are sensitive to the scale of the features and would develop a bias towards features with a larger scale. Common approaches include **min-max scaling** and **z-standardization (z-score)**.

Visualization and data analysis is the third step in the ML life cycle. Data visualization allows data scientists to easily understand visually how data is distributed and what the trends are in the data. **Exploratory Data Analysis (EDA)** allows data scientists to understand the statistical behavior of the data at hand, figure out the information that has predictive power to be included in the modeling process, and eliminate any redundancy in the data, such as duplicated entries, multicollinearity, and unimportant features.

Feature engineering is the fourth step in the ML life cycle. Even with the various sources from which we are collecting data, ML models oftentimes benefit from engineered features that are calculated from existing features. For example, **Body Mass Index (BMI)** is a well-known engineered feature, calculated using the height and weight of a person, and is also an established feature (or risk factor, in clinical terms) that predicts certain diseases rather than height or weight alone. Feature engineering often requires extensive experience in the domain and experimentation to find out what recipes are adding predictive power to the modeling.

Modeling and evaluation

For a data scientist, ML modeling is the most exciting part of the life cycle (I think so; I hope you agree with me). You've formulated the problem in the language of ML. You've collected, processed the data, and looked at the underlying trends that give you enough hints to build an ML model. Now, it's time to build your first model for the dataset, but wait – what model, what algorithm, and what metric do we use to evaluate the performance? Well, that's the core of modeling and evaluation.

The goal is to explore and find out a satisfactory ML model, with an objective metric, from all possible algorithms, feature sets, and hyperparameters. This is definitely not an easy task and requires extensive experience. Depending on the problem type (whether it's classification, regression, or reinforcement learning), data type (as in whether it's tabular, text, or image data), data distribution (is there a class imbalance or outliers?), and domain (medical, financial, or industrial), you can narrow down the choice of algorithms to a handful. With each of these algorithms, there are hyperparameters that control the behavior and performance of the algorithm on the provided data. What is also needed is a definition of an objective metric and a threshold that meets the business requirement, using the metric to guide you toward the best model. You may blindly choose one or two algorithm-hyperparameter combinations for your project, but you may not reach the optimal solution in just one or two trials. It is rather typical for a data scientist to try out hundreds if not thousands of combinations. How is that possible?

This is why establishing a streamlined model training and evaluation process is such a critical step in the process. Once the model training and evaluation is automated, you can simply launch the process that helps you automatically iterate through the experimentations among algorithms and hyperparameters, and compare the metric performance to find out the optimal solution. This process is called **hyperparameter tuning** or **hyperparameter optimization**. If multiple algorithms are the subject of tuning, it can also be called **multi-algorithm hyperparameter tuning**.

Production – predicting, monitoring, and retraining

An ML model needs to be put in use in order to have an impact on the business. However, the production process is different from that of a typical software application. Unlike other software applications where business logic can be pre-written and tested exhaustively with edge cases before production, there is no guarantee that once the model is trained and evaluated, it will be performing at the same level in production as in the testing environment. This is because ML models use probabilistic, statistical, and fuzzy logic to infer an outcome for each incoming data point, and the testing, that is, the model evaluation, is typically done without true prior knowledge of production data. The best a data scientist can do prior to production is to create training data from a sample that closely represents real-world data, and evaluate the model with an out-of-sample strategy in order to get an unbiased idea of how the model would perform on unseen data. While in production, the incoming data is completely unseen by the model; how to evaluate live model performance, and how to take actions on that evaluation, are critical topics for productionizing ML models.

Model performance can be monitored with two approaches. One that is more straightforward is to capture the ground truth for the unseen data and compare the prediction against the ground truth. The second approach is to use the drift in data as a proxy to determine whether the model is going to behave in an expected way. In some use cases, the first approach is not feasible, as the true outcome (the ground truth) may lag behind the event for a long time. For example, in a disease prediction use case, where the purpose of ML modeling is to help a healthcare provider to find a likely outcome in the future, say three months, with current health metrics, it is not possible to gather a true ground truth less than three months or even later, depending on the onset of the disease. It is, therefore, impractical to only fix the model after obtaining it, should it be proven ineffective.

The second approach lies in the premise that an ML model learns statistically and probabilistically from the training data and would behave differently when a new dataset with different statistical characteristics is provided. A model would return gibberish when data does not come from the same statistical distribution. Therefore, by detecting the drift in data, it gives a more real-time estimate of how the model is going to perform. Take the disease prediction use case once again as an example: when data about a group of patients in their 30s is sent to an ML model that is trained on data with an average age of 65 for prediction, it is likely that the model is going to be clueless about these new patients. So we need to take action.

Retraining and updating the model makes sure that it stays performant for future data. Being able to capture the ground truth and detecting the data drift helps create a retraining strategy at the right time. The data that has drifted and the ground truth are the great input into the retraining process, as they will help the model to cover a wider statistical distribution.

Now that we have a clear idea of the basics of the uses and life cycle of ML development, let's take the next step and investigate how it can work with the cloud.

Building ML in the cloud

Cloud computing is a technology that delivers on-demand IT resources that can grow and shrink at any time, depending on the need. There is no more buying and maintaining computer servers or data centers. It is much like utilities in your home, such as water, which is there when you turn on the faucet. If you turn it all the way, you get a high-pressure water stream. If you turn it down, you conserve water. If you don't need it anymore, you turn it off completely. With this model, developers and teams get the following benefits from on-demand cloud computing:

- **Agility**: Quickly spin up resources as you need them. Develop and roll out new apps, experiment with new ideas, and fail quickly without risks.

- **Elasticity**: Scale your resources as you need them. Cloud computing takes away "undifferentiated heavy lifting" – racking up additional servers and planning capacity for the future. These are things that don't help address your core business problems.

- **Global availability**: With a click of a button, you can spin up resources that are closest to your customers/users without relocating your physical compute resources.

How does this impact the field of ML? As compute resources become easier to acquire, information exchange becomes much more frequent. As that happens, more data is generated and stored. And more data means more opportunities to train more accurate ML models. The agility, elasticity, and scale that cloud computing provides accelerates the development and application of ML models from weeks or months down to a much shorter cycle so that developers can now generate and improve ML models faster than ever. Developers are no longer constrained by physical compute resources available to them. With better ML models, businesses can make better decisions and provide better product experiences to customers.

For cloud computing, we will be using Amazon Web Services, which is the provider of Amazon SageMaker Studio, throughout the book.

Exploring AWS essentials for ML

Amazon Web Services (**AWS**) offers cloud computing resources to developers of all kinds to create applications and solutions for their businesses. AWS manages the technology and infrastructure in a secure environment and a scalable fashion, taking away the undifferentiated heavy lifting of infrastructure management from developers. AWS provides a broad range of services, including ML, artificial intelligence, the internet of things, analytics, and application development tools. These are built on top of the following key areas – **compute**, **storage**, **databases**, and **security**. Before we start our journey with Amazon SageMaker Studio, which is one of the ML offerings from AWS, it is important to know the core services that are commonly used while developing your ML projects on Amazon SageMaker Studio.

Compute

For ML in the cloud, developers need computational resources in all aspects of the life cycle. **Amazon Elastic Compute Cloud** (**Amazon EC2**) is the most fundamental cloud computing environment for developers to process, train, and host ML models. Amazon EC2 provides a wide range of compute instance types for many purposes, such as compute-optimized instances for compute-intensive work, memory-optimized instances for applications that have a large memory footprint, and **Graphics Processing Unit** (**GPU**)-accelerated instances for deep learning training.

Amazon SageMaker also offers on-demand compute resources for ML developers to run processing, training, and model hosting. Amazon SageMaker's ML instances build on top of Amazon EC2 instances and equip the instances with a fully managed, optimized versions of popular ML frameworks such as TensorFlow, PyTorch, MXNet, and scikit-learn, which are optimized for Amazon EC2 compute instances. Developers do not need to manage the provisioning and patching of the ML instances, so they can focus on the ML life cycle.

Storage

While conducting an ML project, developers need to be able to access files, store codes, and store artifacts. Reliable storage is crucial to an ML project. AWS provides several types of storage options for ML development. **Amazon Simple Storage Service** (**Amazon S3**) and **Amazon Elastic File System** (**Amazon EFS**) are the two that are most relevant to the development of ML projects in Amazon SageMaker Studio.

Amazon S3 is an object storage service that allows developers to store any amount of data with high security, availability, and scalability. ML developers can store structured and unstructured data, and ML models with versioning on Amazon S3. Amazon S3 can also be used to build a data lake for analytics and to store backups and archives.

Amazon EFS provides a fully managed, serverless filesystem that allows developers to store and share files across users on the filesystem without any storage provisioning, as the filesystem increases and decreases its capacity automatically when you add or delete files. It is often used in a **High-Performance Cluster** (**HPC**) setting and applications where parallel or simultaneous data access across threads, processing tasks, compute instances, and users with high throughput are required. As Amazon SageMaker Studio embeds an Amazon EFS filesystem, each user on Amazon SageMaker Studio gets a home directory for storing and accessing data, codes, and notebooks.

Database and analytics

Besides storage options, where data is saved as a file or an object, AWS users can store and access data at a data point level using database services such as **Amazon Relational Database Service** (**Amazon RDS**) and **Amazon DynamoDB**. AWS Analytics services such as **AWS Glue** and **Amazon Athena** provide capabilities in storing, querying, and data processing that are critical in the early phase of the ML life cycle.

For an ML project, relational databases are a common source of data for modeling. Amazon RDS is a cost-efficient and scalable relational database service in the cloud. It offers six database engines, including open sourced PostgreSQL, MySQL, and MariaDB, and the Oracle and SQL Server commercial databases. Infrastructure provisioning and management are made easy with Amazon RDS.

Another popular database is NoSQL, which uses key-value pairs as the data structure. Unlike relational databases, stringent schema requirements for tables are not required in NoSQL databases. Users can input data with a flexible schema for each row without needing to change the schema. Amazon DynamoDB is a key-value and document database that is fully managed, serverless, and highly scalable.

AWS Glue is a data integration service that has several features to help developers discover and transform data from sources for analytics and ML. The AWS Glue Data Catalog offers a persistent metadata store as a central repository for all your data sources, such as tables in Amazon S3, Amazon RDS, and Amazon DynamoDB. Developers can view all their tables and metadata such as the schema and time of update in one place – AWS Glue Data Catalog. AWS Glue's ETL service helps streamline the extract, transform, and load steps right after data is discovered and cataloged in the AWS Glue Data Catalog.

Amazon Athena is an analytics service that gives developers an interactive and serverless query experience. As a serverless service, developers do not need to think about the infrastructure underneath but instead focus on their data queries. You can easily point Amazon Athena to your data in Amazon S3 with a schema definition to start querying. Amazon Athena integrates natively with the AWS Glue Data Catalog to allow you to quickly and easily query against your data from all sources and services. Amazon Athena is also heavily integrated into several aspects of Amazon SageMaker Studio, which we will talk about in more detail throughout this book.

Security

Security is job zero when you develop your applications, access data, and train ML models on AWS. The access and identity control aspect of the security is governed by the **AWS Identity and Access Management** (**IAM**) service. Any control over services, cloud resources, authentication, and authorization can be granularly managed by AWS IAM.

Key concepts in IAM are the IAM user, group, role, and policy. Each person who logs onto AWS would assume an IAM user. Each IAM user has a list of IAM policies attached that governs the resources and actions in AWS that this IAM user can command and access. An IAM user can also inherit IAM policies from that of an IAM group, a collection of users who have similar responsibilities. An IAM role is similar to an IAM user in that it has a set of permissions to access resources and to perform actions. An IAM role differs from an IAM user in that a role can be assumed by users, applications, or services. For example, you can create and assign an AWS service role to an application in the cloud to permit what services and resources this application can access. An IAM user who has permission to an application can securely execute the application without worrying that the application would reach out to unauthorized resources. More information can be found here: `https://docs.aws.amazon.com/IAM/latest/UserGuide/id_roles.html`.

Setting up an AWS environment

Let's set up an AWS account to start our cloud computing journey. If you already have an AWS account, you can skip this section and move on to the next chapter.

Please go to `https://portal.aws.amazon.com/billing/signup` and follow the instructions to sign up for an account. You will receive a phone call and will need to enter a verification code on the phone keypad as part of the process.

When you first create a new AWS account and log in with your email and password, you will be logged in as an account root user. However, it is best practice to create a new IAM user for yourself with the `AdministratorAccess` policy while logged in as the root user, and then swiftly log out and log in again as the IAM user that you just created. The root user credential shall only be used to perform limited account and service management tasks and shall not be used to develop your cloud applications. You should securely store the root user credential and lock it away from any other people accessing it.

Here are the steps to create an IAM user:

1. Go to the IAM console, select **Users** on the left panel, and then click on the **Add user** button:

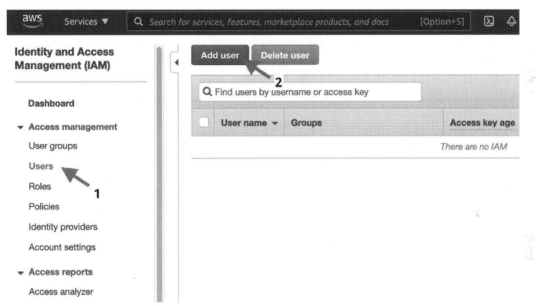

Figure 1.2 – Adding an IAM user in the IAM console

2.   Next, enter a name in **User name** and check the boxes for **Programmatic access** and **AWS Management Console access**. For the password fields, you can leave the default options. Hit the **Next: Permissions** button to proceed:

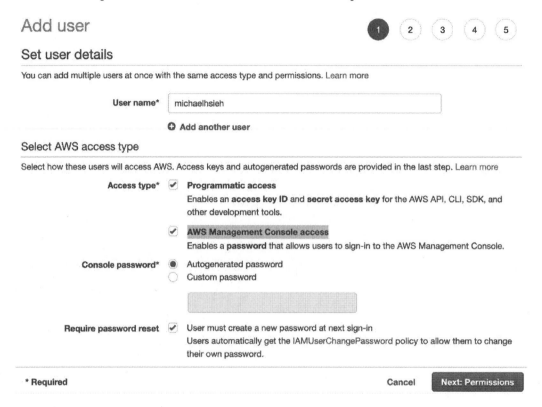

Figure 1.3 – Creating a user name and password for an IAM user

3.   On the next page, choose **Add user to group** under **Set permissions**. In a new account, you do not have any groups. You should click on **Create group**.

4.   In the pop-up dialog, enter Administrator in **Group name**, select AdministratorAccess in the policy list, and hit the **Create group** button:

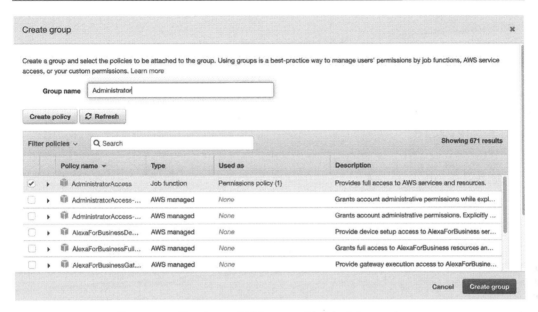

Figure 1.4 – Creating an IAM group with AdministratorAccess

5. The dialog will close. Make sure the new administrator is selected and hit **Next: Tags**. You can optionally add key-value pair tags to the IAM user. Hit **Next: Review** to review the configuration. Hit **Create user** when everything is correct.

   You will see the following information. Please note down the sign-in URL for easy console access, **Access key ID** and **Secret access key** for programmatic access, and the one-time password. You can also download the credential as a CSV file by clicking the **Download .csv** button:

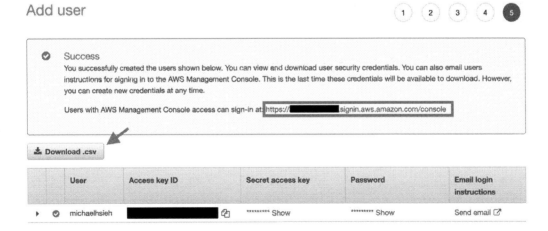

Figure 1.5 – A new IAM user is created

6. After the IAM user creation, you can sign in to your AWS account with the sign-in URL and your IAM user. When you first sign in, you will need to provide the automatically generated password and then set up a new one. Now, you should note in the top-right corner that you are logged in as your newly created IAM user instead of the root user:

Figure 1.6 – Confirm your newly created credentials

If you are new to AWS, don't worry about the cost of trying out AWS. AWS offers a free tier for more than 100 services based on the consumption of the service and/or within a 12-month period. The services we are going to use throughout the book, such as an S3 bucket and Amazon SageMaker, have a free tier for you to learn the skills without breaking the bank. The following table is a summary of the free tier for the services that are going to be covered in this book:

Service name	Free tier amount	Free tier period
Amazon S3	5 GB of standard storage and 20,000/2,000 Get/Put requests	12 months
AWS Lambda	1 million requests per month	Always
Amazon API Gateway	1 million API calls received per month	12 months
Amazon SageMaker Studio notebooks	250 hours of an ml.t3.medium instance	2 months
Amazon SageMaker Data Wrangler	25 hours of an ml.m5.4xlarge instance on Studio Data Wrangler	
Amazon SageMaker Feature Store	10 million write units, 10 million read units, and 25 GB of storage	
Amazon SageMaker training	50 hours of ml.m4.xlarge or ml.m5.xlarge instances	
Amazon SageMaker inference	125 hours of ml.m4.xlarge or ml.m5.xlarge instances	

Figure 1.7 – Notable free trial offers from AWS

Let's finish off the chapter with a recap of what we've covered.

Summary

In this chapter, we've described the concept of ML, the steps in an ML life cycle, and how to approach a business problem with an ML mindset. We also talked about the basics of cloud computing, the role it plays in ML development, and the core services on Amazon Web Services. Lastly, we created an AWS account and set up a user for us to use throughout the fun ride in this book.

In the next chapter, we will learn Amazon SageMaker Studio and its component from a high-level point of view. We will see how each component is mapped to the ML life cycle that we learned in this chapter and will set up our Amazon SageMaker Studio environment together.

2
Introducing Amazon SageMaker Studio

As we just learned in *Chapter 1*, *Machine Learning and Its Life Cycle in the Cloud*, an ML life cycle is complex and iterative. Steps can be quite manual even though most things are done with coding. Having the right tool for an ML project is essential for you to be successful in delivering ML models for production in the cloud. With this chapter, you are in the right place! Amazon SageMaker Studio is a purpose-built ML **Integrated Development Environment** (**IDE**) that offers features covering an end-to-end ML life cycle to make developers' and data scientists' jobs easy in the AWS Cloud.

In this chapter, we will cover the following:

- Introducing SageMaker Studio and its components
- Setting up SageMaker Studio
- Walking through the SageMaker Studio UI
- Demystifying SageMaker Studio notebooks, instances, and kernels
- Using the SageMaker Python SDK

Technical requirements

For this chapter, you will need to have an AWS account. If you don't have one, please revisit the *Setting up AWS environment* section in *Chapter 1, Machine Learning and Its Life Cycle in the Cloud*.

Introducing SageMaker Studio and its components

Amazon SageMaker is an ML service from AWS that has features dedicated to each phase of an ML life cycle that we discussed in *Chapter 1, Machine Learning and Its Life Cycle in the Cloud*. Amazon SageMaker Studio is an ML IDE designed for end-to-end ML development with Amazon SageMaker. You can access Amazon SageMaker features using the SageMaker Studio IDE or using the SageMaker Python SDK, as we will discuss in the *Using SageMaker Python SDK* section. The following chart provides an overview:

PREPARE	BUILD	TRAIN AND TUNE	DEPLOY AND MLOPS
SageMaker Data Wrangler Explore and prepare data for ML	**SageMaker Autopilot** Automatically create ML models with full visibility	**Managed Training** Distributed infrastructure management	**Managed Deployment** Fully managed, ultra-low latency, high throughput
SageMaker Clarify Discover bias and explain model predictions	**SageMaker JumpStart** Pre-built ML solutions and model zoo	**Distributed Training Libraries** Training for large datasets and models	**SageMaker Model Monitor** Maintain accuracy of deployed models
SageMaker Processing Flexible and fully managed data processing	**SageMaker Studio Notebooks** Jupyter notebooks with elastic compute and sharing	**SageMaker Debugger** Debug and profile training runs	**SageMaker Pipelines** Workflow orchestration and automation
SageMaker Feature Store Feature repository for ML training and inferencing	**Training Algorithms** Highly scalable algorithms without coding	**SageMaker Experiments** Capture, organize, and compare every step	**SageMaker Projects and Model Registry** Enable and manage MLOps for ML workflow
Amazon SageMaker Studio (IDE for ML)			

Figure 2.1 – Amazon SageMaker Studio overview – four pillars represent the four stages in the ML life cycle

This chart highlights the SageMaker components that are covered in the book. Let's first walk through at a high level for each component in the ML life cycle stages in this chapter. Then, I will provide pointers to the later chapters.

Prepare

Amazon SageMaker Studio helps data scientists and developers build high-quality datasets for ML quickly. You can use the following features to explore, process, transform, aggregate data, and store processed data or ML features in a central repository.

SageMaker Data Wrangler

Amazon SageMaker Data Wrangler helps developers explore and build a dataset for ML in a fast, easy, and repeatable manner. SageMaker Data Wrangler puts the data preparation workflow – importing from various cloud storage and data warehouses, aggregating multiple tables, understanding data bias and target leakage, and exploring data patterns with visualization – in one easy-to-use graphical interface where you can simply point and click to create a repeatable and portable data recipe. The easy-to-use graphical interface is exclusively in SageMaker Studio. SageMaker Data Wrangler has over 300 built-in data transformations so that you do not need to re-invent the wheel for typical data processing steps in ML. Besides built-in transformation, SageMaker Data Wrangler also supports custom transformation written in Python, SQL, and PySpark to enrich your data engineering steps. We will dive deeper into SageMaker Data Wrangler in *Chapter 3, Data Preparation with SageMaker Data Wrangler*.

SageMaker Clarify

Amazon SageMaker Clarify helps developers discover underlying bias in the training data and explain feature importance from a model prediction. **Data bias** is an imbalance in the training data across different groups and categories, such as age and education level, that is introduced to the training data due to a sampling error or other intricate reasons. Data bias is often neglected until a trained model makes incorrect or unfair predictions against a certain group. It is well understood that a model will learn what is present in the data, including any bias, and will replicate that bias in its inferences. It is more critical than ever to be able to discover the inherent biases in the data early and take action to address them. SageMaker Clarify computes various metrics to measure the bias in the data so that you do not have to be an expert in the science of ML bias. SageMaker Clarify integrates with Amazon SageMaker Data Wrangler so you can detect bias in the preparation phase. SageMaker Clarify also integrates with **Amazon SageMaker Experiments** and **Amazon SageMaker Model Monitor** so that you can identify bias and feature importance in a trained model and inference data in production. We will learn more about SageMaker Clarify in *Chapter 6, Detecting ML Bias and Explaining Models with SageMaker Clarify*.

SageMaker Processing

Amazon SageMaker Processing is a feature that runs your scripts and containers in SageMaker's fully managed compute instances instead of your limited local compute resource. It is designed to make data processing and model evaluation easy and scalable. It is flexible so that developers can use it to run any code at any time in the ML life cycle. SageMaker Processing is also integrated with several SageMaker features as the compute backbone. SageMaker Data Wrangler uses SageMaker Processing to execute your SageMaker Data Wrangler data recipe and save the processed features into storage. SageMaker Clarify uses SageMaker Processing to compute the bias metrics and feature importance. SageMaker Model Monitor, which will be discussed in the *Deploy* section later in this chapter, uses SageMaker Processing to compute the data drift. SageMaker Autopilot, which will be discussed in the *Build* section shortly, uses SageMaker Processing for data exploration and feature engineering.

SageMaker Feature Store

Amazon SageMaker Feature Store is a fully managed ML feature repository that allows ML developers to store, update, query, and share ML features among other ML developers with governance. Having a central feature repository as a single source of features in an organization where many teams are collaborating on feature engineering but go on to create their own models speeds up the development of the models, as features can now be shared and reused across teams, as well as applications for both training and inferencing. It reduces the feature development time and waste of effort for teams. SageMaker Feature Store offers both **online** and **offline feature stores** for real-time, low-latency ML inference use and for querying batch data for model training, respectively. SageMaker Feature Store also has versioning and time travel to allow developers to reuse features and audit past model training and inferences. We will explore more about SageMaker Feature Store in *Chapter 4, Building a Feature Repository with SageMaker Feature Store* .

Build

Amazon SageMaker Studio as an IDE for ML has many features and functionalities that can help you build ML models depending on your use case and project complexity. Heard of an ML algorithm but not sure how to implement it? Amazon SageMaker Studio has **low to no-code options** – automatic ML (**autoML**), pre-built ML solutions, and built-in training algorithms – to help you build a complex ML model and solution by simply plugging in your data. A SageMaker Studio notebook re-invents the way you develop ML models with Jupyter notebooks.

SageMaker Autopilot

Amazon SageMaker Autopilot explores, transforms data, and trains and tunes ML models automatically for your input dataset. You only need to select the dataset location and the target to make SageMaker Autopilot learn and predict in a simple-to-use graphic interface. Then, off it goes. SageMaker Autopilot provides full control and visibility of how the model is built. Jupyter notebooks with code and exploratory data analysis are given to you as well for you to understand how SageMaker Autopilot works under the hood. With the code available to you, you may also improve any step in the process and rerun the job to achieve even better results. When models are trained, the SageMaker Studio user interface makes it easy to browse through and choose the best model. You can view a leader board in SageMaker Studio, compare performance among the choice of an ML algorithm and other hyperparameters, and deploy the best model with just a couple of clicks. We will continue our exploration of SageMaker Autopilot in *Chapter 8, Jumpstarting ML with SageMaker JumpStart and Autopilot.*

SageMaker JumpStart

Amazon SageMaker JumpStart makes it easy to get started with ML by providing a collection of solutions purposefully built for the most common use cases across industries and a model zoo of more than 150 popular open source deep learning models for computer vision and natural language processing use cases. A solution in SageMaker JumpStart is composed of a reference architecture for an end-to-end system, beyond just the ML modeling, that can be deployed to your AWS account. You can simply browse the catalog inside SageMaker Studio IDE for the right solution, deploy with one click, and see how things work together as a production system in the cloud. As for the ML model zoo from SageMaker JumpStart, you can also easily choose a model that meets your use case from the catalog and deploy with one click to perform inferencing on your data or in your applications. You can also fine-tune a model to your use case with your own dataset with training completely managed by SageMaker JumpStart without any coding. We will learn more about how to use SageMaker JumpStart in *Chapter 8, Jumpstarting ML with SageMaker JumpStart and Autopilot.*

SageMaker Studio notebooks

On the topic of building an ML model, developers often write code in a Jupyter notebook for its simplicity and readability, as it captures code. The Amazon SageMaker Studio interface is built on top of JupyterLab, with many additional features designed to enhance the experience. SageMaker Studio notebooks provide an elastic and scalable way to write code and build ML models compared to a regular notebook in stock JupyterLab. For each notebook, not only can developers choose what notebook kernel to run the notebook, but also what compute instance to back the notebook. So, for a data exploration notebook, you can provision an instance that has 2 vCPU and 4 GiB of RAM for plotting and data processing for a modest amount of data. Should you need to load much more data or need a GPU for quick experimentation, you can either create a new notebook with a different compute instance or switch to a different instance on the existing notebook. You can find a list of supported SageMaker instances in the **Studio Notebooks** tab in `https://aws. amazon.com/sagemaker/pricing/`. We will spend more time talking about the infrastructure behind SageMaker Studio notebooks in the *Demystifying SageMaker Studio notebooks, instances, and kernels* section later in this chapter, and in *Chapter 6, Detecting ML Bias and Explaining Models with SageMaker Clarify*.

Training algorithms

Building ML models does not necessarily mean that you need to write lots of code. Amazon SageMaker offers 17 scalable, infrastructure-optimized, built-in algorithms for supervised and unsupervised problem types, and for tabular, computer vision, and Natural Language Processing (NLP) use cases. The **built-in algorithms** are designed to be used with Amazon SageMaker's fully managed compute. When training with the built-in algorithms, you point the algorithm and hyperparameters to a dataset on an S3 bucket, and SageMaker provisions training instances behind the scenes, takes your data and the algorithm as a Docker container to the training instances, and performs the training. By scalable and infrastructure-optimized, we mean the code base behind these algorithms is optimized for AWS compute infrastructure and is capable of running distributed training using multiple instances. The best thing about the built-in algorithms is that you do not need to write extensive code. We will learn more about the built-in algorithms and how to train models with them in *Chapter 5, Building and Training ML Models with SageMaker Studio IDE*.

Training and tuning

Training and tuning ML models perhaps consumes the most time and effort of a data scientist. To help data scientists focus on modeling and not infrastructure, having a fully managed, reliable, and scalable compute environment is critical for them to operate at their best. Amazon SageMaker Studio makes ML training easy and scalable with the following features.

Managed training

SageMaker-managed training enables ML developers to access on-demand compute resources from anywhere and makes model training a near-serverless experience. You can launch a model training job using an optimal compute resource from a wide variety of SageMaker ML instances. You can find a list of training instances under the **Training** tab in `https://aws.amazon.com/sagemaker/pricing/`. For a deep learning model that needs a powerful GPU instance, you can easily specify an **Accelerated Computing** instance that equips with GPU device(s). If you have a linear regression model at hand that utilizes a CPU rather than GPU, you can choose an instance from the **Standard** or **Compute Optimized** instances based on the CPU and memory need. As a SageMaker-managed feature, there is no server provisioning and management for you to do at all. You submit a training job, and SageMaker handles the server provision and shuts down when the training job completes. Monitoring a training job is easy because the training metrics and logs are pushed to **Amazon CloudWatch**. This experience allows you to focus on model building and training rather than the infrastructure. We will learn more about SageMaker managed training and examples of training ML models with popular ML frameworks such as TensorFlow and PyTorch in *Chapter 5, Building and Training ML Models with SageMaker Studio IDE*. SageMaker managed training also supports spot instances so that you can save up to 90% on on-demand instances. We will learn more about SageMaker managed spot training in *Chapter 9, Training ML Models at Scale in SageMaker Studio.*.

Distributed training libraries

As deep learning models are getting bigger and need more data, training a large neural network pushes the need for GPUs beyond a single compute instance. You need to find a way to distribute the training data and the large neural network model to multiple instances. **Amazon SageMaker's distributed training libraries** make it easy to develop your ML training code in a distributed manner. A SageMaker distributed training library has two techniques for scaling – **data parallelism** and **model parallelism**. Data parallelism distributes large datasets to instances to train concurrently. Model parallelism splits models that are too large to fit on a single GPU into portions across multiple GPUs in order to train. SageMaker's distributed training libraries also optimize the distribution framework and partitioning algorithms to train fast on SageMaker's GPU instances, achieving near-linear scaling efficiency. With a few lines of code on top of your training code base, you can turn your model training into a distributed one to efficiently utilize multiple GPU devices on multiple instances. We will dive deeper with examples of how distributed training libraries work in *Chapter 9, Training ML Models at Scale in SageMaker Studio*.

SageMaker Debugger

During a model training job, it is critical to know whether there are problems during training and how your training code is utilizing the compute resource. This feedback information allows you to adjust network architecture, change hyperparameters, and modify other parameters so that you can train a better model and stop failing training jobs without wasting more time and resources. **Amazon SageMaker Debugger** makes it easy to optimize ML models and training instance utilization. SageMaker Debugger is designed to capture training metrics and compute resource utilization in real time and report actionable insights and issues when they arise. SageMaker Debugger creates an interactive dashboard in SageMaker Studio that you can visualize in real time as the training happens. This is especially helpful when training complex neural network models. We will discuss more and show how to use SageMaker Debugger when you are training models at scale in *Chapter 9, Training ML Models at Scale in SageMaker Studio.*

SageMaker Experiments

Amazon SageMaker Experiments is a feature that helps you organize and track your work in the ML life cycle. As you embark on an ML project, you process data, apply a transformation with parameters, and train ML models from various algorithms and hyperparameters. You will realize when the number of trials and experiments grow quickly and become unmanageable. Developers can use the SageMaker Experiments Python SDK to set up trackers to track the data sources, processing steps, and parameters. The SageMaker Studio IDE makes it easy to search the experiments and trials, compare the parameters and model performance, and create charts to visualize the progress. We will go deeper into SageMaker Experiments in *Chapter 5, Building and Training ML Models with SageMaker Studio IDE.*

Deploy

An ML model is created to serve and to make predictions. Deploying an ML model is the starting point of making use of a model. How you serve a model to make inference reliably, at scale, and cost-effectively while creating a feedback loop for your ML application is one of the most important aspects in the ML life cycle, as we learn that, often, 90% or more of ML costs are spent on hosting models for inference.

Managed deployment

SageMaker managed model deployment takes away the heavy lifting of managing, provisioning, and scaling compute instances for model inferencing. Machine learning models can be deployed for real-time inference and for batch inference on SageMaker. Real-time inference is typically required if the ML inference is a part of an online application. The deployed model is also expected to return an inference in a low-latency fashion. With just a couple of lines of code, the **Amazon SageMaker model hosting** feature deploys your model into fully managed ML instance(s) as an endpoint for low latency real-time inference. You can also set up autoscaling of the endpoints so that when the traffic to your model increases, SageMaker will automatically spin up more instances to handle the additional burden so as not to overwhelm the existing instances.

If your ML project requires you to create multiple models for better accuracy for each, say, a geographic area, **SageMaker's multi-model endpoints** are a cost-effective option for you to deploy your models. Instead of hosting 50 models on 50 endpoints for an ML use case with data from 50 US states and paying for 50 endpoints when you know the traffic to some states will be sparser compared to some other states, you can consolidate 50 models into 1 multi-model endpoint to fully utilize the compute capacity for the endpoint and reduce the hosting cost.

As for batch inference, **SageMaker batch transform** is a cost-effective and scalable way to make inferences against your model for a large dataset in batches. SageMaker batch transform handles the data ingestion efficiently so that you do not need to worry about the data size overwhelming the compute instance.

Model deployment and hosting is a big topic, and we will discuss more in *Chapter 7, Hosting ML Models in the Cloud: Best Practices.*

SageMaker Model Monitor

As discussed in *Chapter 1*, *Machine Learning and Its Life Cycle in the Cloud*, closing the ML feedback loop is a step that ensures the model quality and allows developers to take action before it's too late. The **Amazon SageMaker Model Monitor** feature closes the feedback loop by setting up data capture, computing the input data statistic as a baseline, and monitoring the **data drift** for your live endpoints, hosted on SageMaker on a schedule. SageMaker Model Monitor uses a set of statistics and metrics to determine whether the new incoming data is conforming to how the baseline training data looks statistically and schematically. You can also define your own metrics and use them in SageMaker Model Monitor. Once the model monitoring for an endpoint is set up, you can visualize the data drift and any data issues over time in a dashboard in SageMaker Studio IDE. You can also set up alarms and triggers using other AWS services in order to act according to data drift or model performance drift. We will learn more and show how to set up SageMaker model monitoring in *Chapter 10*, *Monitoring ML Models in Production with SageMaker Model Monitor*.

MLOps

Data scientists used to spend too much time and effort maintaining and manually managing an ML pipeline, a process that starts with data processing, model training, and evaluation, and ends with model hosting with ongoing maintenance. SageMaker Studio provides features that aim to streamline this operation with **Continuous Integration** (**CI**) and **Continuous Delivery** (**CD**) as best practices.

SageMaker Pipelines

Amazon SageMaker Pipelines is an orchestration layer that allows you to build workflows for your ML life cycle that can be automated in a production system. You can automate steps, including data processing, model training, tuning, evaluation, and deployment, under one pipeline. You can apply business conditions and logic into a pipeline in order to maintain the model's quality. SageMaker Pipelines creates an audit trail for models because it keeps information of every step in the pipeline in one place. ML pipelines from SageMaker Pipelines can be executed at any time, on a schedule, or in response to trigger events. We will discuss and run an example of SageMaker Pipelines in *Chapter 11*, *Operationalize ML Projects with SageMaker Projects, Pipelines, and Model Registry*.

SageMaker projects and model registry

Amazon SageMaker projects is a feature that helps you bring all your ML artifacts into one place with CI/CD best practices to ensure models in production come with reproducibility, auditability, and governance.

A SageMaker project collects ML code bases, pipelines, experiments, model registry, and deployed endpoints into one single pane of glass. SageMaker provides MLOps templates for you to get started with MLOps in AWS easily. You can choose a built-in template or create your own based on your use case, deploy the template, and start filling in your ML workflow to equip your ML workflow with CI/CD best practices. These include the following:

- Code repositories for version control
- ML pipelines for automating model training
- A code build process that verifies that code commits are working
- A model deployment quality control gate and a model registry for version control
- An automated model deployment process

We will walk through the feature and MLOps best practices in *Chapter 11, Operationalize ML Projects with SageMaker Projects, Pipelines, and Model Registry.*

Now that we've had a brief introduction to the many components of SageMaker Studio, let's get your AWS account ready and learn how to set up SageMaker Studio.

Setting up SageMaker Studio

With the core features out of the way, let's get started with Amazon SageMaker Studio. Please log in to your AWS account with your IAM user and go to the Amazon SageMaker console page from the **Services** drop-down menu. You should be greeted with the page shown in *Figure 2.2*:

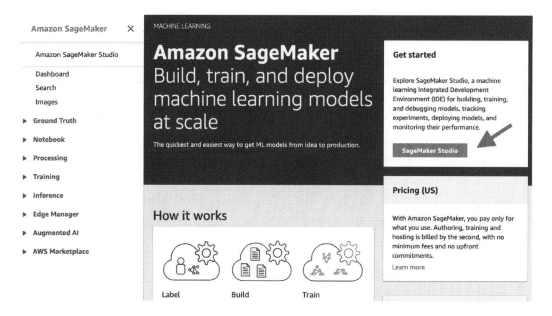

Figure 2.2 – Amazon SageMaker console page

Click on the **SageMaker Studio** button.

Setting up a domain

Because this is our first time with Amazon SageMaker Studio, we need to set up a SageMaker domain and a user profile. There is a quick start setup and a standard setup – which one should you use? Well, it depends on your needs. It is sufficient to use quick start to complete all of the exercises in this book and for most of your personal projects. The standard setup, on the other hand, provides additional options for customizing your compute environment to meet specific security requirements that are often in place in enterprises such as networking and authentication methods.

With the standard setup, you can configure the following:

- *The authentication method*: **Single Sign-On (SSO)** or **AWS Identity and Access Management (IAM)**. SSO is a popular method for enterprise teams that allows you to log in with a single sign-on credential to access software and cloud resources in a portal from anywhere. You do not need to access the AWS console in this case. However, it requires you to first set up an SSO account. The IAM method allows you to set up a domain more quickly and simply. This is also the method used in the quick start setup. You need to first log in to the AWS console using your IAM role in order to access Studio.

- *Permission*: A default execution role defining permissions such as what S3 buckets you are allowed to access and what actions you can perform from within SageMaker Studio for the domain. Note that each new user added to the SageMaker Studio domain can either inherit this default execution role or can have another execution role with different permissions.

- *Notebook-sharing configuration*: Notebook sharing is a key feature when it comes to collaboration. You can configure where the notebook sharing metadata is saved on S3 if you want to encrypt the shareable notebooks and have the ability to share the cell output, or you can disable notebook sharing.

- *SageMaker projects and JumpStart*: Whether you would like to enable the SageMaker project templates and JumpStart for an account and/or users.

- *Network and storage*: SageMaker Studio, as a cloud resource, can be launched inside a **Virtual Private Cloud (VPC)**, a logical virtual network where you can control the route tables, network gateways, public internet access, availability zones, and much more on network security. These options allow enterprises for whom cloud security is crucial to securely run an ML workload in the cloud. You have the option here to choose to host SageMaker Studio in a default VPC created in every AWS account, or your own VPC. You can choose one or more subnets for high availability.

  Many organizations require a well-governed internet access policy in the cloud. You can choose whether the public internet is to be allowed and what set of security groups, which control inbound and outbound rules, should be enforced. Last but not least, you have the option to encrypt the storage used in SageMaker Studio, namely, the EFS filesystem.

- *Tags*: You can add tags in key-value pairs to the Studio domain. This allows you or the administrator to group resources based on tags attached and understand the spending in the cloud.

After reviewing the standard options, let's return to **Quick start**, as this is sufficient and more straightforward for us in the context of this book:

1. Fill in your username.

2. For **Execution role**, we create a new one.

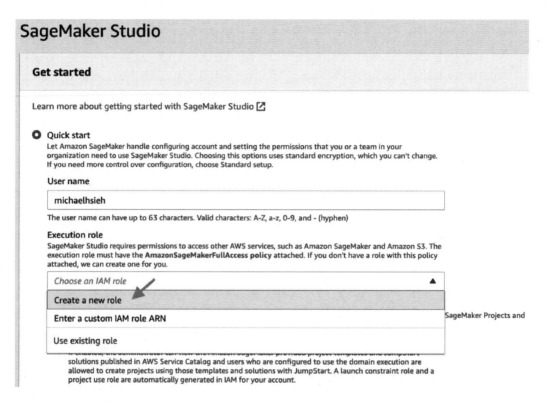

Figure 2.3 – Setting up a SageMaker Studio domain with Quick start

3. You have an option to allow access to any S3 bucket, specific buckets, or no additional buckets, outside of the four other rules listed in the following figure. Let's choose **None** to practice least privilege access. We will be using a SageMaker default bucket that will be created later and satisfies existing rules. Click **Create role**:

Create an IAM role   ✕

Passing an IAM role gives Amazon SageMaker permission to perform actions in other AWS services on your behalf. Creating a role here will grant permissions described by the **AmazonSageMakerFullAccess** ☑ IAM policy to the role you create.

The IAM role you create will provide access to:

⊖ S3 buckets you specify - *optional*

    ○ **Any S3 bucket**
       Allow users that have access to your notebook instance access to any bucket and its contents in your account.

    ○ **Specific S3 buckets**

         | *Example: bucket-name-1, buckε* |

       Comma delimited. ARNs, "*" and "/" are not supported.

    ◉ **None**

⊘ Any S3 bucket with "**sagemaker**" in the name

⊘ Any S3 object with "**sagemaker**" in the name

⊘ Any S3 object with the tag "**sagemaker**" and value "**true**"   See Object tagging ☑

⊘ S3 bucket with a Bucket Policy allowing access to SageMaker   See S3 bucket policies ☑

                                                              Cancel   **Create role**

Figure 2.4 – Creating an IAM role

4.   Before you hit **Submit**, make sure to enable Amazon SageMaker project templates and JumpStart. Choose **Submit**. It will take a few minutes to spin up a domain and a user profile. Feel free to take a quick break and come back later:

Figure 2.5 – SageMaker Studio Control Panel

5.   Once ready, click on **Open Studio**.

A Jupyter Server application will be created when you open it for the first time and this will take a couple of minutes.

Next, let's explore the SageMaker Studio UI.

Walking through the SageMaker Studio UI

Figure 2.6 is a screenshot of the SageMaker Studio UI and the Studio **Launcher** page. You may find the interface very similar to the JupyterLab interface. SageMaker Studio indeed builds on top of JupyterLab and adds many additional features to it to provide you with an end-to-end ML experience within the IDE:

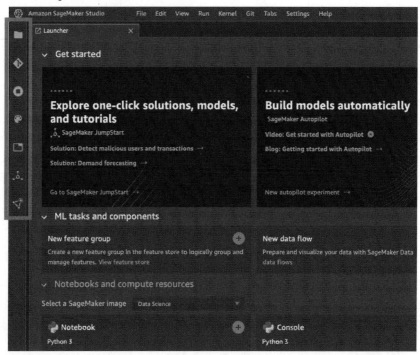

Figure 2.6 – The SageMaker Studio UI – the left sidebar is indicated in the red box

Let's talk about the key components in the Studio UI.

The main work area

The main work area is where the **Launcher** page, the notebooks, code editor, terminals, and consoles go. In addition to these base features from JupyterLab, as you will learn throughout the book, SageMaker Studio's own features, such as Data Wrangler, Autopilot, JumpStart, Feature Store, Pipelines, Model Monitor, and Experiments, also deliver the rich user experience in the main work area. The **Launcher** page is the portal to all the new resources you might like to create, such as a new JumpStart solution, a new feature store, a new MLOps project, a new notebook, and a new terminal.

The sidebar

The sidebar on the left with seven icons (eight when you have a notebook opened) serves as a portal to all of the resources that you have or may need, as indicated in *Figure 2.6*. From top to bottom, they are as follows:

- **File Browser** is where you access files on your home directory on the EFS filesystem and upload new files.

- **Git** is where you can connect to a Git repository and perform Git operations to your code base interactively.

- The **Running Terminals and Kernels** tab allows you to view, access, and shut down compute resources such as notebooks, kernels, and instances.

- **Commands** shows a list of commands and actions you can take in the Studio UI.

- **Network Tools** lets you access a notebook's metadata. It is only shown when a notebook is open in the main work area.

- **Open Tabs** shows a list of open tabs.

- The **SageMaker JumpStart** icon shows launched solutions and associated training jobs and endpoints.

- **SageMaker Components and Registries** lists projects, Data Wrangler files, pipelines, experiments, models, endpoints, and feature stores that you can view and access. There is also a search bar in each component for you to easily find your resources.

The sidebar to the right of the main working area is the **Settings** pane, which allows you to edit table and chart properties when you create a visual analysis from experiments or model monitoring jobs, which is a great feature of SageMaker Studio as well.

"Hello world!" in SageMaker Studio

Let's start with a very basic task – open a notebook, and run a very simple program in Python that every single programming book would use – *"hello world!"*.

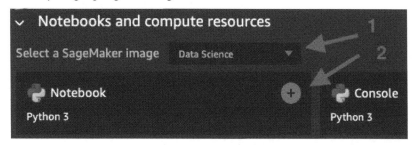

Figure 2.7 – Creating a SageMaker Studio notebook

1. Go to **Notebooks and compute resources, Select a SageMaker image** (optional for now – the **Data Science** default is perfect but you may choose another image), and click on the + icon in the **Notebook | Python 3** box. A new notebook will pop up.

2. If you notice that there is an **Unknown** next to the **Python 3 (Data Science)** in the top right corner, and there is **Kernel: Starting...** in the status bar down at the bottom, as shown in *Figure 2.8*, it means the notebook is still connecting to the compute resource. It should take about a minute. We will talk more in depth about what's happening behind the scenes in the next section, *Demystifying SageMaker Studio notebooks, instances, and kernels*.

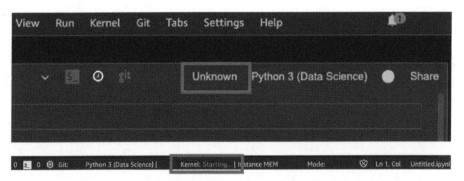

Figure 2.8 – A kernel is starting for a new SageMaker Studio notebook

3. If you see **2 vCPU + 4 GiB** next to the **Python 3 (Data Science)** kernel image, it means that the notebook has finally connected to the instance that has 2 virtual CPUs (**vCPUs**) and 4 GiB of RAM. Let's write our first line of code in the first cell of the notebook:

```
print('hello world!')
```

And now let's execute, as shown in the following screenshot:

Figure 2.9 – The notebook has connected to the kernel and our "hello world!" program is working

Great! We just launched an elastic notebook in SageMaker Studio and executed our "hello world!" example. However, if you went too quickly and executed the code while the status bar at the bottom was still showing **Kernel: Starting…**, you might get the following error:

```
Note: The kernel is still starting. Please execute this cell
again after the kernel is started.
```

What is happening here? Let's switch gears to talk about the infrastructure behind SageMaker Studio.

Demystifying SageMaker Studio notebooks, instances, and kernels

Figure 2.10 is an architectural diagram of the SageMaker Studio domain and how a notebook kernel relates to other components. There are four entities we need to understand here:

- **EC2 instance**: The hardware that the notebook runs on. You can choose what instance type to use based on the vCPU, GPU, and amount of memory. The instance type determines the pricing rate, which can be found in `https://aws.amazon.com/sagemaker/pricing/`.

- **SageMaker image**: A container image that can be run on SageMaker Studio. It contains language packages and other files required to run a notebook. You can run multiple images in an EC2 instance.

- **KernelGateway app**: A SageMaker image runs as a KernelGateway app. There is a one-to-one relationship between a SageMaker image and a KernelGateway app.

- **Kernel**: A process that runs the code in a notebook. There can be multiple kernels in a SageMaker image.

So far, we, as **User1** in the illustration, have logged on to the Studio **JupyterServer App**, the frontend component, in the SageMaker Studio domain. As we open a notebook in the frontend, a new `ipynb` file will be created in the **User1** home directory on the **Amazon EFS filesystem**. SageMaker Studio will attempt to connect the notebook (frontend) to a backend compute resource that satisfies the requirements, namely, the kernel image, and EC2 instance types. In SageMaker Studio, we also call a launched kernel image a KernelGateway app.

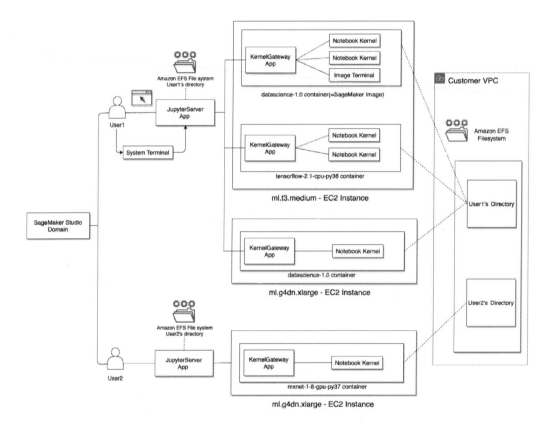

Figure 2.10 – The infrastructure behind the SageMaker Studio IDE

Important Note

Image courtesy of the following link: `https://docs.aws.amazon.com/sagemaker/latest/dg/notebooks.html`.

If the requested compute resource is available, a notebook will connect immediately and become ready for coding. If none are available, as in our case because we just launched our first-ever notebook in the domain, SageMaker Studio spins up a compute instance (`ml.t3.medium`, by default) and attaches the kernel image (the data science image we have chosen) as a container in the compute instance.

That's why we are seeing **Kernel: Starting…** down in the status bar, as shown in *Figure 2.8*. You can also see in your user profile on the SageMaker Studio page of the SageMaker console that a `datascience-1-0-ml-t3-medium-xxxx` KernelGateway app is in a pending state.

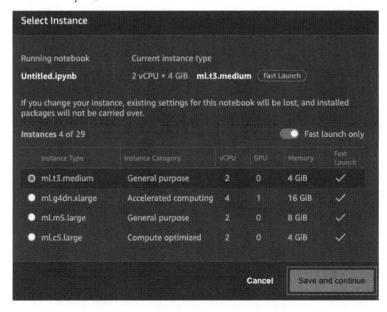

Figure 2.11 – A KernelGateway app is starting up in SageMaker Studio

Once the KernelGateway app is ready, our notebook becomes ready. This innovative mechanism behind the notebooks in SageMaker Studio allows users (multi-tenants) to use the right compute resource for each of the notebooks that we are running under one roof. If you click on **2 vCPU + 4 GiB**, you will be able to see what instance type you are using and what is available to you, as follows:

Figure 2.12 – Selecting an instance for a notebook

There are four commonly used instance types of different categories that are **Fast Launch**, that is, instances that are designed to launch in under 2 minutes. If you uncheck the **Fast launch only** checkbox, you will see all the instance types that are available in SageMaker Studio for your notebook, including the ones that are not of the fast launch type. Feel free to switch to other instance types and kernel images to experiment. You can see all the running instances, apps, and live notebook sessions in **Running Terminals and Kernels** in the left sidebar. You should shut down **RUNNING APPS** and **KERNEL SESSIONS** that you no longer need with the power buttons, as highlighted in the following screenshot, to terminate and recycle the resource on the running instance. Also, you should shut down the **RUNNING INSTANCES** you no longer need to stop incurring charges.

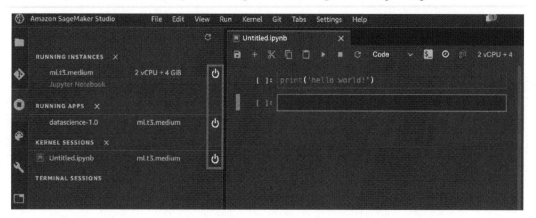

Figure 2.13 – Viewing Running Terminals and Kernels from the left sidebar

Now that we have a good understanding of how notebooks work with instances and kernel images, let's get our hands dirtier with another major resource that we will use throughout the book and your ML development life cycle in SageMaker Studio.

Using the SageMaker Python SDK

SageMaker Studio is more than just a place to run codes in notebooks. Yes, SageMaker Studio is a great place to start coding and training ML models in elastic notebooks, but there are so many more capabilities, as we discussed in the *Introducing SageMaker Studio and its components* section in this chapter.

There are two main ways to communicate and work with SageMaker features. One is through the components that have a UI frontend, such as SageMaker Data Wrangler; the other is through a **Software Development Kit (SDK)**. The SDK enables developers to interact with the world of Amazon SageMaker beyond the interface. You can access SageMaker's scalable, built-in algorithms for your data. You can programmatically run SageMaker Autopilot jobs. If you develop your deep learning models with TensorFlow, PyTorch, or MXNet, you can use the SDK to interact with the SageMaker compute infrastructure for training, processing, and hosting models for them. You can create a feature store with the SDK. And there is so much more. I won't enumerate all the capabilities in this section, as we will mostly use and learn about the SDK for the SageMaker features in future chapters when we need to code.

There are several SDKs from AWS that use SageMaker features, such as the following:

- The **SageMaker Python SDK**, which provides a high-level API that is familiar to data scientists

- **AWS SDK for Python (Boto3)**, which provides low-level access to SageMaker API and other AWS services

- AWS SDK for other programming languages (`https://aws.amazon.com/sagemaker/resources/`), depending on your application

For many data scientists, the SageMaker Python SDK is a more natural choice because of its API design. We will be using the SageMaker Python SDK throughout this book.

The SageMaker Python SDK comes standard in all fully managed SageMaker kernel images, so there is no need for you to install and manage the different versions. You can simply run `import sagemaker` in the code and notebook and use the library. You can also use the SageMaker Python SDK anywhere outside of SageMaker Studio, such as on your laptop or in a serverless application on AWS Lambda, to talk to SageMaker, provided that you have the correct IAM permission configurations.

Because SageMaker is a cloud service in AWS, there are some aspects that you need to take care of before using the service. The following code is a typical method for setting up the SageMaker Python SDK in a given environment. You will see more examples throughout the book:

```
import sagemaker
session = sagemaker.Session()
bucket = session.default_bucket()
role = sagemaker.get_execution_role()
```

This code snippet does the following:

1. Import the SageMaker Python SDK into the runtime.

2. Create a **session** that allows you to interact with the Amazon SageMaker API and any other AWS services.

3. Create a default bucket for use and return the name of the bucket. The bucket has the form of `sagemaker-{region}-{AWS account ID}`.

4. Retrieve the execution role that is available locally. On SageMaker Studio, it is the execution role that we assigned when the user profile was created. A role should have permissions to select S3 buckets and perform SageMaker-related actions in order to properly use the SDK. Our role has the `AmazonSageMakerFullAccess` policy attached to it, so we are covered. If you are using the SDK on your PC, make sure you have an AWS credential with an IAM user that permits you to perform SageMaker-related actions.

You may print out `bucket` and `role` to see what they are. They are string values to an S3 bucket and of an IAM role, respectively. The `role` value is required by all APIs that talk to and perform actions on the cloud. This is important because security is job zero in the cloud. As we discussed in *Chapter 1, Machine Learning and Its Life Cycle in the Cloud*, in AWS, you need to have valid and proper permissions in order to perform and access any cloud resources. When executing actions with SageMaker features, `role` will be used to verify whether you have sufficient permission to do so before proceeding.

As an open source library, you can access the source code here at `https://github.com/aws/sagemaker-python-sdk` and the documentation at `https://sagemaker.readthedocs.io/en/stable/index.html`.

Summary

In this chapter, we introduced the SageMaker Studio features at a high level. We mapped the features to the phases of a typical ML life cycle and discussed why and how SageMaker is used in the ML life cycle. We set up a SageMaker Studio domain and executed our first-ever notebook in SageMaker Studio. We learned the infrastructure of the SageMaker Studio and how to pick the right kernel image and compute instance for a notebook. Lastly, we talked about the basic concepts behind the key tool, the SageMaker Python SDK, and how it interacts with the cloud and SageMaker, as this is the foundation to lots of our future activities inside SageMaker Studio.

In the next chapter, we will jumpstart our ML journey by preparing a dataset with SageMaker Data Wrangler for an ML use case. You will learn how easy it is to prepare and process your data in SageMaker Studio.

Part 2 – End-to-End Machine Learning Life Cycle with SageMaker Studio

In this section of the book, you will gain a working knowledge of each SageMaker Studio component for the **machine learning (ML)** life cycle and how and when to apply SageMaker features in your ML use cases.

This section comprises the following chapters:

- *Chapter 3, Data Preparation with SageMaker Data Wrangler*
- *Chapter 4, Building a Feature Repository with SageMaker Feature Store*
- *Chapter 5, Building and Training ML Models with SageMaker Studio IDE*
- *Chapter 6, Detecting ML Bias and Explaining Models with SageMaker Clarify*
- *Chapter 7, Hosting ML Models in the Cloud: Best Practices*
- *Chapter 8, Jumpstarting ML with SageMaker JumpStart and Autopilot*

3
Data Preparation with SageMaker Data Wrangler

With SageMaker Data Wrangler, you can perform exploratory data analysis and data preprocessing for ML modeling with a point and click experience. You will be able to quickly iterate through data transformation and quick modeling to see if your transform recipe improves model performance, learning if there is implicit bias in the data against sensitive groups, and having a clear record of what transformation has been done on the processed data.

In this chapter, we will be learning how to use **SageMaker Data Wrangler** in the following sections:

- Getting started with SageMaker Data Wrangler for customer churn prediction
- Importing data from sources
- Exploring data with visualization
- Applying transformation
- Exporting data for ML training

Technical requirements

For this chapter, you will need to access materials in `https://github.com/PacktPublishing/Getting-Started-with-Amazon-SageMaker-Studio/tree/main/chapter03`. You need to make sure your IAM execution role has the AmazonAthenaFullAccess policy.

Getting started with SageMaker Data Wrangler for customer churn prediction

Customer churn is a serious problem for businesses. Losing a customer is definitely not something you want to see if you are a business owner. You want to your customers to be happy with your product or service and continue to use them for, well, forever. Customer churn is always going to happen but being able to understand how and why a customer leaves the service or why a customer is not buying your product anymore is critical for your business. Being able to predict ahead of time would be even better.

In this chapter, we will perform exploratory data analysis and data transformation with SageMaker Data Wrangler, and at the end of the chapter, we will be training an ML model using the **XGBoost algorithm** on the wrangled data.

Preparing the use case

We are going to take a synthetic **telecommunication** (**telco**) customer churn dataset for this chapter to demonstrate what it takes to prepare a dataset for machine learning purposes. Please open the `chapter03/1-prepare_data.ipynb` notebook and execute the it. You will get a copy of the data, then perform these steps:

1. Split the data into three data frames, `customer_info`, `account_info`, and `utility`, so that we can demonstrate joining in SageMaker Data Wrangler.

2. Mask out values randomly to create missingness in the data so that we can demonstrate functionalities of SageMaker Data Wrangler.

3. Save the three data frames in an S3 bucket and make `utility` available in Amazon Athena so that we can simulate importing data from multiple sources.

Launching SageMaker Data Wrangler

You can access SageMaker Data Wrangler in any of the following ways:

- Click through **File | New | Data Wrangler Flow** (*Figure 3.1*).

- From the Launcher, click on **New data flow** (*Figure 3.1*).

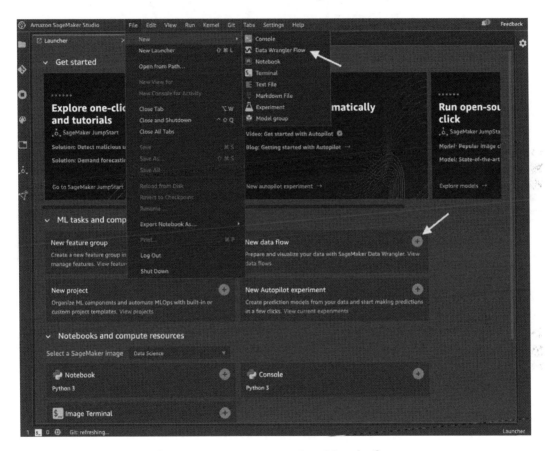

Figure 3.1 – Creating a new Data Wrangler flow

- From the left sidebar, **SageMaker resources**, choose Data Wrangler in the drop-down menu and click **New flow** (*Figure 3.2*).

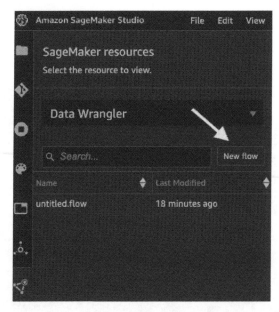

Figure 3.2 – Creating a new Data Wrangler flow file from the registry. You can find all the flow files you have here too

Notably, from **SageMaker Components and registries**, you can also see a list of flow files you have created. Once you create a new data flow file, you will see a new tab in the main working area with a progress bar indicating that it is creating an instance and will take a couple of minutes. At the same time, you will see a new file, untitled.flow, created in the current working directory. A *data flow file*, with the extension .flow, is a file that records all the steps you do with SageMaker Data Wrangler from the UI. It is a JSON-based file that can be easily transferred and reused. SageMaker Studio and Data Wrangler can interpret the content of the JSON file and render the transformations and analyses you do for the dataset. What's happening behind the scenes during this wait time is SageMaker Studio is launching a data wrangler *KernelGateway* app with a dedicated *ml.m5.4xlarge* instance to support the activities we are going to perform inside SageMaker Data Wrangler and to avoid contention with other notebook kernels. Once it's ready, you should see the view presented in *Figure 3.3*.

Figure 3.3 – Starting point of a data wrangling journey with SageMaker Data Wrangler

Before we proceed, let's rename the flow file to `wrangling-customer-churn.flow` or something to your liking by right-clicking on the file in the file explorer and selecting **Rename**.

Now let's get started with SageMaker Data Wrangler.

Importing data from sources

The first step in the data preparation journey is to import data from a source(s). There are four options from which data can be imported: **Amazon S3**, **Amazon Athena**, **Amazon Redshift**, and **Snowflake**. Amazon S3 is an object store service for developers to store virtually any kind of data, including text files, spreadsheets, archives, and ML models. Amazon Athena is an analytic service that gives developers an interactive and serverless SQL-based query experience for data stored in Amazon S3. Amazon Redshift is a data warehouse service that makes it easy to query and process exabytes of data. Snowflake is a data warehouse service from Snowflake Inc. In this chapter, we will be importing data from Amazon S3 and Amazon Athena, which are the two most common data sources. We have two tables in CSV format saved in the SageMaker default S3 bucket and a table available in Amazon Athena as we did in the `chapter03/1-prepare_data.ipynb` notebook.

Importing from S3

Please follow the next steps to import the CSV files into the S3 bucket. We want to load the `customer_info` and `account_info` tables:

1. From the view in *Figure 3.3*, select **Amazon S3** as the source. You should see a list of S3 buckets.

2. Locate the data following the path of the SageMaker default bucket that has the naming convention `sagemaker-<region>-<accountid>`. Then descend into the `sagemaker-studio-book/chapter03/data/` folder to find the CSV files.

3. Select `telco_churn_customer_info.csv` and inspect the data. Make sure the file type is CSV and **First row is header** is checked because our first row is indeed the header or variable names. **Enable sampling** can be left as the default in order to allow Data Wrangler to sample the data. Note that Data Wrangler is backed by an `ml.m5.4xlarge` instance with 16 vCPUs and 64 GiB of RAM. Sampling can be helpful to make sure the dataset fits into the memory when you have a large dataset. Click **Import**.

4. Repeat steps 1–3 for `telco_churn_account_info.csv`.

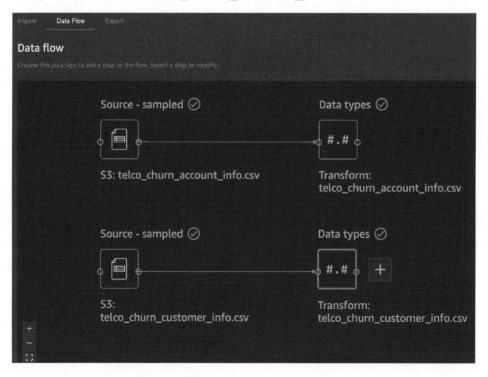

Figure 3.4 – Data flow after two CSV files are imported

Once the two CSV files are loaded, you should see the view in *Figure 3.4* in the **Data flow** tab. Now let's move onto the last table, `utility`.

Importing from Athena

As our `utility` table is being registered as an Amazon Athena table, we can import it from Athena with the following steps:

1. Click on the **Import** tab and select **Amazon Athena** as the source. You should see the view shown in *Figure 3.5*.

2. For the two drop-down options, select **AwsDataCatalog** for **Data catalog** and select **telco_db** for **Database**. And for **Advanced configuration**, you can check/uncheck **Enable sampling**. As shown in **Location of query results**, you can find the output of the query in the location.

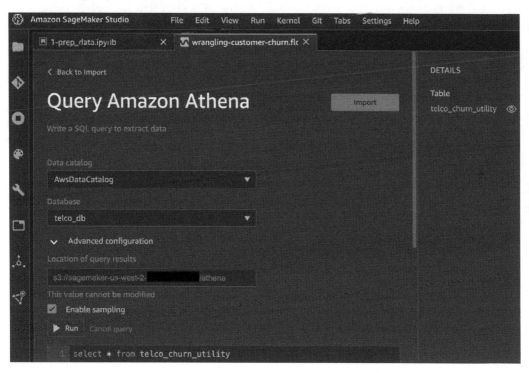

Figure 3.5 – Importing data from Amazon Athena

3. After you select the database, you will see the available tables on the right side in the **DETAILS** section, confirming that we have a `telco_churn_utility` table in our Amazon Athena database. You can click on the eye icon to preview the table so that we know how the table looks, as in *Figure 3.6*, and how to form a more complex query.

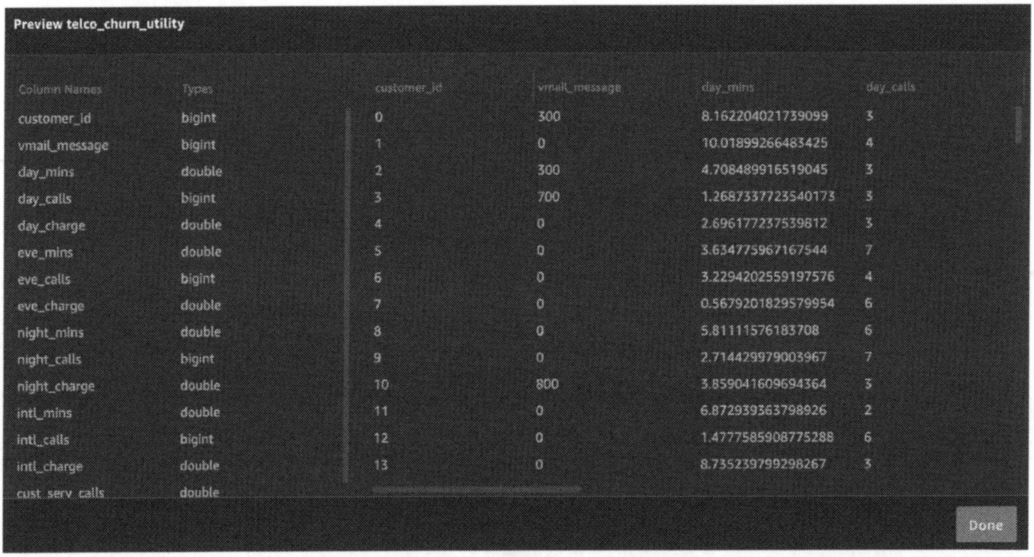

Figure 3.6 – Previewing the table

4. Let's get all the data through a query. Please put the following query statement into the query box. Then click **Run**:

```
select * from telco_churn_utility
```

5. You will find the query result below the query box. We get all the rows and columns with the previous statement. Inspect the data and click on the **Import** button at the top.

6. Provide a dataset name, such as `telco_churn_utility`.

You should see all three tables being loaded into the data flow in the **Data Flow** tab. By clicking on the plus sign when you hover over any of the rightmost nodes, you will see actions that you can perform on such tables, as shown in *Figure 3.7*.

Figure 3.7 – Actions after tables are imported

Next, we should check the data types, or the schema of the tables, to make sure that they are being inferred correctly during the import process.

Editing the data type

The data type dictates how each data column is read by Data Wrangler and how it should be processed. There are **Long**, **Float**, **Boolean**, **String**, and **Date** types in Data Wrangler. **Long** holds data that is in integer form. **Float** allows floating points in the data. **Boolean** represents binary values such as *0/1* and *Yes/No*. **String** makes the data a text-based entry. **Date** holds data that is in the form of text (*dd-MM-yyyy*) but is interpreted as a date instead of a string and allows date-related operations and comparison.

The types of transformation that can be applied to data depends on the data type. For example, you can only apply a numerical operation on columns of the Long and Float types. Therefore, it is important to get the data types correctly defined before proceeding even though Data Wrangler does infer data types while importing.

So, let's check and edit the data types of the imported tables in Data Wrangler:

1. From the view shown in *Figure 3.7*, click on the plus sign next to telco_churn_ account_info.csv and select **Edit data types**.

2. As shown in *Figure 3.8*, **Account Length**, which is all integers in the data, is inferred as the Float type. To avoid unnecessary floating and rounding issues, let's change it to the Long integer type. To change it, in **CONFIGURE TYPES** in the right panel, click on **Type** for the **Account Length** column, and select **Long**.

3. **Int'l Plan** and **VMail Plan** are inferred as String. But they should be of the Boolean type to conserve memory. Change them to Boolean by selecting Boolean in **CONFIGURE TYPES**.

4. Click **Preview** to see how the data looks after the data type change. See *Figure 3.8*.

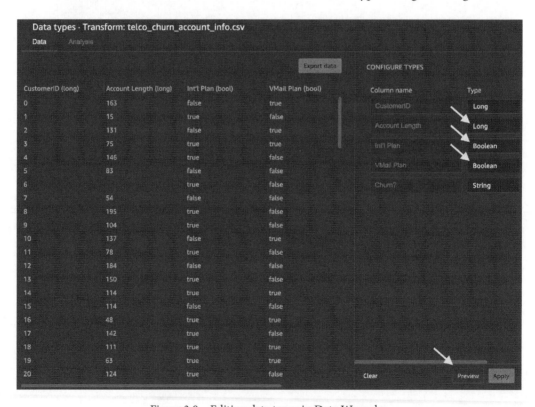

Figure 3.8 – Editing data types in Data Wrangler

We can see that **Account Length** is now of the **Long** type with integer values intact and that **Int'l Plan** and **Vmail Plan** are **Boolean** with yes/no converted to true/false, as shown in the table. Data type conversion does not result in data loss or anything so we can proceed to apply the edit.

5. Click **Apply** to apply the changes to the table.

> **Note**
>
> You can only make the change take effect if you first hit **Preview** then hit **Apply**.
>
> You may be wondering why we do not change the **Churn?** Column, which has True/False. in the column from `String` type to `Boolean` type. This is because the period, ., in the values would invalidate the conversion. You can try changing it and preview the change. You will see the whole column being erased. We will deal with this column with transformation later.

We've changed and confirmed the data type for the first table. We should do the same for the other two tables:

1. Click **Back to data flow** to return to the data flow.
2. Click on the plus sign next to `telco_churn_customer_info.csv` and select **Edit data types**.
3. Change **Area Code** from `Long` to `String`. Though this column has integer values, they should be treated as `locality` rather than numeric features.
4. Click **Preview**, then **Apply**.
5. Click **Back to data flow** to return to the data flow.
6. Click on the plus sign next to the last table, `telco_churn_utility`, then select **Edit data types**.
7. Change `cust_serv_calls` from `Float` to `Long`.
8. Click **Preview**, then **Apply**.
9. Click **Back to data flow** to return to the data flow.

We've verified and fixed the data type for the three tables. Now it is time to join them together as one table.

Joining tables

Joining tables is one of the most common steps when you are working with multiple data sources and the most important step to enrich your features when you are building an ML model. Think on relational database terms. Your tables maintain some sort of relationship that allows you to put them all together to get a big picture. We will be joining the three tables by `customerID` column with Data Wrangler. Please follow the next steps:

1. Click on the plus sign next to `telco_churn_account_info.csv` and select **Join**. You should see the view shown in *Figure 3.9*.

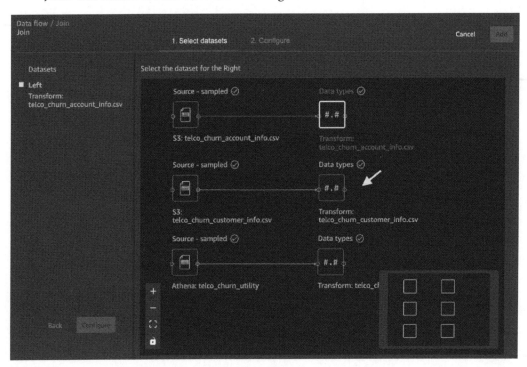

Figure 3.9 – Joining tables in SageMaker Data Wrangler

2. `telco_churn_account_info.csv` is chosen as **Left**. We can now choose the rightmost node of `telco_churn_customer_info.csv` as **Right**. You should see the linkage between the two tables, as shown in *Figure 3.10*.

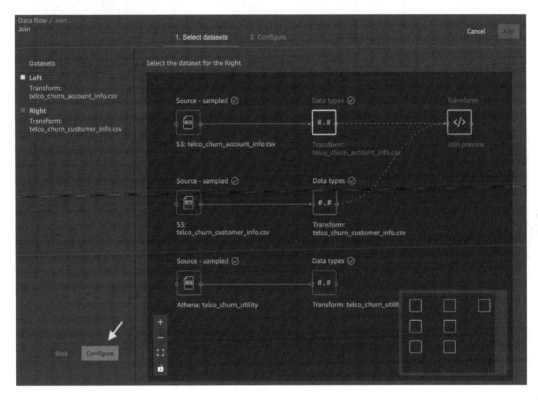

Figure 3.10 – Joining tables

3. Click **Configure** to continue.

4. As shown in *Figure 3.11*, select **Full outer** as the `join` type as we expect to get all the data in, then select **CustomerID** for both **Left** and **Right** as the key to join.

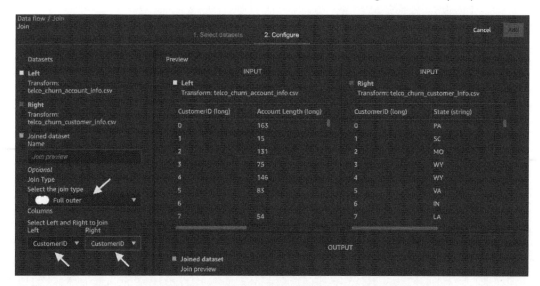

Figure 3.11 – Joining tables with Full outer and select keys

5. Click **Apply** to see the preview on the right, as shown in *Figure 3.12*. Notice that the data is successfully joined but with the joining key duplicated in the table: `CustomerID_0` and `CustomerID_1`. We will deal with this later in the *Applying transformation* section.

6. Click **Add** in the top right to complete the join.

7. Now we need to join the last table. Click on the plus sign next to the joined table and select **Join**.

8. Select `telco_churn_utility` as **Right**, then click **Configure**.

9. Again, select **Full outer** as the join type. Select `CustomerID_0` for **Left** and `customer_id` for **Right** to join.

10. Click **Apply** to preview the joined dataset. Yes, the tables are joined, but with the keys duplicated, which can be addressed later in the *Applying transformation* section. No worries.

11. Click **Add** in the top right to complete the join. You will be brought back to the data flow. You should see the flow, as shown in *Figure 3.12*.

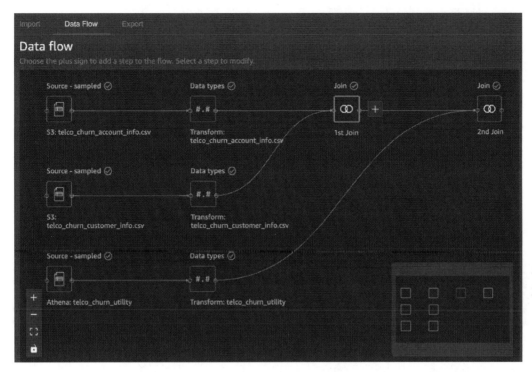

Figure 3.12 – Data flow after joining three tables

> **Note**
>
> If you find anything that was done wrong, don't worry, just click on the plus sign on the node that has the mistake and select **Delete** to remove the node. But do keep in mind that if you delete a node that is not the last node, all the downstream nodes will be deleted too.

We are ready to move on to the next phase: getting to explore the dataset!

Exploring data with visualization

Exploratory data analysis (**EDA**) provides insights into the data at hand and helps us strategize the data transformation so that ML modeling can be the most performant. Analyzing and visualizing data with programming is robust and scalable but it requires lots of coding and development. Using SageMaker Data Wrangler, you can easily create charts and figures in the UI. Currently, SageMaker Data Wrangler supports the following types of chart and analysis that do not require coding: **histogram**, **scatter plot**, **bias report**, **multicollinearity**, **quick model**, **target leakage**, and **table summary**. Let's take a look at how they work one by one.

Understanding the frequency distribution with a histogram

The histogram helps us understand the frequency distribution of a variable whose values are bucketed into discrete intervals with a bar graph. We can use the histogram function in SageMaker Data Wrangler to see, for example, how long callers spend making calls in the daytime. To do this, please follow these steps:

1. Click the plus sign next to the **2nd Join** node and select **Add analysis**. You should see the view shown in *Figure 3.13*.

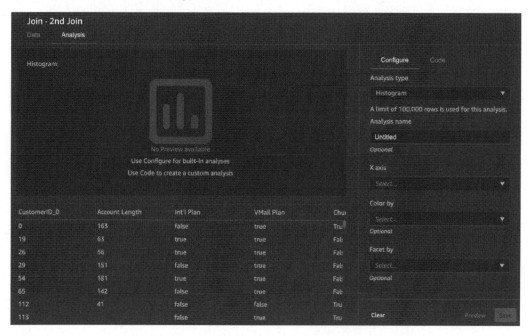

Figure 3.13 – Adding an analysis in SageMaker Data Wrangler

2. Fill in a name for the analysis in **Analysis name**, for example, day_mins_
    histogram.

3. Choose **day_mins** for **X axis**.

4. Click **Preview** to see the chart, as shown in *Figure 3.14*.

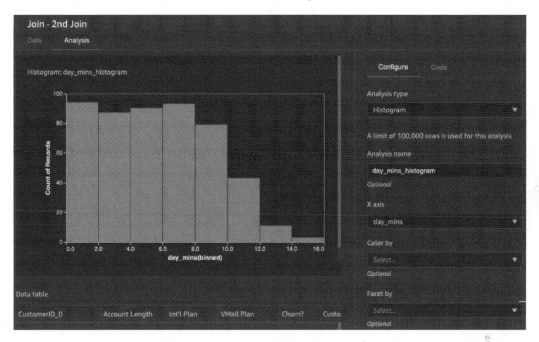

Figure 3.14 – Histogram of minutes of call time in the daytime

This is great! You created your first visualization in SageMaker Data Wrangler to
see the frequency distribution of call time in the daytime among all customers. We
see that most customers' calls are shorter than 8 minutes and few calls are longer
than 12 minutes. But this is an overall view. As a data scientist, you might want to
know how customers who left the service behave differently from the customers
who continue to use the service. We should slice and dice the data based on the
target status: **Churn?**. We can do it through the **Facet by** option. We will proceed to
modify the chart and not save the current chart.

5.   Choose **Churn?** for **Facet by** and click **Preview**. You should see an updated chart, as in *Figure 3.15*.

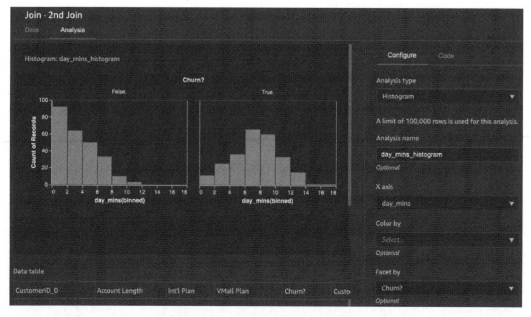

Figure 3.15 – Histogram of the day_mins variable by target

We can conclude that customers who left the service (the **True.** chart) most frequently make calls for around 6-10 minutes while the customers who stayed with the service (the **False.** chart) talk less on calls. What an interesting observation. Let's save the analysis.

6.   Click **Save** to save and return to the page where all analyses are saved.

In the **All Analyses** view, you can see charts and analyses you created for each node at any given state. We have created a histogram. Let's go on to create another chart.

Scatter plots

A data scientist might be wondering if customers who call more in the daytime also call often in the evening. Or you might be curious if any correlation exists between the customer's account length and call time. You can use a **scatter plot** to visualize this characteristic. Let's create a scatter plot for the data:

1.   On the **Analysis** page, click **Create new analysis** at the top right.

2.   Choose **Scatter Plot** for **Analysis type**. Provide a name for the analysis, such as AccountLength_CallTime_Scatter.

3. Choose **Account Length** for **X axis** and **day_mins** for **Y axis**.

4. Click **Preview**. You should see a chart, as shown in *Figure 3.16*.

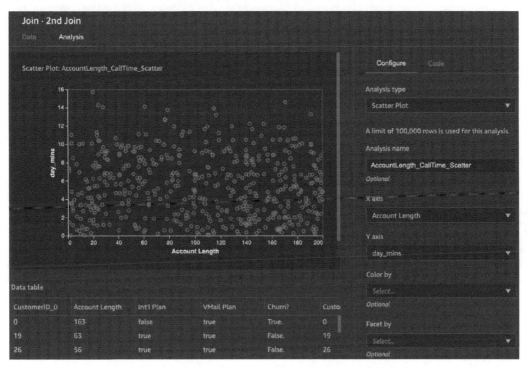

Figure 3.16 – Scatter plot of Account Length versus day_mins

There does not seem to be any correlation visually between the two variables.

Histograms and scatter plots are the two most common tools for EDA that you probably are familiar with. With SageMaker Data Wrangler, you can use ML-oriented analyses such as Quick Model to help you determine your data transformation strategy.

Previewing ML model performance with Quick Model

Quick Model is another tool that helps you quickly get a sense of whether your data provides any predictive power with the variables presented in the data. This tool is useful and can be used frequently. Let's see how it works:

1. On the **Analysis** page, click **Create new analysis** in the top right.

2. Choose **Quick Model** for **Analysis type**.

3.   Add a name in **Analysis name**, such as `first_quickmodel`.

4.   Choose **Churn?** for **Label** and click **Preview**.

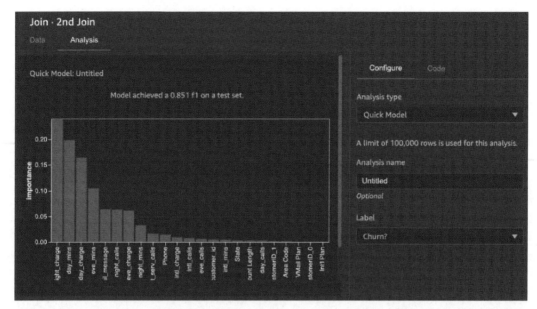

Figure 3.17 – Quick Model result that shows the F1 score of the model performance on a test set and feature importance

SageMaker Data Wrangler takes a minute or so and returns a bar chart, as shown in *Figure 3.17*, showing the feature importance and an F1 score on a randomly split test set from the given dataset. We have not applied any transformation or data cleaning, as you can see in the following data table. SageMaker Data Wrangler employs a popular algorithm called **random forest classification** to train a model and test it out on a hold-out test set. We can see a preliminary result of a 0.851 F1 score, with **night_charge** being the most important feature in predicting customer churn status. We can also see that there are features that do not provide much predictive power, such as **Int'l Plan** and **VMail Plan**. And there are redundant features such as **CustomerID_*** that should not have been included in the modeling. This gives us hints to make sure to include **night_charge** and other high-importance features in the actual modeling and that we can leave out **Int'l Plan** and **VMail Plan** if we are restricted by the number of features we can use. Let's ink the analysis on the paper.

5.   Click **Save** to save the analysis.

As we just did our first quick modeling, to get a sense of the model performance we are getting, it is also a good idea to test whether we are running into any data leakage or target leakage problems.

Revealing target leakage

Target leakage means that there are features in the data that are highly correlated or basically a proxy representation of the target variable. For example, if our dataset contains a column that records the date of termination for each churned customer, then this column is going to contain those who churned, resulting in an extremely high modeling accuracy if we include it in the modeling. The problem in this example is that come prediction time in the real world, it is very unlikely to have the date of termination when the job of the model is to predict future churn. Let's see if our dataset contains any target leakage:

1. On the **Analysis** page, click **Create new analysis** in the top right.

2. Choose **Target Leakage** for **Analysis type**.

3. Add a name in **Analysis name**, such as churn_target_leakage.

4. Input 25 for **Max features** because we have 24 columns in the table.

5. Choose **classification** for **Problem Type**.

6. Choose **Churn?** for **Target** and click **Preview**.

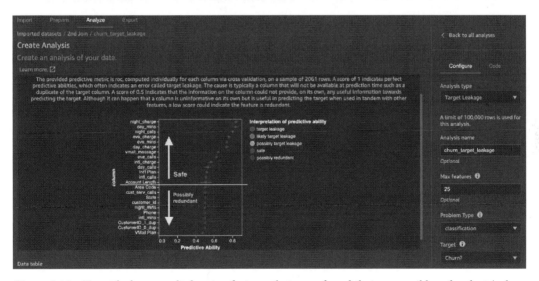

Figure 3.18 – Target leakage result showing features that are safe and that are possibly redundant (color-coded with a legend to the right of the chart)

The target leakage analysis computes the cross-validated area under the ROC for each individual feature against the target, as explained in the text above the chart in *Figure 3.18*. This analysis shows that no feature is determined as potential target leakage, which is a good sign. The result also confirms the conclusions we learned from the quick modeling exercise:

a) `night_charge` is important in predicting churn and provides a high level of predictive ability.

b) `VMail Plan` is providing little predictive ability.

c) `CustomerID_*` is redundant in the dataset.

Let's save the analysis.

7. Click **Save** to save the analysis.

We learned about feature predictive power through the last two analyses. We should also take a look at how we can create a custom visualization with SageMaker Data Wrangler.

Creating custom visualizations

SageMaker Data Wrangler uses **Altair** (https://altair-viz.github.io/) to create visualizations programmatically. We can create any custom visualization with code in SageMaker Data Wrangler as well for greater flexibility. For example, we can create a boxplot for **night_charge** by **Churn?** status to understand the statistical distribution of the two groups:

1. On the **All Analyses** page, click **Create new analysis** in the top right.
2. Click the **Code** tab right next to **Configure**.
3. Add a name, such as `boxplot_night_charge_by_churn`.
4. Input the following code in the coding area. Be sure to import the `altair` library:

```
# Table is available as variable 'df' of pandas dataframe
# Output Altair chart is available as variable 'chart'
import altair as alt
chart=alt.Chart(df).mark_boxplot().encode(
    x='Churn?',
    y='night_charge')
```

5. Click **Preview**.

You should see a box plot representing the distribution of **night_charge** by Churn? status, as shown in *Figure 3.19*. If you hover over the box plot, you can see the descriptive statistics of the data.

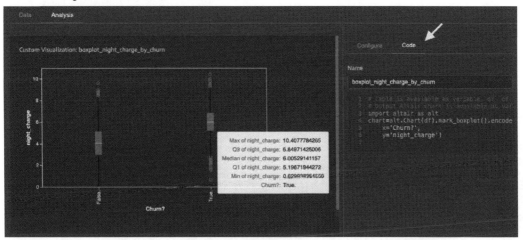

Figure 3.19 – Creating a custom boxplot using the Altair library

6. Click **Save** to save the custom visualization.

What's worth noting is that these analyses and visualizations are saved as part of the flow file so that you can have full visibility of how you wrangle the data.

With these analyses, we now have a good understanding of how we should transform and wrangle the data.

Applying transformation

You can easily apply data transformation using SageMaker Data Wrangler because there are numerous built-in transformations you can use out of the box without any coding. So far, we have observed the following from the analyses that we need to handle next in order to build up an ML dataset:

- Missing data in some features.
- The Churn? column is now in string format with True. and False. as values.
- Redundant CustomerID_* columns after joins.

- Features that are not providing predictive power, including but not limited to `Phone`, `VMail Plan`, and `Int'l Plan`.

  We also would like to perform the following transformations for ML purposes because we want to train an XGBoost model to predict the `Churn?` status afterwards.

- Encoding categorical variables, that is, `State` and `Area Code` features.

Let's get started:

1. In the **Data Flow** tab, click on the plus sign next to the **2nd Join** node, and select **Add transform**. You should see the view shown in *Figure 3.20,* with a table on the left and a list of transformations on the right.

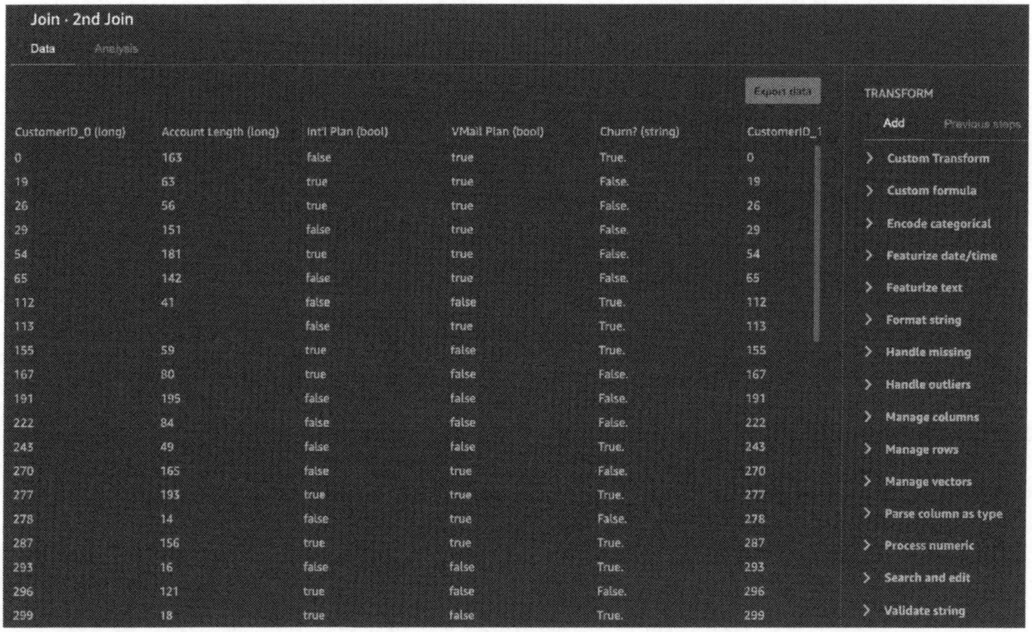

Figure 3.20 – A workspace to transform your data. You can expand each transform on the right side to see options

2. To drop **CustomerID_***, click **Manage columns** to expand the transform, select **Drop column** in **Transform**, and select **CustomerID_0** for **Column to drop**.

3. Click **Preview** to see the effect. CustomerID_0 is now gone, as shown in *Figure 3.21*.

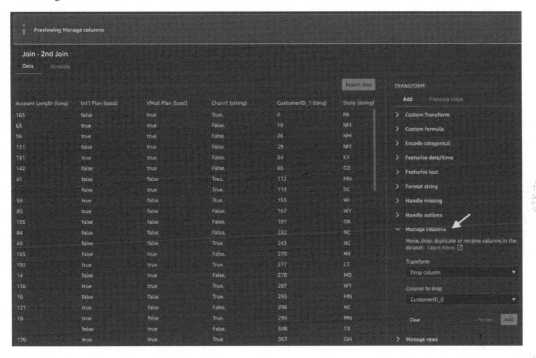

Figure 3.21 – Dropping columns in SageMaker Data Wrangler

4. Click **Add** to put the transformation into effect.

5. Repeat steps 2–4 to drop `CustomerID_1` and `customer_id`.

    If done correctly, you should see four steps applied on the **Previous steps** tab to the right, as shown in *Figure 3.22*.

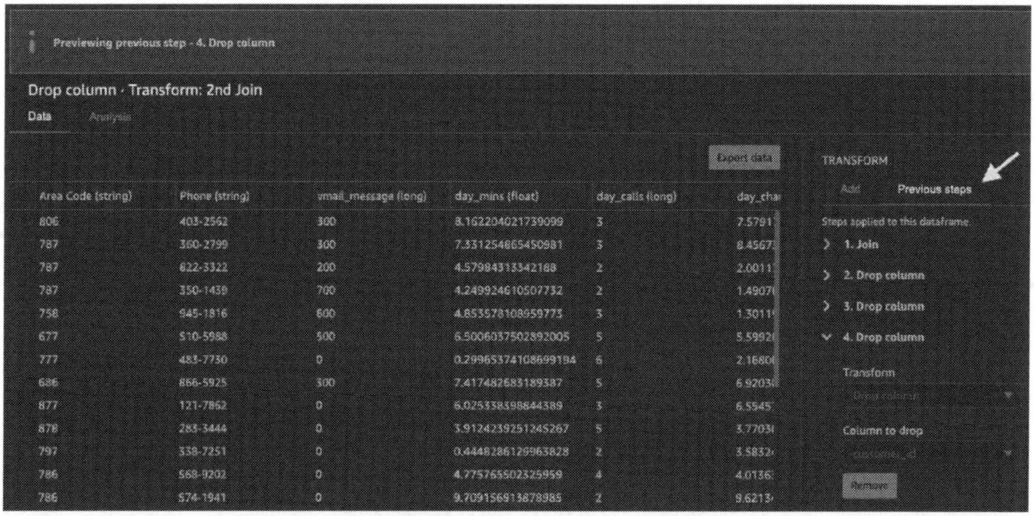

Figure 3.22 – Reviewing previous steps in the Previous steps tab

> **Note**
>
> If you realize you did anything incorrectly and want to revert to a previous transformation, you can **Remove** steps from the last one, one at a time, as shown in *Figure 3.22*.

6. Moving on to handling missing data in **Account Length** and `cust_serv_calls`, expand **Handle missing** in the transform list, select **Impute** for **Transform**, **Numeric** for **Column type**, `Account Length` for **Input column**, and **Approximate Median** for **Imputing strategy**. We can leave **Output column** empty to instruct SageMaker Data Wrangler to overwrite the existing column.

7. Click **Preview**. You should see that a missing cell in the **Account Length** column is filled with the value `102`, as shown in *Figure 3.23*.

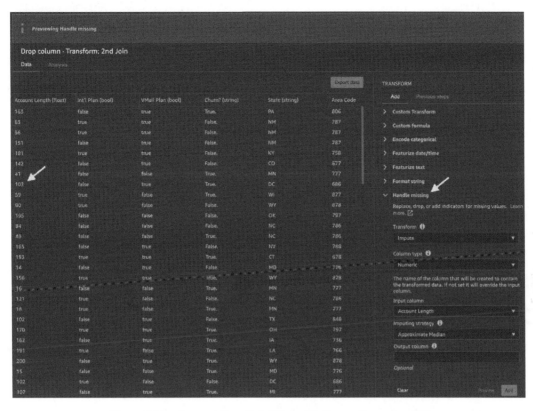

Figure 3.23 – Account Length is filled with the median value, 102

8. Click **Add** to put the transformation into effect.

9. Repeat steps 6–8 for `cust_serv_calls`.

There are features that do not provide much predictive capability based on the quick model and target leakage analyses worth dropping too. `Phone` is one of the features that is shown to contain little to no useful information. Also, as is common knowledge, we know phone numbers are mostly randomly assigned when you sign up for a service. On the other hand, even though `VMail Plan` and `Int'l Plan` provide no predictive information, they are of the simple `Boolean` type and do have real meaning. It might not hurt as much to carry these features into modeling. So, let's drop the `Phone` feature.

10. Repeat steps 2–4 to drop `Phone`.

Moving on to transforming categorical features, we have `State` and `Area Code`, which represent the location of a customer. We could apply one-hot encoding to transform them. However, we may risk the **curse of dimensionality** if one-hot encoding both features could result in too many features. Also, there is a limit of 1,000 columns allowed in SageMaker Data Wrangler. If we are not encoding `Area Code`, the next best action would be to drop it. Let's perform one-hot encoding to `State` and drop `Area Code`.

11. Expand **Encode categorical**, choose **One-hot encode** for **Transform**, select **State** for **Input column**, select **Columns** for **Output style**, and leave other options as their defaults.

12. Click **Preview** to see the transformation. You should see the `State` column is replaced with `State_*` sparse features, with each representing whether customers are of a particular state (0 for false and 1 for true).

13. Click **Add** to put the transformation into effect.

14. Repeat steps 2–4 to drop `Area Code`.

Last but not least, the target feature, `Churn?`, needs some wrangling. It has a weird period that messed up the data type conversion previously. Furthermore, the SageMaker built-in XGBoost algorithm we are going to use for modeling later requires the target feature to be in the first column. Let's apply a text operation and move the column.

15. Expand **Format string**, choose **Remove symbols** for **Transform**, select `Churn?` for **Input column**, and input . (a period) for **Symbols**.

16. Click **Preview** to see the transformation. Now the ending period in `Churn?` has been removed, as shown in *Figure 3.24*. Click **Add** to put the transformation into effect.

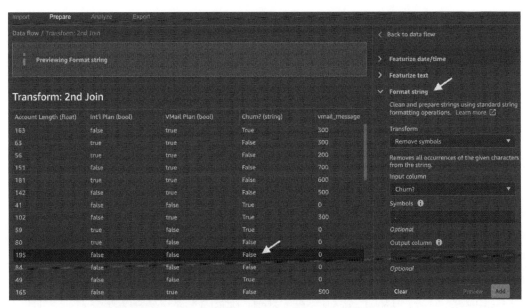

Figure 3.24 – Ending period removed in the Churn? column

17. We can now use the data type parser to convert the True/False into a Boolean representation. Expand **Parse column as type**, choose **Churn?** for **Column**, and select **Boolean** in the **To** drop-down menu.

18. Click **Preview** to see the transformation. Now the **Churn?** column is of the `Boolean` type. Click **Add** to put the transformation into effect.

19. To move **Churn?** to the front, expand **Manage columns**, select **Move column** for **Transform**, select **Move to start** for **Move type**, and choose **Churn?** for **Column to move**.

20. Click **Preview** to see the transformation. Now the **Churn?** column becomes the first feature. Click **Add** to put the transformation into effect.

We've just applied eleven transformations to the dataset. We can run a quick modeling analysis to make sure we are on the right track in terms of modeling.

Exploring performance while wrangling

You can always add an analysis at any point in time while wrangling the data in SageMaker Data Wrangler. This allows you to analyze the data after key transformation and verify the predictive power with Quick Model. Let's add an analysis for the wrangled data:

1. Click the **Analysis** tab.

2. Choose **Quick Model** for **Analysis type**, add a name in **Analysis name**, and select **Churn?** for **Label**.

3. Click **Preview** to see the modeling result, as shown in *Figure 3.25*. The model's F1 score has improved from *0.851* to *0.871*. We are on the right track.

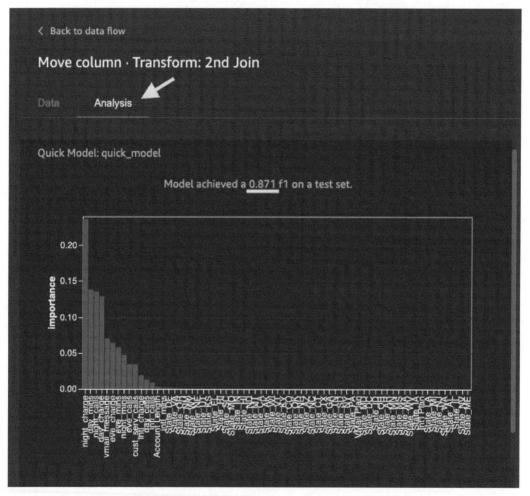

Figure 3.25 – Quick modeling after all transformations

4. Click **Add** to put the analysis on the canvas.

So far, we have used SageMaker Data Wrangler to analyze the telco churn dataset in depth and wrangled the data according to the findings from the analyses. Quick Model is showing an improved F1 score in predicting customer churn. We should move on to see what options we have with this work.

Exporting data for ML training

SageMaker Data Wrangler supports the following export options: **Save to S3**, **Pipeline**, **Python Code**, and **Feature Store**. The data transformations we have applied so far are not really applied to the data yet. The transformation steps need to be executed to get the final transformed data. When we export our flow file with the preceding options, SageMaker Data Wrangler automatically generates code and notebooks to guide you through the execution process so that we do not have to write any code, but it leaves flexibility for us to customize the code.

The four export options satisfy many use cases. **Save to S3** is an obvious one and offers lots of flexibility. If you would like to get the transformed data in an S3 bucket so that you can train an ML model in Amazon SageMaker, you can also download it locally from S3 and import it to other tools if you need to. The **Pipeline** option creates a SageMaker pipeline that can easily be called a repeatable workflow. Such workflows can be configured as event-triggered or time-triggered so that you can automate the data transformation as a pipeline. We will learn more about SageMaker Pipelines in *Chapter 10, Monitoring ML Models in Production with SageMaker Model Monitor*. **Python Code** offers the most visibility and flexibility. You can see how each transformation is implemented by Amazon SageMaker, run the code in a Spark environment, and get the data processed. With the **Feature Store** option, you get an automatically generated Jupyter notebook that will process the data and create a feature group in SageMaker Feature Store. We will learn more about SageMaker Feature Store in *Chapter 5, Building and Training ML Models with SageMaker Studio IDE*.

For this example, I'd like to show you the option **Save to S3**, which includes ML training in the automatically generated notebook:

1. First, save the flow file so that the exported resource will pick up the latest change. In the menu bar, select **File->Save Data Wrangler Flow**.

2. Click on the **Export** tab, click the **Steps** node, and select the last step, **Move column**, in the list of transformations. By clicking a step, all the steps leading to the step chosen will be selected.

3. Click **Export step** in the top right, and click **Save to S3**.

    A new Python Jupyter notebook should pop out. This notebook contains code to process the SageMaker Data Wrangler flow file using SageMaker Processing and to save the processed data in S3. This is our first encounter with SageMaker Processing in action. In short, it allows us to use appropriate compute resources to perform data processing, model evaluation, and statistical analysis. With SageMaker Processing, you are no longer bound by the compute resource available locally in the Studio notebook environment; instead, the processing script and Data Wrangler flow file can be run on a right-size compute instance(s). You can see things in action in the following steps.

4. Please execute all the cells before **(Optional) Next Steps** section.

    > **Note**
    >
    > You may configure the notebook in the section where you see 💡 **Configurable Settings**.

    The SageMaker Processing job may take a couple of minutes. At the end of the processing job, the processed data is available in an S3 bucket. You should see the following output from the cell:

    ```
    Job results are saved to S3 path: s3://sagemaker-us-west-
    2-<account-id>/export-flow-04-01-52-59-xxxxxx/output/
    data-wrangler-flow-processing-04-01-52-59-xxxxxx
    ```

    The following optional sections are the interesting modeling part. Let's run these steps to train an ML model to predict churn using SageMaker's built-in XGBoost algorithm.

5. Reassign the value of `run_optional_steps` to `True`:

    ```
    run_optional_steps = True
    ```

6. The default objective metric, `reg:squarederror`, for XGBoost is for regression use cases. Change it to `binary:logistic` because we have a binary classification use case:

```
hyperparameters = {
    "max_depth":"5",
    "objective": "binary:logistic",
    "num_round": "10",
}
```

7. Execute all the remaining cells in the notebook to start a training job.

The training job will take a minute or two to finish. You can see the actions behind the scenes printed out as output in the last cell. We will learn more about SageMaker training and training algorithms in *Chapter 5, Building and Training ML Models with SageMaker Studio IDE*. Once finished, the model is saved in S3 as well, which can be used in hosting in Amazon SageMaker or the model can be used locally. We will learn more about hosting options in *Chapter 7, Hosting ML Models in the Cloud: Best Practices*

Summary

In this chapter, we showed how to use SageMaker Data Wrangler using a telco customer churn dataset. We learned how to import data from various sources, join tables, analyze with advanced ML-based analyses, and create visualizations with SageMaker Data Wrangler. We then applied transformations easily with built-in transforms available out of the box from SageMaker Data Wrangler without any code. At the end of the chapter, we showed how to export the transformed data to an S3 bucket and how to easily train an ML model using the automatically generated notebook.

In the next chapter, we will learn about the concept of a feature store in a machine learning project, and how to set up a feature store using **SageMaker Feature Store**. SageMaker Feature Store unifies the features across teams so that teams can remove redundant feature engineering pipelines. It also serves as a central repository for both model training and model serving use cases because of its unique design pattern to have an offline store for easy querying for selecting training datasets and an online store for low latency transactions required in the model serving environment.

4
Building a Feature Repository with SageMaker Feature Store

A feature store allows you to store features for **machine learning** (**ML**) training and inference. It serves as a central repository for teams collaborating on ML use cases to prevent duplicating and confusing efforts when creating features. Amazon SageMaker Feature Store makes storing and accessing training and inference data in the cloud easier, faster, and reproducible. With a SageMaker Feature Store instance built for your ML life cycle, you will be able to manage features, which are always evolving, and use them for training and inference with the confidence that you are using the right ones. You will also be able to collaborate with your colleagues more effectively by having a single source of truth when it comes to ML features.

In this chapter, we will be covering the following topics:

- Understanding the concept of a feature store
- Getting started with SageMaker Feature Store
- Accessing features from SageMaker Feature Store

Technical requirements

For this chapter, you need to access the code in `https://github.com/ PacktPublishing/Getting-Started-with-Amazon-SageMaker-Studio/ tree/main/chapter04`. You need to make sure your IAM execution role has the `AmazonSageMakerFeatureStoreAccess` policy.

Understanding the concept of a feature store

Consider the following scenario: you are a data scientist working on an ML project in the automotive industry with a fellow data scientist and a few data engineers. You are responsible for modeling vehicle fuel efficiency, while your fellow data scientist is responsible for modeling vehicle performance. Both of you are using data coming from car manufacturers that your company is working with that is preprocessed and stored in the cloud by the data engineers in the team as input to the models.

The data is stored in disparate sources, such as Amazon S3, Amazon **Relational Database Service** (**RDS**), and a data lake built on AWS, depending on the nature of the source data. You and your fellow data scientist have been reaching out separately to the data engineering team to get the data processed in certain ways that work best for your respective modeling exercises. You do not realize that your fellow data scientist's models actually share some common features, but a new set of features is created and maintained in both of your workspaces.

As the project goes on, the data engineering team is reporting that it has become a challenge to manage the constantly growing data and feature footprint. It is also cumbersome for you to track versions of features when there is a change in the data processing pipeline and/or the car manufacturers amend and update the catalogs. You find yourself in a constant struggle keeping track of what models are trained with what set or versions of features from a multitude of tables and files for your code and notebooks.

Here's a summary of the challenges that the team is facing:

- Data and features are not centrally stored, even though there is a central data engineering team.

- The data scientists do not have visibility and knowledge of features that are created and used by each other; therefore, the default is to create your own.

- Consequently, data and features are duplicated, burdening the data engineering team.

- An update to the feature means another copy of data that someone needs to manage.

- Model and data lineage are difficult to maintain over the iteration of the ML life cycle.

A feature store is a relatively new concept in an ML life cycle that is purposefully designed to address the challenges observed in the preceding scenario. The goal of a feature store is to have a centralized store *for all features, for all models, for training and inference,* and *for all times. For all features* means that we want to have features from various sources to funnel into one central place and to be able to find them easily. *For all models* means that we want teams building various models to use the features from only one central place. *For training and inference* means that we want to retrieve the same features for training and for hosting purposes while meeting different runtime requirements in training and inference applications. *For all times* means that we want to keep versions of features for their entire lifetime, regardless of updates and changes in one single feature store, so that data scientists can access different versions of the features for different time slices.

Let's look at the key components and concepts in SageMaker Feature Store that make it possible.

Understanding an online store

An online store is a feature storage option in SageMaker Feature Store that is designed to stay *online* at all times. *Online* means that the store should behave like an online application, one that responds to data read/write access requests immediately. *Immediately* can be subjective, but in technical terms, it means low response latency so that users do not feel the lapse. In addition to low latency, another aspect that makes the online store "online" is the high throughput of transactions that it can serve at the same time. Imagine hundreds of thousands of users visiting your application; you do not want to disappoint your awesome customers. You want your online application to be capable of handling traffic with high throughput and low latency.

Why do we need an online store that has low latency? In many ML use cases, the ML inference needs to respond to a user's action on the system *immediately* to provide the inference results back to the user. The inference process typically includes querying features for a particular data point and sending the features as a payload to the ML model. For example, an auto insurance online quote application has an ML model that takes a driver's information to predict their risk level and suggest a quote. This application needs to pull vehicle-related features from a feature store based on the car make provided by the user. You'd expect a modern application to return a quote immediately. Therefore, an ideal architecture should keep the latency of both pulling features from a feature store and making an ML inference low. We can't have a system where the ML model responds immediately but takes seconds or minutes to gather features from various databases and locations.

Understanding an offline store

An offline store in SageMaker Feature Store is designed to provide much more versatile functionality by keeping all the records over time for use. You will be able to access features at any given condition and time for a variety of use cases. But this comes at the cost of higher-latency response times for requests to an offline store, because the offline store uses slower and less expensive storage.

An offline store complements the online store for ML use cases where low latency isn't a requirement. For example, when building an ML training dataset to reproduce a particular model for compliance purposes, you need to access historic features in order to build a model that was created in the past. ML training is typically not expected to complete within seconds anyway, so you don't necessarily need sub-second performance when querying a feature store for training data.

Now that we've got a good understanding of the key components and concepts in SageMaker Feature Store, let's get hands-on with a use case.

Getting started with SageMaker Feature Store

Following the scenario we described earlier, we are a data science team in a company in the automotive industry. We are working on a fuel efficiency dataset to create ML models. Let's use an Auto MPG dataset from UCI (`https://archive.ics.uci.edu/ml/datasets/Auto+MPG`), which is a collection of vehicle data and fuel efficiency (measured by miles per gallon) by make from 1970 to 1982, to demonstrate the following:

- How to ingest features into a feature store
- How to access features from an online store and an offline store

- How to update the features year over year and access features using versioning (time travel)

As a prerequisite, please navigate to the code repository and open the `chapter04/01-sagemaker_feature_store.ipynb` notebook. First, execute the notebook until the following code to read the data from the source into a pandas DataFrame:

```
data_url='https://archive.ics.uci.edu/ml/machine-learning-databases/auto-mpg/auto-mpg.data'
col_names=['mpg','cylinders', 'displacement', 'horsepower', 'weight', 'acceleration', 'model_year', 'origin', 'car_name']
df=pd.read_csv(data_url, delimiter='\s+', header=None, names=col_names, na_values='?')
df['car_name']=df['car_name'].astype('string')
```

Additionally, we convert the data type to `string` for the `car_name` column, which is required by SageMaker Feature Store. We will describe what this means later in the *Creating a feature group* section.

We are going to split the DataFrames by year in order to later ingest them to simulate the feature updates over the years. Therefore, it is easier to convert the type for one DataFrame now. The following cell creates a dictionary to hold DataFrames by year and adds a new `event_time` column to encode the time of feature creation. We simulate it by adding a Unix epoch time at 8:00 am on January 1 in each respective year using Python's `datetime` library:

```
d_df = {}
for yr in df['model_year'].unique():
    print(yr)
    d_df[str(yr)]=df[df['model_year']==yr]
    d_df[str(yr)]['event_time']=datetime.datetime(1900+yr, 1, 1, 8, 0, 0).timestamp()
```

> **Important Note**
> A feature that denotes event time, `event_time` in this example, is required for any feature table that goes into a feature group in SageMaker Feature Store. This allows us to perform time travel and versioning of the features by time.

Next, we will start interacting with SageMaker Feature Store.

Creating a feature group

A **feature group** in SageMaker Feature Store defines the metadata, feature definition, unique identifier for the data entries, and other SageMaker Feature Store configurations.

There are two ways to create a feature group – using the SageMaker Python SDK or the Studio UI.

By following these steps (also in the notebook), we can create a feature group in SageMaker Feature Store using the SageMaker Python SDK:

1. Firstly, we create a SageMaker feature group named `auto-mpg-<timestamp>` with the `FeatureGroup` class:

    ```
    from sagemaker.feature_store.feature_group import
    FeatureGroup

    feature_group = FeatureGroup(name=feature_group_name,
    sagemaker_session=sess)
    ```

2. Next, we need to make the SageMaker feature group aware of the data schema and definition. `feature_group.load_feature_definitions()` is an API to load the schema and definition from a pandas DataFrame. The API automatically detects the data type. We also need to make sure that the features in the DataFrame are configured to have the data types supported by SageMaker Feature Store.

    > **Important Note**
    >
    > The data types supported by SageMaker Feature Store are **string**, **fractional**, and **integral**. A pandas DataFrame infers a `data` column with strings as the `object` type for backward-compatibility reasons. With pandas 1.0 onwards, you can explicitly request to use the `string` type for columns containing strings. SageMaker Feature Store works with the `string` type from pandas, not the `object` type. The acceptable data type for the `event_time` column is either `string` or `fractional`. For the `string` type, event time has to be in the ISO-8601 format in UTC time with the *yyyy-MM-dd'T'HH:mm:ssZ* or *yyyy-MM-dd'T'HH:mm:ss.SSSZ* patterns. For the `fractional` type, the values are expected to be in seconds from Unix epoch time with millisecond precision. In our example, we used Unix epoch time returned by the `datetime` library.

We load the feature definition from the first DataFrame. You will see the definition and data types loaded into `feature_group` in the output:

```
feature_group.load_feature_definitions(data_frame=d_
df['70'])
```

```
[FeatureDefinition(feature_name='mpg', feature_
type=<FeatureTypeEnum.FRACTIONAL: 'Fractional'>),
```

```
 FeatureDefinition(feature_name='cylinders', feature_
type=<FeatureTypeEnum.INTEGRAL: 'Integral'>),
```

```
 FeatureDefinition(feature_name='displacement', feature_
type=<FeatureTypeEnum.FRACTIONAL: 'Fractional'>),
```

```
 FeatureDefinition(feature_name='horsepower', feature_
type=<FeatureTypeEnum.FRACTIONAL: 'Fractional'>),
```

```
 FeatureDefinition(feature_name='weight', feature_
type=<FeatureTypeEnum.FRACTIONAL: 'Fractional'>),
```

```
 FeatureDefinition(feature_name='acceleration', feature_
type=<FeatureTypeEnum.FRACTIONAL: 'Fractional'>),
```

```
 FeatureDefinition(feature_name='model_year', feature_
type=<FeatureTypeEnum.INTEGRAL: 'Integral'>),
```

```
 FeatureDefinition(feature_name='origin', feature_
type=<FeatureTypeEnum.INTEGRAL: 'Integral'>),
```

```
 FeatureDefinition(feature_name='car_name', feature_
type=<FeatureTypeEnum.STRING: 'String'>),
```

```
 FeatureDefinition(feature_name='event_time', feature_
type=<FeatureTypeEnum.FRACTIONAL: 'Fractional'>)]
```

3. After the definition is loaded, we can create `feature group` in the system:

```
record_identifier_feature_name = 'car_name'
event_time_feature_name = 'event_time'
feature_group.create(
    s3_uri=f's3://{bucket}/{prefix}',
    record_identifier_name=record_identifier_feature_
name,
    event_time_feature_name=event_time_feature_name,
    role_arn=role,
    enable_online_store=True,
    description=description
)
```

In the create() function, the following is configured for the feature group:

- We specify an S3 bucket location to the s3_uri argument to indicate that we want to set up an offline store at this location for the feature group. We could set it to False to disable the offline store.

- We set enable_online_store to True to create an online store for the feature group. Set it to False if you do not need an online store and avoid unnecessary charges.

- We indicate that the record identifier is the car_name column and the event_time feature is the event_time column in the feature group.

This creation is an asynchronous operation and takes a couple of seconds. The check_feature_group_status() function in the next cell checks the status every 5 seconds and returns the cell once the feature group is created successfully. You can also see a list of feature groups in the Studio UI in the **SageMaker component and registry** tab in the left sidebar, as shown in *Figure 4.1*. If you click on the feature group in the list, you can see all the information associated with the feature group, a description, a feature definition, and example queries:

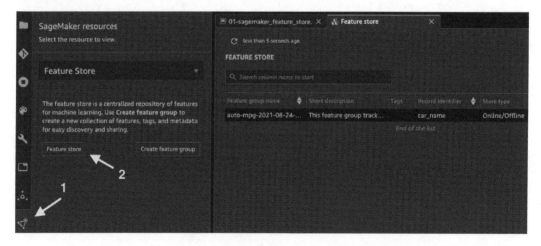

Figure 4.1 – Viewing the feature group in the SageMaker Studio UI

Alternatively, you can also create a feature group from the UI. Because we have the data already in a pandas DataFrame, it was straightforward to load the definition using the SDK. The following steps demonstrate how to create a feature group in Studio UI:

1. Click on **Create feature group**, as shown in *Figure 4.1*.

2. In the first step, as shown in *Figure 4.2*, enter the feature group name, a description, and configurations for the online and offline stores. For the offline store, we put in an S3 bucket location to store the offline store data and an IAM Role ARN that has permission to access the bucket. In this example, we will use the SageMaker execution role that is also attached to the SageMaker Studio user profile. You can see the full ARN from the `role` variable in the notebook. For the **DATA CATALOG** options, let's check the **Auto create AWS Glue table** box and either have SageMaker assign names in the three fields or assign names ourselves. Click **Continue**:

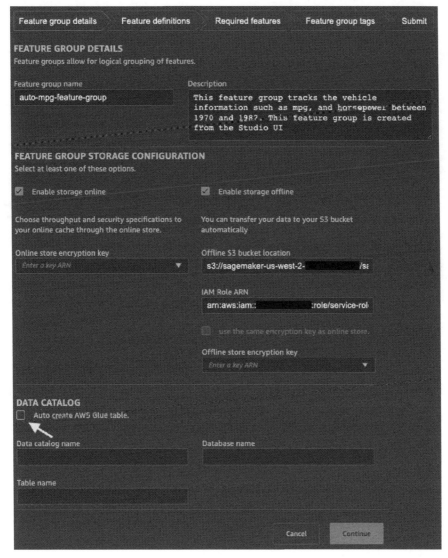

Figure 4.2 – Configuring a feature group in the Studio UI

3. In the second step, we need to create the feature definition. We can use **JSON editor** to paste in definition in bulk, as shown in *Figure 4.3:*

| Feature group details | Feature definitions | Required features | Feature group tags | Submit |

FEATURE DEFINITIONS

Choose unique names and data types for each feature in your group. You can add up to 2500 feature definitions. Definitions can be added in JSON or entered in a table.

JSON editor   Table

```
 1  [
 2      {
 3          "FeatureName": "mpg",
 4          "FeatureType": "Fractional"
 5      },
 6      {
 7          "FeatureName": "car_name",
 8          "FeatureType": "String"
 9      },
10      {
11          "FeatureName": "cylinders",
12          "FeatureType": "Integral"
13      },
14      {
15          "FeatureName": "horsepower",
16          "FeatureType": "Fractional"
17      }
18  ]
```

Figure 4.3 – Editing the feature definitions in JSON editor

4. Or we can use the **Table** tab to edit the feature with an easy-to-use drop-down list, as shown in *Figure 4.4*. Click **Continue** once you've finished:

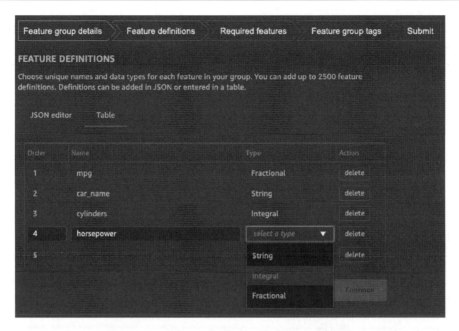

Figure 4.4 – Editing the feature definitions in Table

5. In the third step, as shown in *Figure 4.5*, we need to choose a feature to be a record identifier (car_name) and another feature to identify event time (event_time). Click **Continue** to proceed:

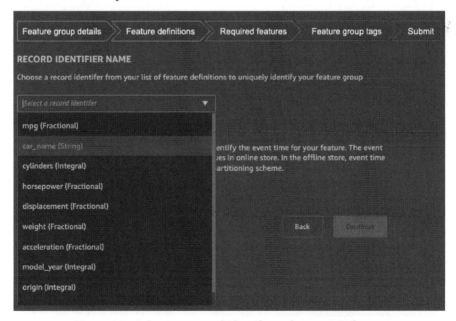

Figure 4.5 – Selecting a record identifier and event time feature

6. Then, we can optionally add tags to the feature group. Click **Create feature group** to continue.

> **Important Note**
> I demonstrated two ways of creating a feature group. We will only need one to proceed. Let's come back to the notebook and use the feature group created from the SageMaker Python SDK.

Once your feature group is created, we are ready to proceed to ingest data to the feature group.

Ingesting data to SageMaker Feature Store

You can ingest data into the SageMaker Feature Store feature group in a batch or streaming fashion. There is an API in the `sagemaker.feature_store` SDK that allows us to ingest pandas DataFrames asynchronously and in batch fashion. For streaming ingestion, the `sagemaker-featurestore-runtime` API makes it easy to put a single record with low latency into a feature group. These two approaches to make feature ingestion flexible can be implemented in different parts of the ML life cycle.

A data engineer or scientist can create a feature group and ingest the first batch of data, which is typically the case in the exploratory phase, using batch ingestion. Once a model is built and is ready to serve, it is critical to think about capturing new data and ingesting it into the feature store so that you can iterate over the model retraining with an enriched dataset. If your data come in batches, you can use batch ingestion that allow ingestion large amount of data efficiently. Alternatively, if your model is deployed as part of a real-time application, you can use the streaming ingestion approach. In this section, we will see how both batch and streaming ingestion work.

In our example, we are simulating data update annually, as we have chopped the dataset by year into multiple DataFrames with distinct `event_time` values for each year's data. We can ingest each DataFrame in a batch with the following code:

```
for yr, df_auto in d_df.items():
    print(yr)
    print(df_auto.shape)
    feature_group.ingest(data_frame=df_auto, max_workers=1,
max_processes = 1, wait=True)
```

We will loop through all the DataFrames in the d_df dictionary and call the feature_group.ingest() method to ingest each DataFrame. You can control the ingestion runtime with the max_workers and max_processes arguments where the max_processes number of processes will be created to ingest different partitions of the DataFrame in parallel, each with the max_worker threads. The wait=True argument in .ingest() waits for the ingestion of a DataFrame to finish before proceeding.

> **Important Note**
>
> While the SageMaker Python SDK allows you to create feature groups, work with feature definitions, ingest data, and query data from the offline store, the sagemaker-featurestore-runtime boto3 SDK allows you to interact (Get and Put) with the online store. Features are available in the online store immediately after ingestion, whereas it takes some time to make features available in the offline store.

After the ingestion, we can quickly verify it by pulling a sample record from the online store, as shown in the following code block, using the get_record function from the sagemaker-featurestore-runtime boto3 API:

```
car_name = 'amc concord'
featurestore_runtime = sess.boto_session.client(service_
name='sagemaker-featurestore-runtime',
                                               region_
name=region)
sample_record = featurestore_runtime.get_record(
    FeatureGroupName=feature_group_name,
RecordIdentifierValueAsString=car_name
)
sample_record
```

To ingest features for a record in a streaming fashion, we could use the put_record API from the sagemaker-featurestore-runtime boto3 API to ingest a single data record, as shown in the following snippet. This API provides low latency that is typically required by a streaming application. Note that record is a list of dictionaries with a FeatureName and ValueAsString pair for each feature in a record:

```
record = [{'FeatureName': 'mpg',
           'ValueAsString': str(mpg)},
          {'FeatureName':'cylinders',
           'ValueAsString': str(cylinders)},
          {'FeatureName':'displacement',
```

```
                    'ValueAsString': str(displacement)},
               {'FeatureName': 'horsepower',
                    'ValueAsString': str(horsepower)},
               {'FeatureName': 'weight',
                    'ValueAsString': str(weight)},
               {'FeatureName': 'acceleration',
                    'ValueAsString': str(acceleration)},
               {'FeatureName': 'model_year',
                    'ValueAsString': str(model_year)},
               {'FeatureName': 'origin',
                    'ValueAsString': str(origin)},
                    'ValueAsString': str(car_name)},
               {'FeatureName': 'event_time',
                    'ValueAsString': str(int(round(time.time())))}]
featurestore_runtime.put_record(FeatureGroupName=feature_group_
name,
                    Record=record)
```

If you have enabled both online and offline stores, as per our example, SageMaker automatically synchronizes features from an online store to an offline store. When we update the feature group with annual data, SageMaker appends the latest values to the offline store to give you a full history of values over time.

We have walked through how to ingest features into a feature group in SageMaker Feature Store in both batch and streaming fashion using the SageMaker Python SDK and the `sagemaker-featurestore-runtime boto3` API respectively. Let's now take a look at another way of ingesting features into SageMaker Feature Store – from **SageMaker Data Wrangler**.

Ingesting from SageMaker Data Wrangler

If you have read *Chapter 3, Data Preparation with SageMaker Data Wrangler*, you may recall that at the end of the journey with SageMaker Data Wrangler, there is an option to export data to SageMaker Feature Store. SageMaker Data Wrangler creates a notebook with all the code automatically so that you can simply execute the cells to ingest data to a feature group. In the notebook, it shows you how SageMaker enables the ingestion by applying **Amazon SageMaker Processing**, which integrates with SageMaker Feature Store as an output destination. To do this, follow these steps:

1. Open the `flow` file created in *Chapter 3, Data Preparation with SageMaker Data Wrangler*.

2. Go to the **Export** tab to select the last transformation step in the flow.

3. Click the **Export step** button in the top right, as shown in *Figure 4.6*, and choose **Feature Store**:

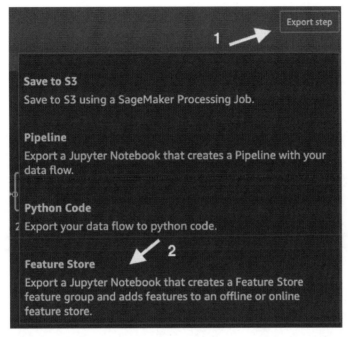

Figure 4.6 – Exporting transformed data to SageMaker Feature Store from SageMaker Data Wrangler

4. A new notebook will pop up. Follow and execute the cells to start a SageMaker Processing job.

At the end of processing, a new feature group will be created and available in SageMaker Feature Store.

After we have created a feature group and ingested features to it, we can move on to see how we can interact with the feature store.

Accessing features from SageMaker Feature Store

Features in a feature store can be accessed programmatically when you are building a training dataset for ML modeling, and when your application is making inferences against a model and is in need of features that are associated with a data point. We will walk through these scenarios to show you how to access features from SageMaker Feature Store.

Accessing a feature group in the Studio UI

In the Studio UI, you can quickly browse through the feature groups in the account on the feature store page. In *Figure 4.1*, you can see a list of feature groups. You can double-click on the line to access further details, such as **Feature group summary**, **Description**, **Feature definitions**, and **Feature group tags**, as shown in *Figure 4.7*:

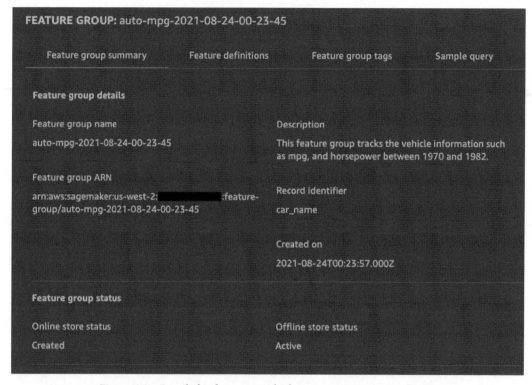

Figure 4.7 – Detailed information of a feature group in the Studio UI

Once you and your team start to use SageMaker Feature Store in more projects, you will have many feature groups in the account. You can use the search bar in the feature group list to search for a feature group of interest:

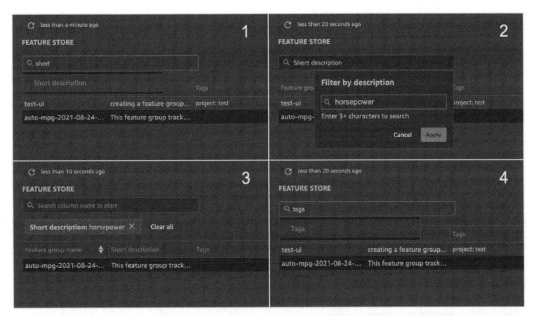

Figure 4.8 – Searching for a feature group in the Studio UI

To use the search bar, as shown in *Figure 4.8*, do the following:

1. Type in the name of the column you want to search, for example, short
    description.

2. Type in the search keyword; for example, I want to find out which feature group
    description contains the word horsepower.

3. The filter is then applied, resulting in only one feature group that satisfies the search
    criteria.

4. You can search by **Tags** or **Feature group name** as well.

Searching by tags is a flexible and powerful tool. In the **Feature group tags** tab, you can add tags on the fly with additional information that will help you identify a feature group. For example, in *Figure 4.9*, I can add up to 50 tags to a feature group to help me organize and search:

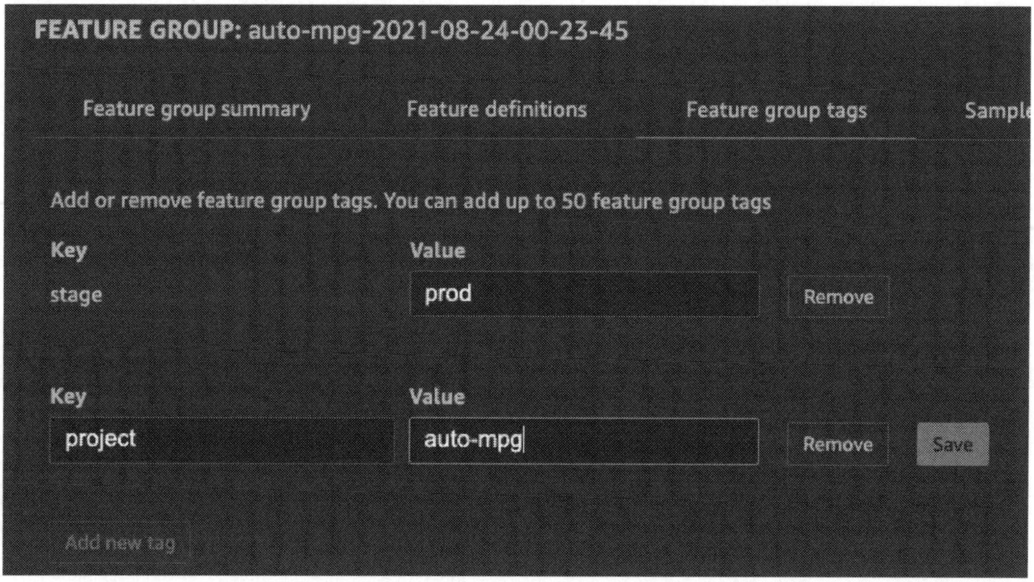

Figure 4.9 – Adding tags to a feature group in the Studio UI

The feature store page in the Studio helps us to identify the right feature group and learn more about feature definition and other configurations before we access the features programmatically. In the next section, we will learn how to access the features.

Accessing an offline store – building a dataset for analysis and training

When building a training dataset, we typically need to be able to access a large number of features, access features of a specific time or version, and combine information from multiple feature groups. The offline store is designed to support such activities.

After ingesting features to a feature group, SageMaker Feature Store stages the data into an S3 bucket, creates a data catalog in the **AWS Glue Catalog**, registers the catalog in **Amazon Athena**, exposes a simple API for a SQL-based query, and returns a pandas DataFrame. We can use the following snippet to turn a query into a pandas DataFrame:

```
query = feature_group.athena_query()
table_name = query.table_name
```

```
query_string = ('SELECT * FROM "%s"' % table_name)
query.run(
        query_string=query_string,
        output_location=f's3://{bucket}/{prefix}/query_
results/')
query.wait()
dataset = query.as_DataFrame()
```

In this snippet, we use the `athena_query()` method from a feature group to create an `AthenaQuery` class instance, which allows us to run a query, saves the query output into an S3 location, and returns a pandas DataFrame. `table_name` refers to the name of the Athena table that we can use in the query string. Here, our query selects all rows and columns from the feature table. You can take a look at the returned `dataset`, which has 398 entries, and note that besides the features that we have defined, there are three additional columns – `write_time`, `api_invocation_time`, and `is_deleted`. These three are also not seen in the output of `featurestore_runtime.get_record()`. They are created specifically for the offline store to enable better governance around the features and versioning. We will see how they can be used later.

Now we understand how to interact and query against the feature store. Let's consider this use case: we want to build training data using all vehicles built before 1979. Our query would look like the following:

```
query_string_2 = '''
SELECT * FROM "%s" WHERE model_year < 79
''' % table_name
```

If we run the query, we get a DataFrame (`dataset_2`) of 280 entries, which is a subset of the full table (398).

Consider another scenario: we would like to build training data using all vehicles built before 1979 but considering only the specs from the latest model year. We can build a point-in-time query, as shown in the following code block. This is also called time travel (going back in time to get the features from that point):

```
query_string_3 = '''
SELECT *
FROM
    (SELECT *,
        row_number()
        OVER (PARTITION BY car_name
```

```
     ORDER BY  event_time desc, Api_Invocation_Time DESC, write_
time DESC) AS row_number
     FROM "%s"
     where event_time < %.f)
WHERE row_number = 1 and
NOT is_deleted
''' % (table_name, datetime.datetime(1979, 1, 1, 8, 0,
0).timestamp())
```

With this query, we get a DataFrame of 212 entries (`dataset_3`). We can compare the entries for the `amc gremlin` car in the last two DataFrames, as shown in *Figure 4.10*:

		mpg	cylinders	displacement	horsepower	weight	acceleration	model_year	origin	car_name	event_time	write_time	api_i
[144]:	dataset_2[dataset_2['car_name']=='amc gremlin']												
	5	21.0	6	199.0	90.0	2648.0	15.0	70	1	amc gremlin	28800.0	2021-08-24 00:31:06.532	
	14	20.0	6	232.0	100.0	2914.0	16.0	75	1	amc gremlin	157795200.0	2021-08-24 00:31:06.538	
	156	19.0	6	232.0	100.0	2634.0	13.0	71	1	amc gremlin	31564800.0	2021-08-24 00:31:06.532	
	275	18.0	6	232.0	100.0	2789.0	15.0	73	1	amc gremlin	94723200.0	2021-08-24 00:31:06.538	
[138]:	dataset_3[dataset_3['car_name']=='amc gremlin']												
	193	20.0	6	232.0	100.0	2914.0	16.0	75	1	amc gremlin	157795200.0	2021-08-24 00:31:06.538	

Figure 4.10 – A point-in-time query (dataset_3) returns the latest data for a vehicle as of 1979 instead of all entries prior to 1979 (dataset_2)

Thanks to the detailed time attribute that is stored in SageMaker Feature Store along with the features, we can perform sophisticated versioning and point-in-time queries against a feature group. We can see that `dataset_3` contains only one entry for the vehicle, whereas `dataset_2` has all the historical entries for the vehicle:

Figure 4.11 – Example queries that can help you perform common tasks with the offline store of a feature group

The offline store in SageMaker Feature Store can be very versatile. In the Feature Store UI, you can find a couple of query examples against the offline store on the **Sample query** tab, as shown in *Figure 4.11*.

Now, let's switch our focus to accessing features from the online store.

Accessing online store – low-latency feature retrieval

SageMaker Feature Store's online store capability offers single-digit millisecond latency and high throughput. This is suitable for use cases where the feature is ingested to the cloud with a streaming architecture and the model inference is of a real-time and streaming nature. Accessing the online store of a feature group can be achieved with the `sagemaker-featurestore-runtime` boto3 API, which is also what we used to verify the feature ingestion in the *Ingesting data to SageMaker Feature Store* section:

```
car_name = 'amc gremlin'
featurestore_runtime =  sess.boto_session.client(service_
name='sagemaker-featurestore-runtime', region_name=region)
amc_gremlin = featurestore_runtime.get_record(
    FeatureGroupName=feature_group_name,
    RecordIdentifierValueAsString=car_name
)
amc_gremlin['Record']
```

```
[{'FeatureName': 'mpg', 'ValueAsString': '20.0'},
 {'FeatureName': 'cylinders', 'ValueAsString': '6'},
 {'FeatureName': 'displacement', 'ValueAsString': '232.0'},
 {'FeatureName': 'horsepower', 'ValueAsString': '100.0'},
 {'FeatureName': 'weight', 'ValueAsString': '2914.0'},
 {'FeatureName': 'acceleration', 'ValueAsString': '16.0'},
 {'FeatureName': 'model_year', 'ValueAsString': '75'},
 {'FeatureName': 'origin', 'ValueAsString': '1'},
 {'FeatureName': 'car_name', 'ValueAsString': 'amc gremlin'},
 {'FeatureName': 'event_time', 'ValueAsString': '157795200.0'}]
```

We take amc gremlin as an example vehicle to retrieve the features. We use the get_record API from boto3 to access the features for the vehicle. The output of the API (amc_gremlin) is a Python dictionary. The feature values are returned in the Record field. If you look closely, you will note that the model_year value for the vehicle is 75. This shows that the online store keeps only the latest entry.

We can also use the batch_get_record API to retrieve multiple records and features in a batch. We can retrieve multiple records with a list of car names and select a subset of features with a list of features that we need. If FeatureNames is not provided, all features are returned:

```
car_names = ['amc gremlin', 'amc concord', 'dodge colt']
feature_names = ['cylinders', 'displacement', 'horsepower']
sample_batch_records=featurestore_runtime.batch_get_record(
    Identifiers=[
        {'FeatureGroupName': feature_group_name,
            'RecordIdentifiersValueAsString': car_names,
            'FeatureNames': feature_names},
    ]
)
sample_batch_records['Records'][0]['Record'] # indexing first
record
[{'FeatureName': 'cylinders', 'ValueAsString': '4'},
 {'FeatureName': 'displacement', 'ValueAsString': '151.0'},
 {'FeatureName': 'horsepower', 'ValueAsString': '90.0'}]
```

You can run these lines of code in your web applications to retrieve features for ML inference with single-digit millisecond latency. With SageMaker Feature Store, you can quickly retrieve features of a given data index quickly and make ML inference in the cloud.

Summary

In this chapter, we learned about the concept of a feature store from an ML perspective. We described the functionality of Amazon SageMaker Feature Store and walked through several feature store use cases when developing an ML model using a public automotive dataset. In the example code, we showed you how to create a feature group in SageMaker Feature Store and how to ingest and update features and data to a feature group. We also showed you how to access features from the offline store for model training purposes and how to perform a point-in-time (time travel) feature query, which is useful when you need to access features in the past. Finally, we showed you how to access features from the online store for ML inference purposes.

In the next chapter, we will move into the topic of building and training ML models with the SageMaker Studio IDE. Building and training ML models can be challenging in a typical ML life cycle, as it is time-consuming and is compute resource-intensive. You will learn ways to build and train ML models with ease using the SageMaker Studio IDE.

5
Building and Training ML Models with SageMaker Studio IDE

Building and training a **machine learning** (**ML**) model can be easy with SageMaker Studio. It is an **integrated development environment** (**IDE**) designed for ML developers for building and training ML models at scale and efficiently. In order to train an ML model, you may previously have dealt with the cumbersome overhead of managing compute infrastructure for yourself or for your team to train ML models properly. You may also have experienced compute resource constraints, either on desktop machines or with cloud resources, where you are given a fixed-size instance. When you develop in SageMaker Studio, there is no more frustration with provisioning and managing compute infrastructure because you can easily make use of elastic compute in SageMaker Studio and its wide support of sophisticated ML algorithms and frameworks for your ML use case.

In this chapter, we will be covering the following topics:

- Training models with SageMaker's built-in algorithms
- Training with code written in popular frameworks
- Developing and collaborating using SageMaker Notebook

Technical requirements

For this chapter, you need to access the code provided at `https://github.com/PacktPublishing/Getting-Started-with-Amazon-SageMaker-Studio/tree/main/chapter05`.

Training models with SageMaker's built-in algorithms

When you want to build an ML model from a notebook in SageMaker Studio for your ML use case and data, one of the easiest approaches is to use one of SageMaker's built-in algorithms. There are two advantages of using built-in algorithms:

- The built-in algorithms do not require you to write any sophisticated ML code. You only need to provide your data, make sure the data format matches the algorithms' requirements, and specify the hyperparameters and compute resources.
- The built-in algorithms are optimized for AWS compute infrastructure and are scalable out of the box. It is easy to perform distributed training across multiple compute instances and/or enable GPU support to speed up training time.

SageMaker's built-in algorithm suite offers algorithms that are suitable for the most common ML use cases. There are algorithms for the following categories: **supervised learning**, **unsupervised learning**, **image analysis**, and **textual analysis**. Most notably, there is **XGBoost** and **k-means** for tabular data for supervised learning and unsupervised learning, respectively, as well as **image classification**, **object detection**, and **semantic segmentation** for image analysis. For textual analysis, we have the **word2vec**, **text classification**, and **sequence-to-sequence** algorithms. These are just example algorithms for each category we've mentioned. There are more useful algorithms available but I am not listing them exhaustively. You can visit `https://docs.aws.amazon.com/sagemaker/latest/dg/algos.html` to see a full list and further details.

> **Note**
> GPU support and distributed training capability for algorithms vary. Please
> visit `https://docs.aws.amazon.com/sagemaker/latest/`
> `dg/common-info-all-im-models.html` for GPU and distributed
> training support for each algorithm.

Let's take a use case and an algorithm to demonstrate how to use SageMaker's
built-in algorithms.

Training an NLP model easily

Training an ML model does not require writing any ML codes with SageMaker's built-in
algorithms. We will look at an NLP use case to classify sentences into categories using the
DBpedia Ontology Dataset from *DBpedia* (`https://www.dbpedia.org/`), which
consists of 560,000 training samples and 70,000 testing samples of the titles and abstracts
of Wikipedia articles. Please open the notebook in `chapter05/01-built_in_`
`algorithm_text_classification.ipynb` from the repository using the **Python 3
(Data Science)** kernel and the **ml.t3.medium** instance.

In the notebook, we first download the dataset and inspect it to understand how we need
to process the data, as shown in the following snippet:

```
!wget -q https://github.com/le-scientifique/torchDatasets/raw/
master/dbpedia_csv.tar.gz
```
```
!tar -xzf dbpedia_csv.tar.gz
```
```
!head dbpedia_csv/train.csv -n 3
```
```
!cat dbpedia_csv/classes.txt
```

We see that the data, `dbpedia_csv/train.csv`, is formatted as `<class
index>,<title>,`. There is also a file called `dbpedia_csv/`
`classes.txt` documenting the classes in an order that corresponds to the class index
seen in `dbpedia_csv/train.csv`.

This is a text classification problem: given the abstract of an article, we want to build a
model to predict and classify the classes this abstract belong to. This is a common use case
when working with a large number of text documents, such as articles on the Wikipedia
site from which this dataset is sourced. It is almost impossible to use human review to
organize all the documents.

One of the built-in algorithms that is suitable for this use case is **BlazingText**. BlazingText has highly optimized implementations for both Word2vec (unsupervised) and text classification (supervised). The Word2vec algorithm can convert text into a vector representation, or **word embedding**, for any downstream NLP usage, such as sentiment analysis or named entity recognition. Text classification can classify documents into categories. This is perfect for our use case and dataset.

Getting the data ready for training is key when using SageMaker's built-in algorithm. Using BlazingText for text classification requires each data point to be formatted as __ label__ <class> text.... Here's an example:

```
__label__latin Lorem ipsum dolor sit amet , consectetur
adipiscing elit , sed do eiusmod tempor incididunt ut labore et
dolore magna aliqua .
```

We use a `preprocess` function, which calls the `transform_text` function to tokenize each row of the abstract. We use a sentence tokenizer, `punkt`, from the `nltk` library inside the `transform_text` function. We preprocess both train and test files. To keep the processing time manageable, we use only 20% of the training data, as shown in the following code snippet:

```
preprocess("dbpedia_csv/train.csv", "dbpedia.train", keep=0.2)
preprocess("dbpedia_csv/test.csv", "dbpedia.validation")
!head -n 1 dbpedia.train
__label__Company automatic electric automatic electric
company ( ae ) was the largest of the manufacturing units of
the automatic electric group . it was a telephone equipment
supplier for independent telephone companies in north america
and also had a world-wide presence . with its line of automatic
telephone exchanges it was also a long-term supplier of
switching equipment to the bell system starting in 1919.
```

We can see that now we have the data in the expected format. Feel free to expand the training set to a higher percentage using the `keep` argument in `preprocess`. After preprocessing, we are ready to invoke the built-in algorithm.

SageMaker's built-in algorithms are fully managed containers that can be accessed with a simple SDK call. The following code allows us to use the BlazingText algorithm for text classification:

```
image=sagemaker.image_uris.retrieve(framework='blazingtext',
                                     region=region,
                                     version='1')
```

```
print(image)
433757028032.dkr.ecr.us-west-2.amazonaws.com/blazingtext:1
```

After execution, we get a string in a variable called `image`. You may be wondering, what is this string that looks like a URL path? How is this an algorithm for model training?

Container technology is the core of SageMaker managed training. Container technology allows SageMaker the flexibility to work with algorithms from any framework and any runtime requirements. Instead of using the runtime setup in the notebook and using the compute resource behind the notebook for model training, SageMaker takes the data you supply and a container image that has the runtime setup and the code base to a separate SageMaker-managed compute infrastructure to conduct model training.

The path in `image` points to a container image stored in **Amazon Elastic Container Registry** (**ECR**) that has the BlazingText ML algorithm. We can use it to start a model training job with a SageMaker estimator.

SageMaker estimator is a key construct for the fully managed model training that enables us to command various aspects of a model training job with a simple API. The following snippet is how we set up a training job with SageMaker's BlazingText algorithm:

```
estimator = sagemaker.estimator.estimator(
        image,
        role,
        instance_count=1,
        instance_type='ml.c5.2xlarge',
        volume_size=30,
        max_run=360000,
        input_mode='File',
        enable_sagemaker_metrics=True,
        output_path=s3_output_location,
        hyperparameters={
            'mode': 'supervised',
            'epochs': 20,
            'min_count': 2,
            'learning_rate': 0.05,
            'vector_dim': 10,
            'early_stopping': True,
            'patience': 4,
            'min_epochs': 5,
```

```
                    'word_ngrams': 2,
           },
)
```

Most notably, the arguments that go into the estimator are as follows:

- The algorithm as a container, `image`

- `hyperparameters` for the training job

- The compute resources needed for the job, `instance_type`, `instance_count`, and `volume_size`

- The IAM execution role, `role`

As you can see, not only do we specify algorithmic options, but also instruct SageMaker what cloud compute resources we need for this model training run. We request one `ml.c5.2xlarge` instance, a compute-optimized instance that has high-performance processors, with 30 GB storage for this training job. It allows us to use a lightweight, cheap instance type (`ml.t3.medium`) for the notebook environment during prototyping and do full-scale training on a more powerful instance type to get the job done faster.

We have set up the algorithm and the compute resource; next, we need to associate the estimator with the training data. After we have prepared the data, we need to upload the data into an S3 bucket so that the SageMaker training job can access the `ml.c5.4xlarge` instance. We start the training by simply calling `estimator.fit()` with the data:

```
train_channel = prefix + '/train'
validation_channel = prefix + '/validation'
sess.upload_data(path='dbpedia_csv/dbpedia.train',
bucket=bucket, key_prefix=train_channel)
sess.upload_data(path='dbpedia_csv/dbpedia.validation',
bucket=bucket, key_prefix=validation_channel)
s3_train_data = f's3://{bucket}/{train_channel}'
s3_validation_data = f's3://{bucket}/{validation_channel}'
print(s3_train_data)
print(s3_validation_data)
data_channels = {'train': s3_train_data,
                 'validation': s3_validation_data}
exp_datetime = strftime('%Y-%m-%d-%H-%M-%S', gmtime())
jobname = f'dbpedia-blazingtext-{exp_datetime}'
```

```
estimator.fit(inputs=data_channels,
              job_name=jobname,
              logs=True)
```

You can see the job log in the notebook and observe the following:

- SageMaker spins up one `ml.c5.2xlarge` instance for this training job.
- SageMaker downloads the data from S3 and the BlazingText container image from ECR.
- SageMaker runs the model training and logs the training and validation accuracy in the cell output shown here:

```
#train_accuracy: 0.9961
Number of train examples: 112000
#validation_accuracy: 0.9766
Number of validation examples: 70000
```

The cell output from the training job is also available in **Amazon CloudWatch Logs**. The metrics of the training job, such as CPU utilization and accuracy measures, which we enabled in `estimator(..., enable_sagemaker_metrics=True)`, are sent to **Amazon CloudWatch Metrics** automatically. This gives us governance of the training jobs even if the notebooks are accidentally deleted.

Once the training job finishes, you can access the trained model in `estimator.model_data`, which can later be used for hosting and inferencing either in the cloud, which is a topic we will explore in depth in the next chapter, or on a computer with the `fastText` program. You can access the model with the following code block:

```
!aws s3 cp {estimator.model_data} ./dbpedia_csv/
%%sh
cd dbpedia_csv/
tar -zxf model.tar.gz
# Use the model archive with fastText
# eg. fasttext predict ./model.bin test.txt
```

> **Note**
>
> BlazingText is a GPU-accelerated version of FastText. FastText (`https://fasttext.cc/`) is an open source library that can perform both word embedding generation (unsupervised) and text classification (supervised). The models created by BlazingText and FastText are compatible with each other.

We have just created a sophisticated text classification model that is capable of classifying the category of documents from DBpedia at an accuracy of 0.9766 on the validation data with minimal ML code.

Let's also set up an ML experiment management framework, **SageMaker Experiments**, to keep track of jobs we launch in this chapter.

Managing training jobs with SageMaker Experiments

As data scientists, we might have all encountered a tricky situation where the number of model training runs can grow very quickly to such a degree that it becomes difficult to track the best model in various experiment settings, such as dataset versions, hyperparameters, and algorithms. In SageMaker Studio, you can easily track the experiments among the training runs with **SageMaker Experiments** and visualize them in the experiments and trials component UI. SageMaker Experiments is an open source project (https://github.com/aws/sagemaker-experiments) and can be accessed programmatically through the Python SDK.

In SageMaker Experiments, an **Experiment** is a collection of **trial** runs that are executions of an ML workflow that can contain **trial components** such as data processing and model training.

Let's continue with the chapter05/01-built_in_algorithm_text_classification.ipynb notebook and see how we can set up an experiment and trial with SageMaker Experiments to track training jobs with different learning rates in the following snippet so that we can compare the performance from the trials easily in SageMaker Studio:

1. First, we install the sagemaker-experiments SDK in the notebook kernel:

    ```
    !pip install -q sagemaker-experiments
    ```

2. We then create an experiment named dbpedia-text-classification that we can use to store all the jobs related to this model training use case using the smexperiments library:

    ```
    from smexperiments.experiment import Experiment
    from smexperiments.trial import Trial
    from botocore.exceptions import ClientError
    from time import gmtime, strftime
    import time
    experiment_name = 'dbpedia-text-classification'
    try:
    ```

```
    experiment = Experiment.create(
        experiment_name=experiment_name,
        description='Training a text classification model
using dbpedia dataset.')
except ClientError as e:
    print(f'{experiment_name} experiment already exists!
Reusing the existing experiment.')
```

3. Then we create a utility function, `create_estimator()`, with an input argument, `learning_rate`, for ease of use later when we iterate over various learning rates:

```
def create_estimator(learning_rate):
    hyperparameters={'mode': 'supervised',
                     'epochs': 40,
                     'min_count': 2,
                     'learning_rate': learning_rate,
                     'vector_dim': 10,
                     'early_stopping': True,
                     'patience': 4,
                     'min_epochs': 5,
                     'word_ngrams': 2}
    estimator = sagemaker.estimator.estimator(
                     image,
                     role,
                     instance_count=1,
                     instance_type='ml.c4.4xlarge',
                     volume_size=30,
                     max_run=360000,
                     input_mode='File',
                     enable_sagemaker_metrics=True,
                     output_path=s3_output_location,
                     hyperparameters=hyperparameters)
    return estimator
```

4. Let's run three training jobs in a `for` loop with varying learning rates in order to understand how the accuracy changes:

```
for lr in [0.1, 0.01, 0.001]:
    exp_datetime = strftime('%Y-%m-%d-%H-%M-%S',
gmtime())
    jobname = f'dbpedia-blazingtext-{exp_datetime}'
    exp_trial = Trial.create(
        experiment_name=experiment_name,
        trial_name=jobname)
    experiment_config={
        'ExperimentName': experiment_name,
        'TrialName': exp_trial.trial_name,
        'TrialComponentDisplayName': 'Training'}
    estimator = create_estimator(learning_rate=lr)
    estimator.fit(inputs=data_channels,
            job_name=jobname,
            experiment_config=experiment_config,
            wait=False)
```

In the `for` loop, we create unique training job names, `dbpedia-blazingtext-{exp_datetime}`, to be associated with a trial, `exp_trial`, and an experiment configuration, `experiment_config`, to store information. Then we pass `experiment_config` into the `estimator.fit()` function and SageMaker will track the experiments for us automatically.

> **Note**
>
> We put `wait=False` in the `estimator.fit()` call. This allows the training job to run asynchronously, meaning that the cell is returned immediately as opposed to being held by the process until the training is completed. In effect, our jobs with different learning rates are run in parallel, each using its own separate SageMaker-managed instances for training.

In SageMaker Studio, you can easily compare the results of these training jobs with SageMaker Experiments. We can create a chart to compare the accuracies of the three jobs with varying learning rates in the SageMaker Studio UI:

1. Click on the **SageMaker Components and registries** in the left sidebar, as shown in *Figure 5.1*:

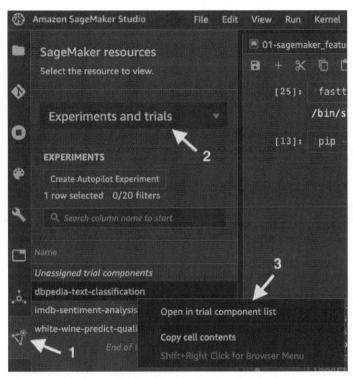

Figure 5.1 – Viewing experiments and trials from the left sidebar

2. Select **Experiments and trials** in the drop-down menu, as shown in *Figure 5.1*.

3. Right-click on the **dbpedia-text-classification** experiment entry and choose **Open in trial component list**.

4. A new view in the main working area will pop up. You can configure the columns to show the accuracies and learning rates as shown in *Figure 5.2*. We can see **validation:accuracy**, and **train:accuracy** with respect to the three **learning_rate** settings. With **learning_rate** set to **0.01**, we have the most balanced training and validation accuracies. A learning rate of 0.1 is overfitted, while a learning rate of 0.001 is underfitted.

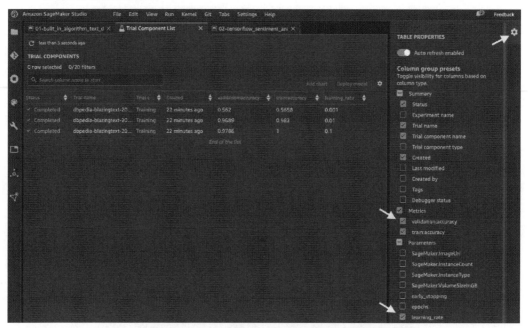

Figure 5.2 – Viewing and comparing training jobs

5. We can create a line chart of **validation:accuracy** versus **learning_rate**. Multi-select the three trial components and click **Add chart** in the top right. A new view will pop up. Configure the chart properties as shown in *Figure 5.3*. You will get a chart that shows the relationship between **validation:accuracy** and **learning_rate**.

Figure 5.3 – Comparing and charting validation accuracy versus learning rate

SageMaker Experiments is useful for managing jobs and resources and comparing performance as you start building an ML project at scale in SageMaker Studio.

> **Note**
>
> Training and processing jobs that do not have `experiment_config` will be placed in **Unassigned trial components**.

More often than not, you already have some ML projects that use popular frameworks such as TensorFlow and PyTorch to train models. You can also run them with SageMaker's fully managed training capability.

Training with code written in popular frameworks

SageMaker's fully managed training works with your favorite ML frameworks too, thanks to the container technology we mentioned previously. You may have been working with `Tensorflow`, `PyTorch`, `Hugging Face`, `MXNet`, `scikit-learn`, and many more. You can easily use them with SageMaker so that you can use its fully managed training capabilities and benefit from the ease of provisioning right-sized compute infrastructure. SageMaker enables you to use your own training scripts for custom models and run them on prebuilt containers for popular frameworks. This is known as **Script Mode**. For frameworks not covered by the prebuilt containers, you also can use your own container for virtually any framework of your choice.

Let's look at training a sentiment analysis model written in TensorFlow as an example to show you how to use your own script in SageMaker to run with SageMaker's prebuilt TensorFlow container. Then we will describe a similar process for other frameworks.

TensorFlow

TensorFlow is an open source framework for ML, specifically for deep neural networks. You can run TensorFlow code using SageMaker's prebuilt TensorFlow training and inference containers, available through the SageMaker SDK's `sagemaker.tensorflow`. Please open the notebook in `chapter05/02-tensorflow_sentiment_analysis.ipynb` from the repository using the **Python 3** (**TensorFlow 2.3 Python 3.7 CPU Optimized**) kernel and the `ml.t3.medium` instance. The objective in this example is to train and predict the sentiment (positive/negative) from movie reviews from the IMDb movie database using a neural network built with TensorFlow layers. You could run the neural network training inside a notebook, but this will require you to have a compute instance that is capable of training a deep neural network with a large amount of data at all times, even when you are just exploring data and writing code. But with SageMaker, you can optimize the compute usage by using a smaller instance for code building and only using a GPU instance for full-scale training.

In `chapter06/02-tensorflow_sentiment_analysis.ipynb`, we first install the library we need and get the Sagemaker session set up. Then we load the IMDb dataset from `tensorflow.python.keras.datasets`, run minimal data preprocessing, and save the training and test splits to the local filesystem and then to an S3 bucket.

Assuming we have previously developed a neural network architecture that works on this IMDb dataset, as shown in the following code block, we can easily take it into SageMaker to train.

```
embedding_layer = tf.keras.layers.Embedding(max_features,
                                            embedding_dims,
                                            input_
length=maxlen)
sequence_input = tf.keras.Input(shape=(maxlen,), dtype='int32')
embedded_sequences = embedding_layer(sequence_input)
x = tf.keras.layers.Dropout(args.drop_out_rate)(embedded_
sequences)
x = tf.keras.layers.Conv1D(filters, kernel_size,
padding='valid', activation='relu', strides=1)(x)
x = tf.keras.layers.MaxPooling1D()(x)
x = tf.keras.layers.GlobalMaxPooling1D()(x)
x = tf.keras.layers.Dense(hidden_dims, activation='relu')(x)
x = tf.keras.layers.Dropout(drop_out_rate)(x)
preds = tf.keras.layers.Dense(1, activation='sigmoid')(x)
model = tf.keras.Model(sequence_input, preds)
optimizer = tf.keras.optimizers.Adam(learning_rate)
model.compile(loss='binary_crossentropy', optimizer=optimizer,
metrics=['accuracy'])
```

SageMaker can take a TensorFlow script into a Docker container and train the script with the data. To do so, SageMaker requires the script to be aware of environmental variables set in the container, the compute infrastructure, and, optionally, the script needs to be able to take inputs from the execution, such as hyperparameters. Here are the steps:

1. Create a script to put in the model architecture and data loading functions (get_model, get_train_data, get_test_data, and so on).

2. Create an argument parser that takes in parameters such as hyperparameters and training data location from script execution. SageMaker is going to run the script as an executable in the container with arguments specified from a SDK call. The training data location is passed into the script with a default from environmental variable SageMaker set up in the container (SM_CHANNEL_*). The argument parser is defined in a parse_arg() function, shown as follows:

```
def parse_args():
    parser = argparse.ArgumentParser()
```

```
    # hyperparameters sent by the client are passed as
command-line arguments to the script
    parser.add_argument('--epochs', type=int, default=1)
    parser.add_argument('--batch_size', type=int,
default=64)
    parser.add_argument('--learning_rate', type=float,
default=0.01)
    parser.add_argument('--drop_out_rate', type=float,
default=0.2)
    # data directories
    parser.add_argument('--train', type=str, default=os.
environ.get('SM_CHANNEL_TRAIN'))
    parser.add_argument('--test', type=str, default=os.
environ.get('SM_CHANNEL_TEST'))
    # model directory /opt/ml/model default set by
SageMaker
    parser.add_argument('--model_dir', type=str,
default=os.environ.get('SM_MODEL_DIR'))
    return parser.parse_known_args()
```

> **Note**
>
> The TRAIN or TEST suffix in the SM_CHANNEL_* environmental variable
> has to match that of the dictionary key provided in the input data channel in
> the estimator.fit() call. So, later, when we specify the data channel, we
> need to create a dictionary whose keys are TRAIN and TEST, case-insensitive.

3. Put in the training steps as part of if __name__ == "__main__"::

```
if __name__ == "__main__":
    args, _ = parse_args()
    x_train, y_train = get_train_data(args.train)
    x_test, y_test = get_test_data(args.test)
    model = get_model(args)
    history = model.fit(x_train, y_train,
            batch_size=args.batch_size,
            epochs=args.epochs,
            validation_data=(x_test, y_test))
    save_history(args.model_dir + "/history.p", history)
```

```
# create a TensorFlow SavedModel for deployment to a
SageMaker endpoint with TensorFlow Serving
model.save(args.model_dir + '/1')
```

4. Make sure to replace the variables in the network with that from the argument parser. For example, change `tf.keras.optimizers.Adam(learning_rate)` to `tf.keras.optimizers.Adam(args.learning_rate)`.

5. In our notebook, we write out the script to `code/tensorflow_sentiment.py`.

6. Create a TensorFlow estimator using `sagemaker.tensorflow.TensorFlow`, which is an extension of the `estimator` class we used previously to work exclusively with ML training written in TensorFlow:

```
from sagemaker.tensorflow import TensorFlow
exp_datetime = strftime('%Y-%m-%d-%H-%M-%S', gmtime())
jobname = f'imdb-tf-{exp_datetime}'
model_dir = f's3://{bucket}/{prefix}/{jobname}'
code_dir = f's3://{bucket}/{prefix}/{jobname}'
train_instance_type = 'ml.p3.2xlarge'
hyperparameters = {'epochs': 10, 'batch_size': 256,
'learning_rate': 0.01 , 'drop_out_rate': 0.2 }
estimator = TensorFlow(source_dir='code',
                       entry_point='tensorflow_sentiment.py',
                       model_dir=model_dir,
                       code_location=code_dir,
                       instance_type=train_instance_type,
                       instance_count=1,
                       enable_sagemaker_metrics=True,
                       hyperparameters=hyperparameters,
                       role=role,
                       framework_version='2.1',
                       py_version='py3')
```

Some of the key arguments here in TensorFlow estimator are `source_dir`, `entry_point`, `code_location`, `framework_version`, and `py_version`. `source_dir`, and `entry_point` is where we specify where the training script is located on the EFS filesystem (`code/tensorflow_sentiment.py`). If you need to use any additional Python libraries, you can include the libraries in a `requirements.txt` file, and place the text file in a directory specified in `source_dir` argument. SageMaker will first install libraries listed in the `requirements.txt` before executing the training script. `code_location` is where the script will be staged in S3. `framework_version` and `py_version` allow us to specify the TensorFlow version and Python version that the training script is developed in.

> **Note**
>
> You can find supported versions of TensorFlow at `https://github.com/aws/deep-learning-containers/blob/master/available_images.md`. You can find the TensorFlow estimator API at `https://sagemaker.readthedocs.io/en/stable/frameworks/tensorflow/sagemaker.tensorflow.html`.

7. Create a data channel dictionary:

```
data_channels = {'train':train_s3, 'test': test_s3}
```

8. Create a new experiment in SageMaker Experiments:

```
experiment_name = 'imdb-sentiment-analysis'
try:
    experiment = Experiment.create(
        experiment_name=experiment_name,
        description='Training a sentiment classification
model using imdb dataset.')
except ClientError as e:
    print(f'{experiment_name} experiment already exists!
Reusing the existing experiment.')
# Creating a new trial for the experiment
exp_trial = Trial.create(
```

```
        experiment_name=experiment_name,
    trial_name=jobname)
experiment_config={
    'ExperimentName': experiment_name,
    'TrialName': exp_trial.trial_name,
    'TrialComponentDisplayName': 'Training'}
```

9. Call the `estimator.fit()` function with data and experiment configurations:

```
estimator.fit(inputs=data_channels,
              job_name=jobname,
              experiment_config=experiment_config,
              logs=True)
```

The training on one ml.p3.2xlarge instance, which has one high-performance NVIDIA® V100 Tensor Core GPU, takes about 3 minutes. Once the training job finishes, you can access the trained model from `model_dir` on S3. This model is a Keras model and can be loaded in by Keras' `load_model` API. You can then evaluate the model the same way you would in TensorFlow:

```
!mkdir ./imdb_data/model -p
!aws s3 cp {estimator.model_data} ./imdb_data/model.tar.gz
!tar -xzf ./imdb_data/model.tar.gz -C ./imdb_data/model/
my_model=tf.keras.models.load_model('./imdb_data/model/1/')
my_model.summary()
loss, acc=my_model.evaluate(x_test, y_test, verbose=2)
print('Restored model, accuracy: {:5.2f}%'.format(100 * acc))
782/782 - 55s - loss: 0.7448 - accuracy: 0.8713
Restored model, accuracy: 87.13%
```

We have successfully trained a custom TensorFlow model to predict IMDb review sentiment using SageMaker's fully managed training infrastructure. For other frameworks, it is rather a similar process to adopt a custom script to SageMaker. We will take a look at the estimator API for PyTorch, Hugging Face, MXNet, and scikit-learn, which share the same base class: `sagemaker.estimator.Framework`.

PyTorch

PyTorch is a popular open source deep learning framework that is analogous to TensorFlow. Similar to how SageMaker supports TensorFlow, SageMaker has an estimator dedicated to PyTorch. You can access it with the `sagemaker.pytorch.PyTorch` class. The API's documentation is available at `https://sagemaker.readthedocs.io/en/stable/frameworks/pytorch/sagemaker.pytorch.html`. Follow *steps 1-9* in the *TensorFlow* section to use your PyTorch training script, but instead of `framework_version`, you would specify the PyTorch version to access the specific SageMaker-managed PyTorch training container image.

Hugging Face

Hugging Face is an ML framework dedicated to natural language processing use cases. It helps you train complex NLP models easily with pre-built architecture and pre-trained models. It is compatible with both TensorFlow and PyTorch, so you can train with the framework that you are most familiar with. You can access the estimator with the `sagemaker.huggingface.HuggingFace` class. The API's documentation is available at `https://sagemaker.readthedocs.io/en/stable/frameworks/huggingface/sagemaker.huggingface.html`. Follow *steps 1-9* in the *TensorFlow* section to use your scripts. The major difference compared with TensorFlow/PyTorch estimators is that there is an additional argument, `transformers_version`, for the **transformer** library from Hugging Face. Another difference is that depending on your choice of underlying framework, you need to specify `pytorch_version` or `tensorflow_version` instead of `framework_version`.

MXNet

MXNet is a popular open source deep learning framework that is analogous to TensorFlow. You can access the MXNet estimator with the `sagemaker.mxnet.MXNet` class. The API documentation is available at `https://sagemaker.readthedocs.io/en/stable/frameworks/mxnet/sagemaker.mxnet.html`. Follow *steps 1-9* in the *TensorFlow* section to use your MXNet training script, but instead of `framework_version`, you need to specify the MXNet version to access the specific SageMaker-managed container image.

Scikit-learn

Scikit-learn (**sklearn**) is a popular open source ML framework that is tightly integrated with NumPy, SciPy, and matplotlib. You can access the sklearn estimator with the `sagemaker.sklearn.SKLearn` class. The API's documentation is available at `https://sagemaker.readthedocs.io/en/stable/frameworks/sklearn/sagemaker.sklearn.html`. Follow *steps 1-9* in the *TensorFlow* section to use your sklearn training script, but instead of `framework_version`, you need to specify the sklearn version to access the specific SageMaker-managed container image.

While developing in SageMaker Studio, it is common that you need to be able to collaborate with your colleague and be able to run ML and data science code with diverse Python libraries. Let's see how we can enrich our model-building experience in SageMaker Studio.

Developing and collaborating using SageMaker Notebook

The SageMaker Studio IDE makes collaboration and customization easy. Besides the freedom of choosing the kernel and instance backing a SageMaker notebook, you could also manage Git repositories, compare notebooks, and share notebooks.

Users can interact with a Git repository easily in SageMaker Studio, and you may have already done so to clone the sample repository from GitHub for this book. Not only can you clone a repository from a system terminal, you can also use the Git integration in the left sidebar in the UI to graphically interact with your code base, as shown in *Figure 5.4*. You can conduct actions you would normally do in Git with the UI: switching branches, pull, commit, and push.

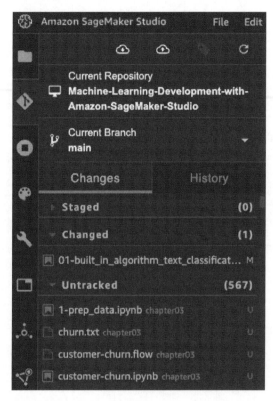

Figure 5.4 – Graphical interface of Git integration in the SageMaker Studio IDE

You can also perform *notebook diff* on a changed file by right-clicking on the changed file and selecting **Diff**, as shown in *Figure 5.5*. A new view will appear in the main working area to display the changes in the cell in the notebook. This is more powerful than the command-line tool $ `git diff`. For example, in *Figure 5.5*, we can see clearly that `instance_type` has been changed since the last commit:

Figure 5.5 – Visualizing changes in a notebook in Git

Another powerful collaboration feature in SageMaker Studio is sharing a notebook with your colleagues so that they can directly work on the notebook you created. You can share a notebook with output and Git repository information with a click of the **Share** button in the top right of a notebook, as shown in *Figure 5.6*:

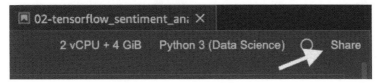

Figure 5.6 – Sharing a notebook in SageMaker Studio with another user

You will be prompted to choose the level of information to be included and will be provided with a URL such as `https://<sm-domain-id>.studio.<region>. sagemaker.aws/jupyter/default/lab?sagemaker-share- id=xxxxxxxxxxxxxxxxxxxx` for anyone who has a user profile in the same SageMaker Studio domain. Once your colleague opens the URL, they will see the read-only notebook, snapshot details, and an option to create a copy to be able to edit the notebook, as shown in *Figure 5.7*:

Figure 5.7 – Another user's view of the shared notebook

> **Note**
>
> The notebook-sharing feature requires configuration when the domain is created. Notebook sharing is enabled if you set up the domain using **Quickstart**, as described in *Chapter 2, Introducing Amazon SageMaker Studio*. If you use the Standard setup, you need to explicitly enable notebook sharing.

Summary

In this chapter, we explained how you can train a ML model in a notebook in SageMaker Studio. We ran two examples, one using SageMaker's built-in BlazingText algorithm to train a text classification model, and another one using TensorFlow as a deep learning framework to build a network architecture to train a sentiment analysis model to predict the sentiment in movie review data. We learned how SageMaker's fully managed training feature works and how to provision the right amount of compute resources from the SageMaker SDK for your training script.

We demonstrated SageMaker Experiments' ability to manage and compare ML training runs in SageMaker Studio's UI. Besides training with TensorFlow scripts, we also explained how flexible SageMaker training is when working with various ML frameworks, such as PyTorch, MXNet, Hugging Face, and scikit-learn. Last but not least, we showed you how SageMaker's Git integration and notebook-sharing features can help boost your productivity.

In the next chapter, we will learn about **SageMaker Clarify** and how to apply SageMaker Clarify to detect bias in your data and ML models and to explain how models make decisions. Understanding bias and model explainability is essential to creating a fair ML model. We will dive deep into the approaches, metrics SageMaker Clarify uses to measure the bias and how Clarify explains the model.

6

Detecting ML Bias and Explaining Models with SageMaker Clarify

Machine learning (ML) models are increasingly being used to help make business decisions across industries, such as in financial services, healthcare, education, and human resources (HR), thanks to the automation ML provides, with improved accuracy over humans. However, ML models are never perfect. They can make poor decisions—even unfair ones if not trained and evaluated carefully. An ML model can be biased in a way that hurts disadvantaged groups. Having an ability to understand bias in data and ML models during the ML life cycle is critical for creating a socially fair ML model. **SageMaker Clarify** computes ML biases in datasets and in ML models to help you gain an understanding of the limitation of ML models so that you can take appropriate action to mitigate these biases.

ML models have long been considered as black box operations because it is rather difficult to see how a prediction is made. SageMaker Clarify computes feature attribution to help you explain how an ML model makes a decision so that it is no longer a black box to us. SageMaker Clarify integrates with SageMaker Studio so that you can easily review the results while building ML models. With SageMaker Clarify, you will be able to know more about your ML models, promote fairness and explainability in your ML use cases, and meet regulatory requirements if required.

In this chapter, we will be learning about the following topics:

- Understanding bias, fairness in ML, and ML explainability

- Detecting bias in ML

- Explaining ML models using **SHapley Additive exPlanations** (**SHAP**) values

Technical requirements

For this chapter, you need to access the code provided at `https://github.com/PacktPublishing/Getting-Started-with-Amazon-SageMaker-Studio/tree/main/chapter06`.

Understanding bias, fairness in ML, and ML explainability

There are two types of bias in ML that we can analyze and mitigate to ensure fairness—**data bias** and **model bias**. **Data bias** is an imbalance in the training data across different groups and categories that can be introduced into an ML solution simply due to a sampling error, or intricately due to inherent reasons that are unfortunately ingrained in society. Data bias, if neglected, can translate into poor accuracy in general and unfair prediction against a certain group in a trained model. It is more critical than ever to be able to discover inherent biases in the data early and take action to address them. **Model bias**, on the other hand, refers to bias introduced by model prediction, such as the distribution of classification and errors among advantaged and disadvantaged groups. Should the model favor an advantaged group for a particular outcome or disproportionally predict incorrectly for a disadvantaged group, causing undesirable consequences in real-world ML applications such as loan-approval prediction systems, we as data scientists need to take action to understand why this has happened and mitigate the behavior.

Ensuring fairness in ML starts with understanding the data and detecting biases within it. Data bias may lead to model bias, as it is well understood that the model will learn what is presented in the data, including any bias, and will replicate that bias in its inferences. Quantifying biases using metrics that are developed and accepted by the ML community is key to detection and choosing mitigation approaches.

Being able to explain how the model makes a decision is another key factor to ensure fairness in ML models. People had long thought that ML is a magical black box—it predicts things better than humans can, but nobody knows why or how. But ML researchers have developed frameworks to help unbox the black box, the most notable one being SHAP. SHAP computes and assigns an importance score for each feature for a particular prediction. This importance score is called a **Shapley value** and is an implementation of cooperative game theory to allocate credit for a model's output among its input features. With the Shapley values for each feature for a prediction, we can describe how and why the model makes such a prediction and which feature contributes the most to this. Should there be a sensitive feature that contributes significantly to model prediction, we need to take action to address this effect.

Amazon SageMaker Clarify helps developers discover underlying bias in the training data and model prediction and explain feature importance for an ML model. SageMaker Clarify computes various metrics to measure bias in the data so that you do not have to be an expert in the science of ML bias. You can use SageMaker Clarify with the SageMaker **software development kit (SDK)** to analyze data and models from a notebook, which we will focus on in this chapter. SageMaker Clarify also integrates with Amazon SageMaker Data Wrangler so that you can detect bias using a simple graphical interface. SageMaker Clarify further integrates with **Amazon SageMaker Experiments** to provide graphical results for each experiment and **Amazon SageMaker Model Monitor** so that you can identify bias and feature importance in a trained model and in inference data in production.

Let's get started with an ML example to see how we can detect bias using SageMaker Clarify.

Detecting bias in ML

For this chapter, I'd like to use an ML adult census income dataset from the **University of California Irvine** (**UCI**) ML repository (`https://archive.ics.uci.edu/ml/datasets/adult`). This dataset contains demographic information from census data and income level as a prediction target. The goal of the dataset is to predict whether a person earns over or below **United States dollars** (**USD**) **$50,000** (**$50K**) per year based on the census information. This is a great example and is the type of ML use case that includes socially sensitive categories such as gender and race, and is under the most scrutiny and regulation to ensure fairness when producing an ML model.

In this section, we will analyze the dataset to detect data bias in the training data, mitigate if there is any bias, train an ML model, and analyze whether there is any model bias against a particular group.

Detecting pretraining bias

Please open the notebook in `Getting-Started-with-Amazon-SageMaker-Studio/chapter06/01-ml_fairness_clarify.ipynb` and follow the next steps:

1. We will use SageMaker Experiments to organize the analysis and training job. Therefore, we install `sagemaker-experiments` in the first cell, and we set up the SageMaker session and import the required libraries in the following two cells.

2. In the fourth cell, we load the train and test datasets from the UCI ML repository. The `orig_columns` values are parsed from `https://archive.ics.uci.edu/ml/machine-learning-databases/adult/adult.names`. The original dataset has both string representation and ordinal representation for education level in the `education` and `education-num` features. Let's just keep the ordinal representation and drop the `education` column. We also move the `target` column to the first column because we will use SageMaker's built-in `XGBoost` algorithm to train an ML model to predict the target. The `target` column contains the label for income greater than $50K (`>50K`) and less than and equal to $50K (`<=50K`). You can see an illustration of this in the following screenshot:

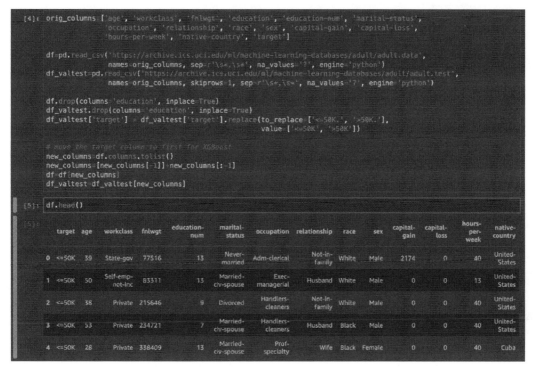

Figure 6.1 – Screenshot of the DataFrame after step 2

3. We encode the categorical features in the train data (`df`) and test data (`df_valtest`) with `OrdinalEncoder` from `sklearn` to make the dataset compatible with the XGBoost algorithm. After the encoding, the `target` variable of values >50K and <=50K are encoded as 1 and 0, respectively; there is a potentially sensitive `sex` category with `Male` and `Female` values encoded as 1 and 0, respectively. We further take 10% of the test dataset as the validation dataset for model training.

4. With this dataset, there are many angles from which we can analyze the data for bias and fairness. Intuitively, gender equality in income would be one angle we could start with. Let's make some visualizations to understand it qualitatively, as follows:

```
df['sex'].value_counts(sort=False).plot(kind='bar',
title='Total count by sex', rot=0)
```

```
plt.xlabel('Sex (0: Female, 1: Male)')
```

```
df['target'].value_counts(sort=False).plot(kind='bar',
title='Target distribution', rot=0)
```

```
plt.xlabel('target (0: <=50K, 1: >50K)')
```

```
df[df['target']==1]['sex'].value_counts(sort=False).
plot(kind='bar', title='Earning >$50K by sex', rot=0)
plt.xlabel('Sex (0: Female, 1: Male)')
```

In the next screenshot, we can observe the following:

- The total number of females is about half that of males.

- There are many more people whose earnings are below $50K.

- There are more males than females who earn more than $50K.

You can see the output here:

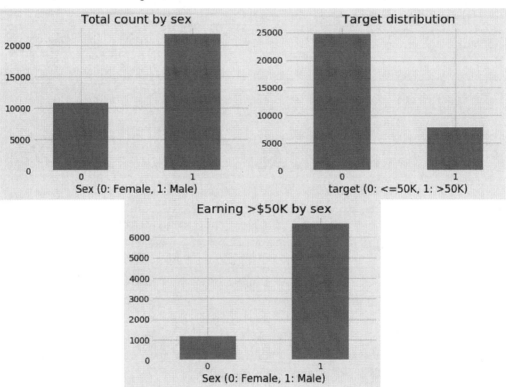

Figure 6.2 – Output of the plotting, showing the distribution of sex and income level; an imbalanced distribution in sex and income level can be observed

This distribution may be reflective of social inequality, but how do we quantify these skewed distributions so that we can be more aware of the bias in the dataset automatically and programmatically? This is where SageMaker Clarify comes into play.

SageMaker Clarify from the SageMaker SDK (`sagemaker.clarify`) uses a dedicated container and SageMaker Processing to compute ML bias and explain ML predictions. We can start by instantiating `sagemaker.clarify.SageMakerClarifyProcessor` with the type of compute resource that fits the dataset, as follows:

```
from sagemaker import clarify
clarify_processor = clarify.SageMakerClarifyProcessor(
        role=role,
        instance_count=1,
        instance_type='ml.m5.xlarge',
        sagemaker_session=sess)
```

5. We will use `SageMakerClarifyProcessor.run_pre_training_bias()` specifically to compute the data bias prior to training an ML model. The metrics it returns allow us to quantify data bias based on the target and facet we choose and allow us to take action to mitigate the bias. But first, `run_pre_training_bias()` requires two configurations: a **data configuration** and a **bias configuration**. In a data configuration, we specify the input training data and the feature-heading information in `clarify.DataConfig()`, as shown in the following code block:

```
pretraining_bias_report_output_path = f's3://{bucket}/
{prefix}/{experiment_name}-{exp_trial_1.trial_name}/
clarify-pretraining-bias'

bias_data_config = clarify.DataConfig(
    s3_data_input_path=train_s3_uri,
    s3_output_path=pretraining_bias_report_output_path,
    label='target',
    headers=df.columns.tolist(),
    dataset_type='text/csv')
```

Because the training data in `train_s3_uri` does not contain column headers, the feature columns are provided in the `headers` argument. In the `label` argument, we specify the target variable from the dataset, which has to be one of the column names in what's input in the `headers` argument.

In a bias configuration, we specify the facets—that is, the sensitive categories that we would like to analyze using `clarify.BiasConfig()`, as follows:

```
bias_config = clarify.BiasConfig(
    label_values_or_threshold=[1],
    facet_name=['sex', 'race'],
    facet_values_or_threshold=[[0], None])
```

We would like to analyze how much gender bias (the `sex` column) there is in the dataset and, in particular, how the outcome (the `target` column) is impacted by gender. To do so, we specify a positive class (`>50K` or `1`) from the target in a list to the `label_values_or_threshold` argument. We specify the facet(s) to be `sex` and `race`. Although in this example we are mostly focused on gender bias, we are adding a `race` feature to showcase that you can use multiple features as facets and that SageMaker Clarify would analyze bias in all the facets at once. The last required argument, `facet_values_or_threshold`, is there to specify the sensitive category in the facets for SageMaker Clarify to focus on when quantifying the bias. `facet_values_or_threshold=[[0], None]` corresponds to `facet_name=['sex', 'race']`. This means that we are asking Clarify to only calculate the bias metrics for class `0` in `sex`, which is female, while not specifying a class (`None`) for `race`, which will force Clarify to calculate bias metrics for all classes in `race`.

6. Once the setup is complete, we can run the processing job with the configurations, as follows:

```
clarify_processor.run_pre_training_bias(
    data_config=bias_data_config,
    data_bias_config=bias_config,
    methods='all',
    job_name=jobname,
    experiment_config=experiment_config)
```

We ask Clarify to compute all possible pretraining bias with `methods='all'`. SageMaker Clarify integrates with SageMaker Experiments, so we also provide an experiment and trial configuration for this job. In the notebook, we name the experiment `experiment_name = 'adult-income-clarify'`.

7. We can visualize the Clarify results in the **Experiments and trials** dropdown in the left sidebar, where we can find the experiment we created for this example. Double-click the `adult-income-clarify` entry, and right-click the new trial entry whose name is a timestamp to select **Open in trial component list**, as shown in the following screenshot:

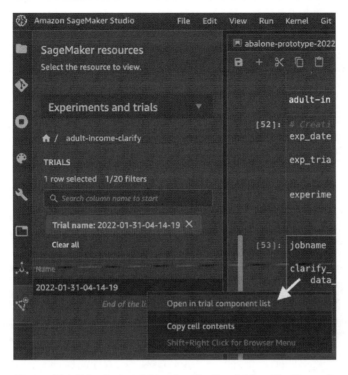

Figure 6.3 – Selecting a trial to view the SageMaker Clarify result

A new page with a **TRIAL COMPONENTS** list will show up in the main working area. We can open the **Trial details** page to see the result by right-clicking on the entry and selecting **Open in trial details**, as shown in the following screenshot:

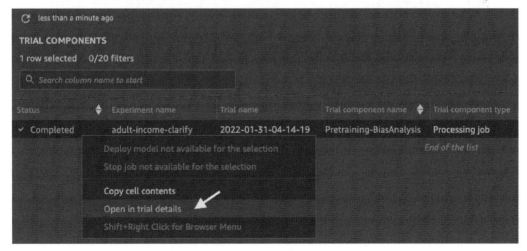

Figure 6.4 – Selecting a trial component to view the SageMaker Clarify result

8. On the **Trial components** page, move to the **Bias report** tab to find the analysis results, as shown in the following screenshot. Here, you can find metrics calculated by SageMaker Clarify:

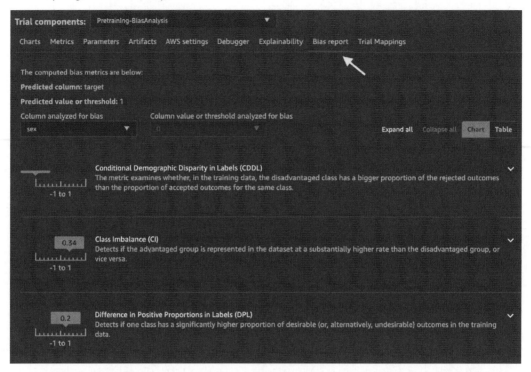

Figure 6.5 – Reviewing the pretraining bias report on the trial details page in SageMaker Studio

With each metric, you can see a description to understand what it means. For further information, you can expand a line item to see how the metric is calculated, with an example and interpretation. Furthermore, you can find additional papers in the details' descriptions to read more about the mathematical definition for all metrics.

> **Note**
>
> For convenience, this **Uniform Resource Locator** (**URL**) takes you to the technical whitepaper: `https://pages.awscloud.com/ rs/112-TZM-766/images/Amazon.AI.Fairness.and. Explainability.Whitepaper.pdf`. This is a good read if you are interested in the math behind the metrics.

Let's review the bias in the data. Most notably, it is reported that there is **Class Imbalance (CI)**, which was measured as 0.34, and **Difference in Positive Proportions in Labels (DPL)**, which was measured as 0.2. **Class Imbalance (CI)** reveals the imbalance between males and females (`sex` feature) as there are 0.34 or 34% fewer females compared to males. **Difference in Positive Proportions in Labels (DPL)** quantifies how much more of a positive outcome (>50K) there is for males compared to females. There are 0.2 or 20% more males who earn >50K in the dataset than females. These two metrics alone not only confirm the imbalance we saw in the chart we plotted in the notebook but also quantify the imbalance.

> **Note**
>
> There is no valid result for **Conditional Demographic Disparity in Labels (CDDL)** because we did not specify a conditional group in `clarify.BiasConfig(group_name=None)`.
>
> You can view the analysis for other facets and categories we have specified in `clarify.BiasConfig()`—race, for example—by toggling the **Column analyzed for bias** and **Column value or threshold analyzed for bias** drop-down lists.
>
> SageMaker Clarify also saves a copy of the analysis in **Portable Document Format (PDF)**, **HyperText Markup Language (HTML)**, and IPYNB formats in **Simple Storage Service (S3)**. You can find the S3 path stored in `pretraining_bias_report_output_path` variable.

This imbalance in the data, if left unmitigated, could very well be ingrained into an ML model after training and it could start repeating what it learned from the biased data. Let's see how to mitigate it.

Mitigating bias and training a model

There are a couple of data science approaches to mitigate the data imbalance, such as matching, oversampling, and undersampling. In this example, let's try a simple matching in terms of gender and target outcome to balance the male and female samples and the proportion in a positive outcome (>50K). We'll proceed as follows:

1. Coming back to the notebook, we continue to work with the data to address the bias, as follows:

```
max_female_sample=df.groupby(['sex', 'target'],
          group_keys=False).count().loc[(0, 1)]['age']
df_sampled=df.groupby(['sex', 'target'],
```

```
group_keys=False).apply(lambda x: x.sample(max_female_
sample))
```

This generates a sampled and matched dataset that has an equal amount of both genders and an equal proportion in the target outcome.

2. We can verify the effectiveness of this approach by plotting the same charts and creating another pretraining bias analysis using SageMaker Clarify for this sampled and matched dataset with an identical bias configuration. Note that we are creating another trial in SageMaker Experiments to track this run and direct the output to a different output S3 location. The code is illustrated in the following snippet:

```
pretraining_bias_report_output_path = f's3://{bucket}/
{prefix}/{experiment_name}-{exp_trial_2.trial_name}/
clarify-pretraining-bias'
bias_data_config = clarify.DataConfig(
    s3_data_input_path=train_sampled_s3_uri,
    s3_output_path=pretraining_bias_report_output_path,
    label='target',
    headers=df_sampled.columns.tolist(),
    dataset_type='text/csv')
```

We then use the same `bias_config` and call the `clarify_processor.` `run_pre_training_bias()` method as we did before to run a pre-training bias analysis job after bias mitigation.

3. After the SageMaker Clarify job is done, we can open the **Bias report** feature on the trial details page for the new pretraining bias analysis job. You can see that **Class Imbalance (CI)** and **Difference in Positive Proportions in Labels (DPL)** are now both zeros. In fact, there are zeros across all the bias metrics.

4. We have successfully zeroed out the data bias we observed previously. Let's get the model training started with SageMaker's built-in XGBoost algorithm, which is a great tool for structured data such as we have. We run this training job as a new trial component in the second trial, `exp_trial_2`. For the hyperparameter, we choose a `binary:logistic` objective for binary classification, `error` as an evaluation metric, and `50` rounds of optimization. The code is illustrated in the following snippet:

```
experiment_config={'ExperimentName': experiment_name,
                    'TrialName': exp_trial_2.trial_name,
                    'TrialComponentDisplayName':
'Training'}
```

```
...
xgb = sagemaker.estimator.Estimator(
        image,
        role,
        instance_type='ml.m5.xlarge',
        instance_count=1,
        output_path=train_s3_output,
        enable_sagemaker_metrics=True,
        sagemaker_session=sess)
xgb.set_hyperparameters(objective='binary:logistic',
                        eval_metric='error',
                        num_round=50)
...
data_channels={'train': train_input, 'validation': val_
input}
xgb.fit(inputs=data_channels,
        job_name=jobname,
        experiment_config=experiment_config,
        wait=True)
```

The training job completes in about 5 minutes, including the infrastructure provisioning.

5. We create a SageMaker model from the training job so that later, we can use it in SageMaker Clarify jobs to analyze model bias. Here's the code to do this:

```
model = xgb.create_model(name=model_name)
container_def = model.prepare_container_def()
sess.create_model(model_name, role, container_def)
```

After the model is trained, we can use SageMaker Clarify to detect and measure biases that occur in the prediction.

Detecting post-training bias

The following steps analyze biases in prediction and data after the model is trained. To run a post-training bias analysis with SageMaker Clarify, we need to prepare three configurations: a **data configuration**, a **bias configuration**, and a **model configuration**. Proceed as follows:

1. Create a new `clarify.DataConfig()` instance to analyze the matched training data and direct the output to a different output S3 location, as follows:

    ```
    posttraining_bias_report_output_path = f's3://{bucket}/
    {prefix}/{experiment_name}-{exp_trial_2.trial_name}/
    clarify-posttraining-bias'
    bias_data_config = clarify.DataConfig(
        s3_data_input_path=train_sampled_s3_uri,
        s3_output_path=posttraining_bias_report_output_path,
        label='target',
        headers=df_sampled.columns.tolist(),
        dataset_type='text/csv')
    ```

2. The bias configuration remains the same as what we used in the pretraining bias analysis. We continue to analyze how model prediction is impacted by `sex`, `race`, and `target` distribution.

3. When a post-training analysis job is started, a SageMaker real-time endpoint with the ML model is created to make a prediction on the input data for a short duration of time to avoid additional traffic to your production endpoint, if any. This endpoint is also called a shadow endpoint and will be deprovisioned once the analysis job finishes. For the model configuration, we specify a model and configure the endpoint. `accept_type` denotes the endpoint response payload format, and `content_type` indicates the payload format of the request to the endpoint.

We also specify a probability threshold of 0.5 to convert the probability output from the XGBoost model to binary hard labels, as follows:

```
model_config = clarify.ModelConfig(
    model_name=model_name,
    instance_type='ml.m5.xlarge',
    instance_count=1,
    accept_type='text/csv',
    content_type='text/csv')
predictions_config = clarify.
ModelPredictedLabelConfig(probability_threshold=0.5)
```

A prediction above 0.5 is predicted as 1 (>50K); otherwise, it is 0 (<=50K).

4. Finally, we run the job with the configurations. We request to compute all valid post-training bias metrics, as follows:

```
clarify_processor.run_post_training_bias(
    data_config=bias_data_config,
    data_bias_config=bias_config,
    model_config=model_config,
    model_predicted_label_config=predictions_config,
    methods='all',
    job_name=jobname,
    experiment_config=experiment_config)
```

5.   We can also review the results on the trial details page of the second trial (`exp_trial_2.trial_name`), as shown in the following screenshot. We see a different set of metrics are shown compared to a pretraining bias analysis. A post-training bias job focuses on analyzing predicted labels or comparing the predictions with the observed target values in the data with respect to groups with different attributes:

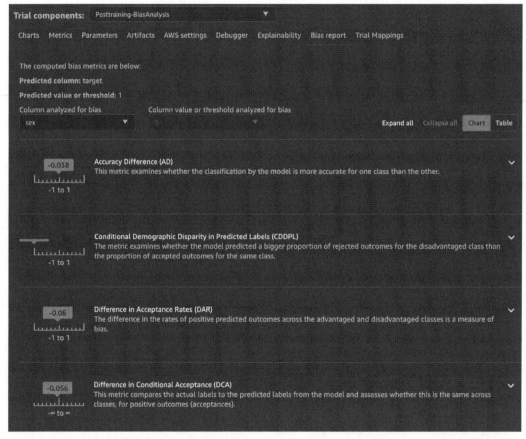

Figure 6.6 – Reviewing the post-training bias report on the trial details page in SageMaker Studio

There is very low bias in most of the measures such as **Accuracy Difference (AD)**, meaning that the model is equally accurate in predicting the income level for the two sexes. However, there is one metric that has rather high biases: **Treatment Equality (TE)**. This measures whether a *Type 1* error (false positive) and a *Type 2* error (false negative) are affecting the two genders in the same way. This is the difference in the ratio of false negatives to false positives between the male and female groups. A positive value translates to females having a lower ratio of false negatives to false positives. That means that the model is more often incorrectly predicting a female to be a high-income earner when in fact they are not; rather, it is the other way around. Having a higher false-positive rate for females compared with males is somewhat concerning and could lead to unfair consequences with such models.

> **Note**
> The technical whitepaper I shared in the *Detecting pretraining bias* section also has many more details on the post-training metrics. You can find the paper here: `https://pages.awscloud.com/rs/112-TZM-766/images/Amazon.AI.Fairness.and.Explainability.Whitepaper.pdf`.

After understanding how to measure the bias, both pretraining and post-training, we should also explore how the ML model makes decisions in the way it does with SageMaker Clarify.

Explaining ML models using SHAP values

SageMaker Clarify also computes model-agnostic feature attribution based on the concept of Shapley values. Shapley values can be used to determine the contribution each feature makes to model predictions. Feature attribution helps explain how a model makes decisions. Having a quantifiable approach to describe how a model makes decisions enables us to have trust in an ML model that meets regulatory requirements and supports the human decision-making process.

Similar to setting up configurations to run bias analysis jobs using SageMaker Clarify, it takes three configurations to set up a model explainability job: a **data configuration**, a **model configuration**, and an **explainability configuration**. Let's follow the next steps from the same notebook:

1. Create a data configuration with the training dataset (matched). This is similar to the data configurations we created before. The code is illustrated in the following snippet:

```
explainability_data_config = clarify.DataConfig(
    s3_data_input_path=train_sampled_s3_uri,
    s3_output_path=explainability_output_path,
    label='target',
    headers=df_sampled.columns.tolist(),
    dataset_type='text/csv')
```

2. Create or reuse the `model_config` argument that was created before for the post-training bias analysis job.

3. Create a `clarify.SHAPConfig()` instance with a baseline. A baseline is an instance of a data point that would be used to compute the Shapley values with the input data. For the same model, you can expect to get different explanations with respect to different baselines, so the choice of a baseline is crucial. It is desirable to select a general baseline with very low information content, such as an average or median feature vector. In this case, in our example, we would interpret the model attribution as to why a particular person is predicted as a high-income earner compared to an average person. Alternatively, you can choose to explain the model with respect to a particular type of data. For example, we can choose a baseline from a similar demographic that represents the people in the inference. The code is illustrated in the following snippet:

```
baseline = df_sampled.query('target == 1').mode().iloc[0,
1:].astype(int).tolist()
shap_config = clarify.SHAPConfig(
    baseline=[baseline],
    num_samples=15,
    agg_method='mean_abs')
```

In our example, let's simulate an "average" high-income (>50K) person from the training data using `mode` for the baseline. The `num_samples` argument is used to determine the size of the generated synthetic dataset to compute the SHAP values. You can also leave it empty to make Clarify choose a number automatically. `agg_method='mean_abs'` denotes how to aggregate for global SHAP values.

4. Afterward, we start the analysis job with the configurations, as follows:

```
clarify_processor.run_explainability(
    data_config=explainability_data_config,
    model_config=model_config,
    explainability_config=shap_config,
    job_name=jobname,
    experiment_config=experiment_config,
    wait=False,
    logs=False)
```

5. Once the processing job completes, we can view the results on the trial details page in SageMaker Experiments under the **Explainability** tab, as shown in the following screenshot. Here, we see the global feature attribution in SHAP values for the top 10 features in the dataset. The `education-num` feature, which represents the highest education level, contributes the most to predicting the income level (>50K or <=50K):

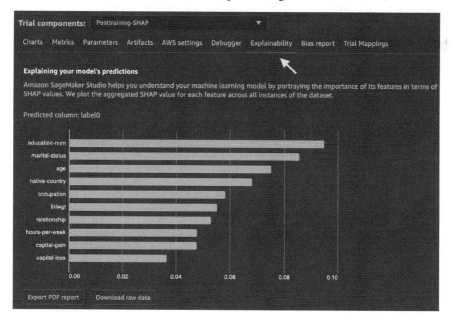

Figure 6.7 – Reviewing the model explainability results in SHAP values in SageMaker Studio

6. Besides global SHAP values, we can also review local SHAP explanations for any given data point to explain how a model makes predictions on this particular data point. SageMaker Clarify computes and saves local explanations for the entire dataset that is provided in `clarify.DataConfig()` in a **comma-separated values (CSV)** file in the output S3 location `explainability_output_path`. We can plot the local SHAP values for each feature for a particular data point (the 500th row) with the following code:

```python
S3Downloader.download(f'{explainability_output_path}/
explanations_shap/out.csv', './', sagemaker_session=sess)
local_explanations_out = pd.read_csv('out.csv')
feature_names = [str.replace(c, '_label0', '') for c in
local_explanations_out.columns.to_series()]
local_explanations_out.columns = feature_names
selected_example = 500
print(f'Example number: {selected_example}')
print(f'with model prediction: {sum(local_explanations_
out.iloc[selected_example]) > 0}')
print()
print(f'Feature values: \n{df_sampled.iloc[selected_
example].to_frame().T}')

local_explanations_out.iloc[selected_example].plot(
    kind='barh',
    title=f'Local explanation for the {selected_example}
th example.',
    rot=0)
```

As shown in *Figure 6.8*, we can see how the XGBoost model predicts this data point as <=50K. The marital-status, education-num, and capital-gain factors are the top three factors that the model thinks of this person as a low-income earner. Thanks to SHAP values computed by SageMaker Clarify, we can understand and explain how the model makes the prediction on an individual basis too.

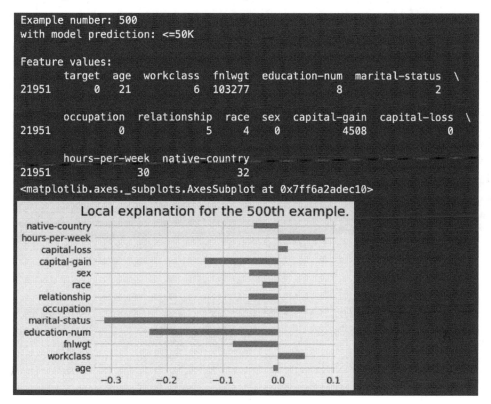

Figure 6.8 – Explaining individual prediction

Let's summarize the chapter after you've completed the example

Summary

In this chapter, we explored biases in ML and ML explainability with an adult income example. We learned that the data could contain unfair biases against a certain group or category in the dataset, which could translate into an ML model making unfair predictions. We worked through an adult income-level prediction example in SageMaker Studio to analyze and compute any bias prior to model training using **SageMaker Clarify**. Clarify produces metrics to quantify imbalance in the dataset that could potentially lead to unfair biases. We mitigated the imbalances using sampling and matching techniques and proceeded to train an ML model. We further analyzed the resulting ML model for potential bias in predictions using SageMaker Clarify. Finally, we reviewed how the ML model makes decisions using SageMaker Clarify and SHAP values.

In the next chapter, we will learn where to go after training an ML model in SageMaker. Hosting an ML model in the cloud is critical for most ML use cases, and being able to use the right tool for model hosting from SageMaker is key to successful ML adoption for your organization. We will learn about various options for hosting an ML model and how to optimize compute resources and cost using SageMaker's hosting features.

7
Hosting ML Models in the Cloud: Best Practices

After you've successfully trained a model, you want to make the model available for inference, don't you? ML models are often the product of a business that is ML-driven. Your customers consume the ML prediction from your model, not your training jobs or processed data. How do you provide a satisfying customer experience, starting with a good experience with your ML models?

SageMaker has several options for ML hosting and inferencing, depending on your use case. Options are welcomed in many aspects of life, but it can be difficult to find the best option. This chapter will help you understand how to host models for batch inference and for online real-time inference, how to use multi-model endpoints to save costs, and how to conduct resource optimization for your inference needs.

In this chapter, we will be covering the following topics:

- Deploying models in the cloud after training
- Inferencing in batches with batch transform
- Hosting real-time endpoints
- Optimizing your model deployment

Technical requirements

For this chapter, you need to access the code at `https://github.com/ PacktPublishing/Getting-Started-with-Amazon-SageMaker-Studio/ tree/main/chapter07`. If you did not run the notebooks in the previous chapter, please run the `chapter05/02-tensorflow_sentiment_analysis.ipynb` file from the repository before proceeding.

Deploying models in the cloud after training

ML models can primarily be consumed in the cloud in two ways, **batch inference** and **live inference**. Batch inference refers to model inference performed on data that is in batches, often large batches, and asynchronous in nature. It fits use cases that collect data infrequently, that focus on group statistics rather than individual inference, and that do not need to have inference results right away for downstream processes. Projects that are research oriented, for example, do not require model inference to be returned for a data point right away. Researchers often collect a chunk of data for testing and evaluation purposes and care about overall statistics and performance rather than individual predictions. They can conduct the inference in batches and wait for the prediction for the whole batch to complete before they move on.

Live inference, on the other hand, refers to model inference performed in real time. It is expected that the inference result for an incoming data point is returned immediately so that it can be used for subsequent decision-making processes. For example, an interactive chatbot would require a live inference capability to support such a service. No one would want to wait until the end of the conversation to get responses from the chatbot model, nor would people want to wait for more than even a couple of seconds. Companies looking to provide the best customer experience would want an inference to be made and returned to the customer instantly.

Given the different requirements, the architecture and deployment choices also differ between batch inference and live inference. Amazon SageMaker has it covered as it provides various fully managed options for your inference use cases. **SageMaker batch transform** is designed to perform batch inference at scale and is cost-effective as the compute infrastructure is fully managed and is de-provisioned when your inference job is complete. **SageMaker real-time endpoints** aim to provide a robust live hosting option for your ML use cases. Both the SageMaker hosting options are fully managed, meaning you do not have to worry much about the cloud infrastructure.

Let's first take a look at SageMaker batch transform, how it works, and when to use it.

Inferencing in batches with batch transform

SageMaker batch transform is designed to provide offline inference for large datasets. Depending on how you organize the data, SageMaker batch transform can split a single large text file in S3 by lines into a small and manageable size (mini-batch) that would fit into the memory before making inference against the model; it can also distribute the files by S3 key into compute instances for efficient computation. For example, it could send `test1.csv` to instance 1 and `test2.csv` to instance 2.

To demonstrate SageMaker batch transform, we can pick up from our training example in the previous chapter. In *Chapter 6, Detecting ML Bias and Explaining Models with SageMaker Clarify*, we showed you how to train a TensorFlow model using SageMaker managed training for a movie review sentiment prediction use case in `Getting-Started-with-Amazon-SageMaker-Studio/chapter05/02-tensorflow_sentiment_analysis.ipynb`. We can deploy the trained model to make a batch inference using SageMaker batch transform in the following steps:

1. Please open the `Getting-Started-with-Amazon-SageMaker-Studio/chapter07/01-tensorflow_sentiment_analysis_batch_transform.ipynb` notebook and use the **Python 3 (TensorFlow 2.3 Python 3.7 CPU Optimized)** kernel.

2. Run the first three cells to set up the SageMaker SDK, import the libraries, and prepare the test dataset. There are 25,000 documents in the test dataset. We save the test data as a CSV file and upload the CSV file to our S3 bucket. The file is 27 MB.

> **Note**
> SageMaker batch transform expects the input CSV files to *not* contain headers. That is, the first row of the CSV should be the first data point.

3. We retrieve the training TensorFlow estimator from a training job we did in *Chapter 6, Detecting ML Bias and Explaining Models with SageMaker Clarify*. We need to grab the training job name for the `TensorFlow.attach()` method. You can find it in **Experiments and trials** in the left sidebar, as shown in *Figure 7.1*, thanks to the experiments we used when training. In **Experiments and trials**, left-click on **imdb-sentiment-analysis** and you should see your training job as a trial in the list.

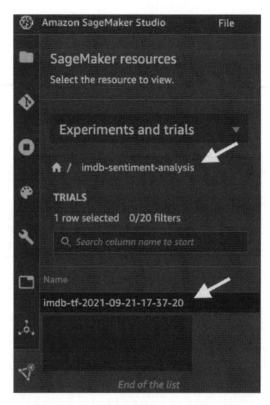

Figure 7.1 – Obtaining training job name in Experiments and trials

You should replace `training_job_name` in the following code with your own:

```
from sagemaker.tensorflow import TensorFlow
training_job_name='<your-training-job-name>'
estimator = TensorFlow.attach(training_job_name)
```

Once you have replaced `training_job_name` and attached it to reload `estimator`, you should see the history of the job printed in the output.

4. To run SageMaker batch transform, you only need two lines of SageMaker API code:

```
transformer = estimator.transformer(instance_count=1,
                                instance_type='ml.
c5.xlarge',
                                max_payload = 2, # MB
                                accept =
'application/jsonlines',
                                output_path = s3_
output_location,
                                assemble_with =
'Line')

transformer.transform(test_data_s3,
                content_type='text/csv',
                split_type = 'Line',
                job_name = jobname,
                experiment_config = experiment_
config)
```

The `estimator.transformer()` method creates a `Transformer` object with the compute resource desired for the inference. Here we request one `ml.c5.xlarge` instance for predicting 25,000 movie reviews. The `max_payload` argument allows us to control the size of each mini-batch that SageMaker Batch Transform is splitting. The `accept` argument determines the output type. SageMaker managed Tensorflow serving container supports `'application/json'`, and `'application/jsonlines'`. `assemble_with` controls how you assemble the inference results that are in mini-batches. Then we provide the S3 location of the test data (`test_data_s3`) in the `transformer.transform()`, and indicate that the input content type to be of `'text/csv'` as the file is of CSV format. `split_type` determines how the input files will be split by SageMaker Batch Transform into mini-batch. We put in a unique job name and SageMaker Experiments configuration so that we can track the inference to the associated training job in the same trial. The Batch Transform job would take around 5 minutes to complete. Like a training job, SageMaker manages the provisioning, computation, and de-provisioning of the instances once the job finishes.

5. After the job completes, we should take a look at the result. SageMaker batch transform saves the results after assembly to the specified S3 location with .out appended to the input filename. You can access the full S3 path in `transformer.output_path` attribute. SageMaker uses TensorFlow Serving, a model serving framework developed by TensorFlow, for model serving, the model output is written in JSON format. The output has the sentiment probabilities in an array with predictions as the JSON key. We can inspect the batch transform results with the following code:

```
output = transformer.output_path
output_prefix = 'imdb_data/test_output'
!mkdir -p {output_prefix}
!aws s3 cp --recursive {output} {output_prefix}
!head {output_prefix}/{csv_test_filename}.out
{    "predictions": [[0.00371244829], [1.0], [1.0],
[0.400452465], [1.0], [1.0], [0.163813606], [0.10115058],
[0.793149233], [1.0], [1.0], [6.37737814e-14],
[2.10463966e-08], [0.400452465], [1.0], [0.0], [1.0],
[0.400452465], [2.65155926e-29], [4.04420768e-11], ......]}
```

We then collect all 25,000 predictions into a `results` variable:

```
results=[]
with open(f'{output_prefix}/{csv_test_filename}.out',
'r') as f:
    lines = f.readlines()
    for line in lines:
        print(line)
        json_output = json.loads(line)
        result = [float('%.3f'%(item)) for sublist in
json_output['predictions']
                                        for item in
sublist]
        results += result

print(results)
```

6. The rest of the notebook displays one original movie review, the predicted sentiment, and the corresponding ground truth sentiment. The model returns the probabilities of the reviews being positive or negative. We take a 0.5 threshold and mark probabilities over the threshold to be positive and below 0.5 to be negative.

7. As we logged the batch transform job in the same trial as the training job, we can find it easily in **Experiments and trials** in the left sidebar, as shown in *Figure 7.2*. You can see more information about this batch transform job in this entry.

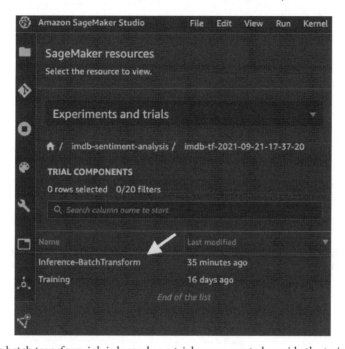

Figure 7.2 – The batch transform job is logged as a trial component alongside the training component

That's how easy it is to make use of SageMaker batch transform to generate inferences on a large dataset. You may wonder, why can't I just use the notebook to make inferences? What's the benefit of using SageMaker batch transform? Yes, you can use the notebook for quick analysis. The advantages of SageMaker batch transform are as follows:

- Fully managed mini-batching helps make inferences on a large dataset efficiently.

- You can use a separate SageMaker-managed compute infrastructure that is different from your notebook instance. You can easily run prediction with a cluster of instances for faster prediction.

- You only pay for the runtime of a batch transform job, even with a much larger compute cluster.

- You can schedule and kick off a model prediction independently in the cloud with SageMaker batch transform. It is not necessary to use a Python notebook in SageMaker Studio to start a prediction job.

Next, let's see how we can host ML models in the cloud for real-time use cases.

Hosting real-time endpoints

SageMaker real-time inference is a fully managed feature for hosting your model(s) on compute instance(s) for real-time low-latency inference. The deployment process consists of the following steps:

1. Create a model, container, and associated inference code in SageMaker. The model refers to the training artifact, `model.tar.gz`. The container is the runtime environment for the code and the model.

2. Create an HTTPS endpoint configuration. This configuration carries information about compute instance type and quantity, models, and traffic patterns to model variants.

3. Create ML instances and an HTTPS endpoint. SageMaker creates a fleet of ML instances and an HTTPS endpoint that handles the traffic and authentication. The final step is to put everything together for a working HTTPS endpoint that can interact with client-side requests.

Hosting a real-time endpoint faces one particular challenge that is common when hosting a website or a web application: it can be difficult to scale your compute instances when you have a spike in traffic to your endpoint. You may have 1,000 customers visiting your website per minute in a particular hour and then have 100,000 customers in the next hour. If you only deploy one instance behind your endpoint that is capable of handling 5,000 requests per minute, it would work well in the first hour and would struggle in the next. Autoscaling is a technique in the cloud to help you scale out instances automatically when certain criteria are met so that your application can handle the load at any time.

Let's walk through a SageMaker real-time endpoint example. Like the batch transform example, we continue the ML use case in *Chapter 5, Building and Training ML Models with SageMaker Studio IDE* and 05/02-tensorflow_sentiment_analysis. ipynb. Please open the notebook in `Getting-Started-with-Amazon-SageMaker-Studio/ chapter07/02-tensorflow_sentiment_analysis_inference.ipynb` and use the **Python 3 (TensorFlow 2.3 Python 3.7 CPU Optimized)** kernel. We will deploy a trained model to SageMaker as a real-time endpoint, make some predictions as an example, and finally apply an autoscaling policy to help scale the compute instances behind the endpoint. Please follow these steps:

1. In the first four cells, we set up the SageMaker session, load the Python libraries, load the test data that we created in `01-tensorflow_sentiment_analysis_ batch_transform.ipynb`, and retrieve the training job that we trained previously using its name.

2. We then deploy the model to an endpoint:

```
predictor = estimator.deploy(
                    instance_type='ml.c5.xlarge',
                    initial_instance_count=1)
```

Here, we choose `ml.c5.xlarge` for `instance_type` argument. `initial_ instance_ count` argument refers to the number of ML instances behind the endpoint when we make this call. Later, we will show you how to use the autoscaling feature, which is designed to help us scale out the instance fleet when the initial settings become insufficient. The deployment process takes about 5 minutes.

3. We can test the endpoint with some sample data. The TensorFlow Serving framework in the container handles the data interface and takes the NumPy array as input so we can pass an entry into the model directly. We can get a response from the endpoint in JSON format, which gets converted to a dictionary in Python in the `prediction` variable:

```
prediction=predictor.predict(x_test[data_index])
print(prediction)
{'predictions': [[1.80986511e-11]]}
```

The next two cells retrieve the review in text and print out the ground truth sentiment and the predicted sentiment with a threshold of 0.5, just like in the batch transform example.

4. (Optional) You may be wondering: Can I ask the endpoint to predict the entire `x_test` of 25,000 data points? To find out, feel free to try out the following line:

```
predictor.predict(x_test)
```

This line will run for a couple of seconds and eventually fail. This is because a SageMaker endpoint is designed to take on requests that are 6 MB in size one at a time. You can request inferences for multiple data points, for example, `x_test[:100]`, but not 25,000 all in one call. In contrast, batch transform does the data splitting (mini-batching) automatically and is better suited to handle large datasets.

5. Next, we can apply SageMaker's autoscaling feature to this endpoint using the `application-autoscaling` client from the `boto3` SDK:

```
sagemaker_client = sess.boto_session.client('sagemaker')
autoscaling_client = sess.boto_session.
client('application-autoscaling')
```

6. It is a two-step process to configure autoscaling for computing instances in AWS. First, we run `autoscaling_client.register_scalable_target()` to register the target with the desired minimum/maximum capacity for our SageMaker endpoint:

```
resource_id=f'endpoint/{endpoint_name}/variant/
AllTraffic'
response = autoscaling_client.register_scalable_target(
    ServiceNamespace='sagemaker',
    ResourceId=resource_id,
ScalableDimension='sagemaker:variant:
DesiredInstanceCount',
    MinCapacity=1,
    MaxCapacity=4)
```

Our target, the SageMaker real-time endpoint, is denoted with `resource_id`. We set the minimum capacity to 1 and the maximum to 4, meaning that when the load is at the lowest, there will be at least one instance running behind the endpoint. Our endpoint is capable of scaling out to four instances at the most.

7. Then we run `autoscaling_client.put_scaling_policy()` to instruct *how* we want to autoscale:

```
response = autoscaling_client.put_scaling_policy(
    PolicyName='Invocations-ScalingPolicy',
    ServiceNamespace='sagemaker',
    ResourceId=resource_id,
    ScalableDimension='sagemaker:variant:
DesiredInstanceCount',
    PolicyType='TargetTrackingScaling',
    TargetTrackingScalingPolicyConfiguration={
        'TargetValue': 4000.0,
        'PredefinedMetricSpecification': {
            'PredefinedMetricType':
                'SageMakerVariantInvocationsPerInstance'},
        'ScaleInCooldown': 600,
        'ScaleOutCooldown': 300})
```

In this example, we employ a scaling strategy called **target tracking scaling**. Target tracking scaling aims to scale in and out the instances based on a specific target metric, such as instance CPU load, or the number of inference requests per instance per minute. We use the latter (SageMakerVariantInvocationsPerInstance) in this configuration to make sure each instance can share 4,000 requests per minute before scaling out another instance. ScaleInCooldown and ScaleOutCooldown refer to the period of time in seconds after the last scaling activity before autoscaling can scale in and out again. With our configuration, SageMaker will not scale in (remove an instance) within 600 seconds of the last scale-in activity, and will not scale out (add an instance) within 300 seconds of the last scale-out activity.

> **Note**
>
> There are two commonly used advanced scaling strategies for PolicyType: **step scaling** and **scheduled scaling**. In step scaling, you can define the number of instances to scale in/out based on the size of the alarm breaches of a certain metric. Read more about step scaling at https://docs.aws.amazon. com/autoscaling/ec2/userguide/as-scaling-simple-step.html. In scheduled scaling, you can set up the scaling based on the schedule. This is particularly useful if the traffic is predictable or has some seasonality. Read more about scheduled scaling at https://docs.aws. amazon.com/autoscaling/ec2/userguide/schedule_ time.html.

8. We can verify the configuration of the autoscaling policy with the following code:

```
response = autoscaling_client.describe_scaling_policies(
        ServiceNamespace='sagemaker')
for i in response['ScalingPolicies']:
    print('')
    print(i['PolicyName'])
    print('')
    if('TargetTrackingScalingPolicyConfiguration' in i):

print(i['TargetTrackingScalingPolicyConfiguration'])
    else:
        print(i['StepScalingPolicyConfiguration'])
    print('')
```

```
Invocations-ScalingPolicy
{'TargetValue': 4000.0, 'PredefinedMetricSpecification':
{'PredefinedMetricType':
'SageMakerVariantInvocationsPerInstance'},
'ScaleOutCooldown': 300, 'ScaleInCooldown': 600}
```

9. In **Amazon SageMaker Studio**, you can easily find the details of an endpoint in the **Endpoints** registry in the left sidebar, as shown in *Figure 7.3*. If you double-click on an endpoint, you can see more information in the main working area:

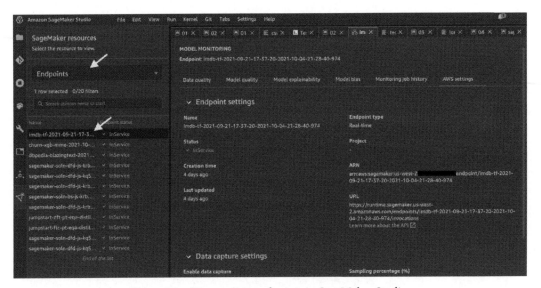

Figure 7.3 – Discovering endpoints in SageMaker Studio

The purpose of hosting an endpoint is to serve the ML models in the cloud so that you can integrate ML as a microservice into your applications or websites. Your model has to be available at all times as long as your main product or service is available. You can imagine that there is a great opportunity and incentive for you to optimize the deployment to minimize the cost while maintaining performance. We just learned how to deploy an ML model in the cloud; we should also learn how to optimize the deployment.

Optimizing your model deployment

Optimizing model deployment is a critical topic for businesses. No one wants to be spending a dime more than they need to. Because deployed endpoints are being used continuously, and incurring charges continuously, making sure that the deployment is optimized in terms of cost and runtime performance can save you a lot of money. SageMaker has several options to help you reduce costs while optimizing the runtime performance. In this section, we will be discussing multi-model endpoint deployment and how to choose the instance type and autoscaling policy for your use case.

Hosting multi-model endpoints to save costs

A multi-model endpoint is a type of real-time endpoint in SageMaker that allows multiple models to be deployed behind the same endpoint. There are many use cases in which you would build models for each customer or for each geographic area, and depending on the characteristics of the incoming data point, you would apply the corresponding ML model. Take the telecommunications churn prediction use case that we tackled in *Chapter 3, Data Preparation with SageMaker Data Wrangler,* as an example. We may get more accurate ML models if we train them by state because there may be regional differences in terms of competition among local telecommunication providers. And if we do train ML models for each US state, you can also easily imagine that the utilization of each model might not be completely equal. Actually, quite the contrary.

Model utilization is inevitably proportional to the population of each state. Your New York model is going to be used more frequently than your Alaska model. In this scenario, if you host an endpoint for each state, you will have to pay for instances, even for the least utilized endpoint. With multi-model endpoints, SageMaker helps you reduce costs by reducing the number of endpoints needed for your use case. Let's take a look at how it works with the telecommunications churn prediction use case. Please open the `Getting-Started-with-Amazon-SageMaker-Studio/chapter07/03-multimodel-endpoint.ipynb` notebook with the Python 3 (Data Science) kernel and follow the next steps:

1. We define the SageMaker session, load up the Python libraries, and load the churn dataset in the first three cells.

2. We do minimal preprocessing to convert the binary columns from strings to 0 and 1:

```
df[["Int'l Plan", "VMail Plan"]] = df[["Int'l Plan",
"VMail Plan"]].replace(to_replace=['yes', 'no'],
value=[1, 0])
df['Churn?'] = df['Churn?'].replace(to_replace=['True.',
'False.'], value=[1, 0])
```

3. We leave out 10% of the data for ML inference later on:

```
from sklearn.model_selection import train_test_split
df_train, df_test = train_test_split(df_processed,
        test_size=0.1, random_state=42, shuffle=True,
        stratify=df_processed['State'])
```

4. After the data is prepared, we set up our state-wise model training process in the function `launch_training_job()` with SageMaker Experiments integrated. The training algorithm we use is SageMaker's built-in XGBoost algorithm, which is fast and accurate for structural data like this. For binary classification, we use a `binary:logtistic` objective with num_round set to 20:

```
def launch_training_job(state, train_data_s3, val_data_
    s3):
    ...
    xgb = sagemaker.estimator.Estimator(image, role,
            instance_count=train_instance_count,
            instance_type=train_instance_type,
            output_path=s3_output,
            enable_sagemaker_metrics=True,
            sagemaker_session=sess)
    xgb.set_hyperparameters(
            objective='binary:logistic',
            num_round=20)


    ...
    xgb.fit(inputs=data_channels,
            job_name=jobname,
            experiment_config=experiment_config,
            wait=False)
    return xgb
```

5. With `launch_training_job()`, we could easily create multiple training jobs in a `for` loop for states. For demonstration purposes, we only train five states in this example:

```
dict_estimator = {}
for state in df_processed.State.unique()[:5]:
    print(state)
```

```
        output_dir = f's3://{bucket}/{prefix}/{local_prefix}/
by_state'
        df_state = df_train[df_train['State']==state].
drop(labels='State', axis=1)
        df_state_train, df_state_val = train_test_split(df_
state, test_size=0.1, random_state=42,

shuffle=True, stratify=df_state['Churn?'])

        df_state_train.to_csv(f'{local_prefix}/churn_{state}_
train.csv', index=False)
        df_state_val.to_csv(f'{local_prefix}/churn_{state}_
val.csv', index=False)
        sagemaker.s3.S3Uploader.upload(f'{local_prefix}/
churn_{state}_train.csv', output_dir)
        sagemaker.s3.S3Uploader.upload(f'{local_prefix}/
churn_{state}_val.csv', output_dir)

        dict_estimator[state] = launch_training_job(state,
out_train_csv_s3, out_val_csv_s3)
        time.sleep(2)
```

Each training job should take no more than 5 minutes. We will wait for all of them to complete before proceeding to use the `wait_for_training_job_to_complete()` function.

6. After the training is done, we finally deploy our multi-model endpoint. It's a bit different to deploying a single model to an endpoint from a trained estimator object. We use the `sagemaker.multidatamodel.MultiDataModel` class for deployment:

```
model_PA = dict_estimator['PA'].create_model(
        role=role, image_uri=image)
mme = MultiDataModel(name=model_name,
        model_data_prefix=model_data_prefix,
        model=model_PA,
        sagemaker_session=sess)
```

`MultiDataModel` initialization needs to understand the common model configuration, such as the container image and the network configurations, to configure the endpoint configuration. We pass in the model for PA. Afterward, we deploy the model to one `ml.c5.xlarge` instance and configure the `serializer` and `deserializer` to take CSV as input and produce JSON as output, respectively:

```
predictor = mme.deploy(
        initial_instance_count=hosting_instance_count,
        instance_type=hosting_instance_type,
        endpoint_name=endpoint_name,
        serializer = CSVSerializer(),
        deserializer = JSONDeserializer())
```

7. We can then dynamically add models to the endpoint. Note that at this time, there is no model deployed behind an endpoint:

```
for state, est in dict_estimator.items():
    artifact_path = est.latest_training_job.describe()
['ModelArtifacts']['S3ModelArtifacts']
    model_name = f'{state}.tar.gz'
    mme.add_model(model_data_source=artifact_path,
                  model_data_path=model_name)
```

That's it. We can verify that there are five models associated with this endpoint:

```
list(mme.list_models())
['MO.tar.gz', 'PA.tar.gz', 'SC.tar.gz', 'VA.tar.gz', 'WY.
tar.gz']
```

8. We can test out the endpoint with some data points from each state. You can specify which model to make inference with using the `target_model` argument in `predictor.predict()`:

```
state='PA'
test_data=sample_test_data(state)
prediction = predictor.predict(data=test_data[0],
                                target_model=f'{state}.
tar.gz')
```

In this cell and onwards, we also set up a timer to measure the time it takes models for other states to respond in order to illustrate the nature of dynamic loading of the model from S3 to the endpoint. When the endpoint is first created, there is no model located behind the endpoint. With `add_model()`, it merely upload the models to an S3 location, `model_data_prefix`. When a model is first requested, SageMaker dynamically downloads the requested model from S3 to the ML instance and loads it into the inference container. This process has a longer response time when we first run the prediction for each of the state models, up to 1,000 milliseconds. But once the model is loaded into the memory in the container behind the endpoint, the response time is greatly reduced, to around 20 milliseconds. When a model is loaded, it is persisted in the container until the memory of the instance is exhausted by having too many models loaded at once. Then SageMaker unloads models that are not being used anymore from memory while still keeping `model.tar.gz` on disk in the instance for the next request to avoid downloading it from S3.

In this example, we showed how to host a SageMaker multi-model endpoint that is flexible and cost-effective because it drastically reduces the number of endpoints needed for your use case. So, instead of hosting and paying for five endpoints, we would only host and pay for one endpoint. That's an easy 80% cost saving. With hosting models trained for 50 US states in 1 endpoint instead of 50, that's a 98% cost saving!

With SageMaker multi-model endpoints, you can host as many models as you can in an S3 bucket location. The number of simultaneous models you can load in an endpoint depends on the memory footprint of your models and the amount of RAM on the compute instance. Multi-model endpoints are suitable for use cases where you have models that are built in the same framework (XGBoost in this example), and where it is tolerable to have latency on less frequently used models.

> **Note**
>
> If you have models built from different ML frameworks, for example, a mix of TensorFlow, PyTorch, and XGBoost models, you can use a multi-container endpoint, which allows hosting up to 15 distinct framework containers. Another benefit of multi-container endpoints is that they do not have latency penalties as all containers are running at the same time. Find out more at `https://docs.aws.amazon.com/sagemaker/latest/dg/multi-container-endpoints.html`.

The other optimization approach is using a technique called load testing to help us choose the instance and autoscaling policy.

Optimizing instance type and autoscaling with load testing

Load testing is a technique that allows us to understand how our ML model hosted in an endpoint with a compute resource configuration responds to online traffic. There are factors such as model size, ML framework, number of CPUs, amount of RAM, autoscaling policy, and traffic size that affect how your ML model performs in the cloud. Understandably, it's not easy to predict how many requests can come to an endpoint over time. It is prudent to understand how your model and endpoint behave in this complex situation. Load testing creates artificial traffic and requests to your endpoint and stress tests how your model and endpoint respond in terms of model latency, instance CPU utilization, memory footprint, and so on.

In this section, let's run some load testing against the endpoint we created in `chapter07/02-tensorflow_sentiment_analysis_inference.ipynb` with some scenarios. In the example, we hosted a TensorFlow-based model to an `ml.c5.xlarge` instance, which has 4 vCPUs and 8 GiB of memory.

First of all, we need to understand the model's latency and capacity as a function of the type of instance and the number of instances before an endpoint becomes unavailable. Then we vary the instance configuration and autoscaling configuration until the desired latency and traffic capacity has been reached.

Please open the `Getting-Started-with-Amazon-SageMaker-Studio/chapter07/04-load_testing.ipynb` notebook with the **Python 3 (Data Science)** kernel and an `ml.t3.xlarge` instance and follow these steps:

1. We use a Python load testing framework called **locust** to perform the load testing in SageMaker Studio. Let's download the library first in the notebook. You can read more about the library at `https://docs.locust.io/en/stable/index.html`.

2. As usual, we set up the SageMaker session in the second cell.

3. Create a load testing configuration script, `load_testing/locustfile.py`, which is required by locust. The script is also provided within the repository. This cell overwrites the file. In this configuration, we instruct locust to create simulated users (the `SMLoadTestUser` class) to run model inference against a SageMaker endpoint (the `test_endpoint` class function) provided by the environment variable with a data point loaded from `imdb_data/test/test.csv`. Here, the response time, `total_time`, is measured in **milliseconds (ms)**.

4. In the next cell, we start our first load testing job on our already-deployed SageMaker endpoint with an `ml.c5.xlarge` instance. Remember we applied the autoscaling policy in `chapter07/02-tensorflow_sentiment_analysis_inference`? Let's first reverse the policy by setting `MaxCapacity` to 1 to make sure the endpoint does not scale out to multiple instances during our first test:

```
sagemaker_client = sess.boto_session.client('sagemaker')
autoscaling_client = sess.boto_session.
client('application-autoscaling')
endpoint_name = '<endpoint-with-ml.c5-xlarge-instance>'
resource_id = f'endpoint/{endpoint_name}/variant/
AllTraffic'
response = autoscaling_client.register_scalable_target(
    ServiceNamespace='sagemaker',
    ResourceId=resource_id,
    ScalableDimension='sagemaker:variant:
DesiredInstanceCount',
    MinCapacity=1,
    MaxCapacity=1)
```

5. Then we test the endpoint with locust. We set up two-worker distributed load testing on two CPU cores in the following snippet. We instruct `locust` to create 10 users (the `-r 10` argument) per second up to 500 online users (`-u 500`), each making calls to our endpoint for 60 seconds (`-t 60s`). Please replace the `ENDPOINT_NAME` string with your SageMaker endpoint name. You can find the endpoint name in the **Endpoints** registry, as shown in *Figure 7.3*:

```
%%sh --bg
export ENDPOINT_NAME='<endpoint-with-ml.c5-xlarge-
instance>'
bind_port=5557
locust -f load_testing/locustfile.py --worker --loglevel
ERROR --autostart --autoquit 10 --master-port ${bind_
port} &

locust -f load_testing/locustfile.py --worker --loglevel
ERROR --autostart --autoquit 10 --master-port ${bind_
port} &
```

```
locust -f load_testing/locustfile.py --headless -u 500 -r
10 -t 60s \
        --print-stats --only-summary --loglevel ERROR \
        --autostart --autoquit 10 --master --expect-
workers 2 --master-bind-port ${bind_port}
```

As it is running, let's navigate to the **Amazon CloudWatch** console to see what's happening from the endpoint's perspective. Please copy the following URL and replace <endpoint-with-ml.c5-xlarge-instance> with your endpoint name and replace the region if you use a region other than us-west-2:

```
https://us-west-2.console.aws.amazon.com/cloudwatch/
home?region=us-west-2#metricsV2:graph=~(metrics~(~(~'AW
S*2fSageMaker~'InvocationsPerInstance~'EndpointName~'<
endpoint-with-ml.c5-xlarge-instance>~'VariantName~'All
Traffic)~(~'.~'ModelLatency~'.~'.~'.~'.~(stat~'Average
))~(~'.~'Invocations~'.~'.~'.~'.)~(~'.~'OverheadLatenc-
y~'.~'.~'.~'.~(stat~'Average))~(~'.~'Invoca
tion5XXErrors~'.~'.~'.~'.)~(~'.~'Invocation4XXErrors~'.~'
.~'.~'.))~view~'timeSeries~stacked~false~region~'us-west-
2~stat~'Sum~period~60~start~'-PT3H~end~'P0D
);query=~'*7bAWS*2fSageMaker*2cEndpointName*2cVariantName*
7d*20<endpoint-with-ml.c5-xlarge-instance>
```

You can see a dashboard in *Figure 7.4*. The dashboard has captured the most important metrics regarding our SageMaker endpoint's health and status. **Invocations** and **InvocationsPerInstance** show the total number of invocations and per-instance counts. **Invocation5XXErrors** and **Invocation4XXErrors** are error counts with HTTP codes 5XX and 4XX respectively. **ModelLatency** (in microseconds) is the time taken by a model inside the container behind a SageMaker endpoint to return a response. **OverheadLatency** (in microseconds) is the time taken for our SageMaker endpoint to transmit a request and a response. Total latency for a request is **ModelLatency** plus **OverheadLatency**. These metrics are emitted by our SageMaker endpoint to Amazon CloudWatch.

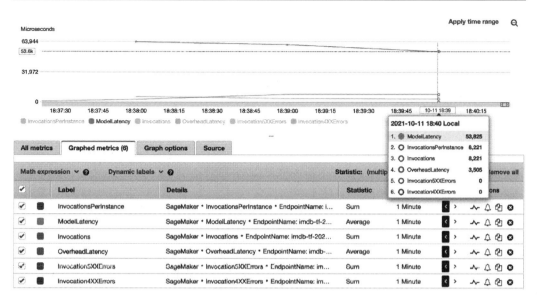

Figure 7.4 – Viewing load testing results on one ml.c5.xlarge instance in Amazon CloudWatch

In the first load test (*Figure 7.4*), we can see that there are around 8,221 invocations per minute, 0 errors, with an average **ModelLatency** of **53,825** microseconds, or 53.8 milliseconds.

With these numbers in mind as a baseline, let's scale up the instance, that is, let's use a larger instance.

6. We load up the previous IMDb sentiment analysis training job and deploy the TensorFlow model to another endpoint with one ml.c5.2xlarge instance, which has 8 vCPU and 16 GiB of memory, twice the capacity of ml.c5.xlarge:

```
from sagemaker.tensorflow import TensorFlow
training_job_name='<your-training-job-name>'
estimator = TensorFlow.attach(training_job_name)
predictor_c5_2xl = estimator.deploy(
        initial_instance_count=1,
        instance_type='ml.c5.2xlarge')
```

The deployment process takes a couple of minutes. Then we retrieve the endpoint name with the next cell, predictor_c5_2xl.endpoint_name.

7. Replace `ENDPOINT_NAME` with the output of `predictor_c5_2xl.endpoint_ name` and run the cell to kick off another load test against the new endpoint:

```
export ENDPOINT_NAME='<endpoint-with-ml.c5-2xlarge-
instance>'
```

8. In Amazon CloudWatch (replacing `<endpoint-with-ml.c5-xlarge- instance>` in the long URL in *step 4* or clicking the hyperlink generated in the next cell in the notebook), we can see how the endpoint responds to traffic in *Figure 7.5*:

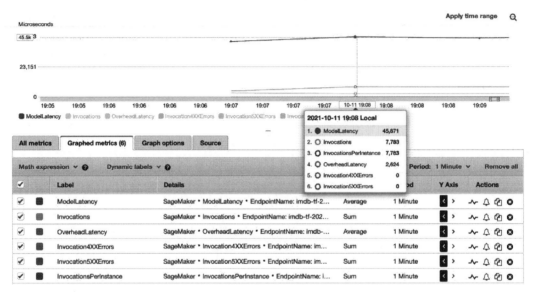

Figure 7.5 – Viewing load testing results on one ml.c5.2xlarge instance in Amazon CloudWatch

Similarly, the traffic that locust was able to generate is around 8,000 invocations per minute (**7,783** in *Figure 7.5*). **ModelLatency** clocks at **45,871** microseconds (45.8 milliseconds), which is 15% faster than the result from one `ml.c5.xlarge` instance.

9. Next, we deploy the same model to an `ml.g4dn.xlarge` instance, which is a GPU instance dedicated to model inference use cases. G4dn instances are equipped with NVIDIA T4 GPUs and are cost-effective for ML inference and small neural network training jobs:

```
predictor_g4dn_xl = estimator.deploy(
        initial_instance_count=1,
        instance_type='ml.g4dn.xlarge')
```

10. We set up a load testing job similar to the previous ones. The result can also be found on the Amazon CloudWatch dashboard by replacing `<endpoint-with-ml.c5-xlarge- instance>` in the long URL in *step 4* or clicking the hyperlink generated in the next cell in the notebook. As shown in *Figure 7.6*, with around 6,000 invocations per minute, the average **ModelLatency** is **2,070** microseconds (2.07 milliseconds). This is significantly lower than the previous compute configurations, thanks to the GPU device in the `ml.g4dn.xlarge` instance making inference much faster.

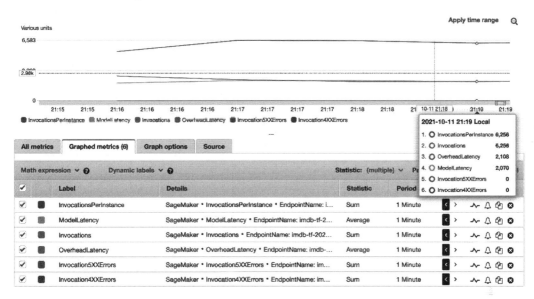

Figure 7.6 – Viewing the load test results on one ml.g4dn.xlarge instance in Amazon CloudWatch

11. The last approach we should try is autoscaling. Autoscaling allows us to spread the load across instances, which in turns helps improve the CPU utilization and model latency. We once again set the autoscaling to `MaxCapacity=4` with the following cell:

```
endpoint_name = '<endpoint-with-ml.c5-xlarge-instance>'
resource_id=f'endpoint/{endpoint_name}/variant/
AllTraffic'
response = autoscaling_client.register_scalable_target(
    ServiceNamespace='sagemaker',
    ResourceId=resource_id,
    ScalableDimension='sagemaker:variant:
DesiredInstanceCount',
```

```
MinCapacity=1,
MaxCapacity=4)
```

You can confirm the scaling policy attached with the next cell in the notebook.

12. We are ready to perform our last load testing experiment. Replace ENDPOINT_ NAME with <endpoint-with-ml.c5-xlarge-instance>, and run the next cell to kick off the load test against the endpoint that is now able to scale out up to four instances. This load test needs to run longer in order to see the effect of autoscaling. This is because SageMaker first needs to observe the number of invocations to decide how many new instances are based on our target metric, SageMakerVariantInvocationsPerInstance=4000. With our traffic at around 8,000 invocations per minute, SageMaker will spin up one additional instance to have a per-instance invocation at the desired value, 4,000. Spinning up new instances takes around 5 minutes to complete.

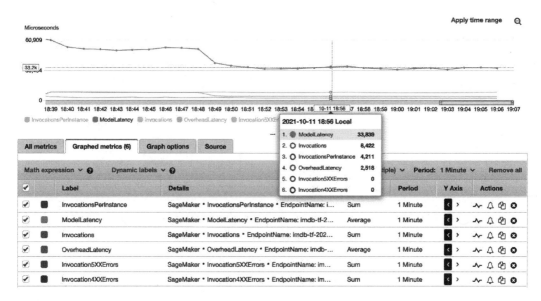

Figure 7.7 – Viewing load testing results on an ml.c5.xlarge instance with autoscaling in Amazon CloudWatch

We can see the load test result on the Amazon CloudWatch dashboard, as shown in *Figure 7.7*. We can see an interesting pattern in the chart. We can clearly see something happened between 18:48 and 18:49. The **ModelLatency** dropped significantly from around 50,000 microseconds (50 milliseconds) to around 33,839 microseconds (33.8 milliseconds). And the **InvocationsPerInstance** was cut to half the number of **Invocations**. We are seeing the effect of SageMaker's autoscaling. Instead of one single instance taking all 8,000 invocations, SageMaker determines that two instances are more appropriate to achieve a target of `SageMakerVariantInvocationsPerInstance=4000` and splits the traffic into two instances. A lower **ModelLatency** is the preferred outcome of having multiple instances to share the load.

After the four load testing experiments, we can conclude that at a load of around 6,000 to 8,000 invocations per minute, the following takes place:

- Single-instance performance is measured by average **ModelLatency**. `ml.g4dn.xlarge` with 1 GPU and 4 vCPUs gives the smallest **ModelLatency** at 2.07 milliseconds. Next is the `ml.c5.2xlarge` instance with 8 vCPUs at 45.8 milliseconds. Last is the `ml.c5.xlarge` instance with 4 vCPUs at 53.8 milliseconds.

- With autoscaling, two `ml.c5.xlarge` instances with 8 vCPUs achieves 33.8 milliseconds' **ModelLatency**. This latency is even better than having one `ml.c5.2xlarge` with the same number of vCPUs.

If we consider another dimension, the cost of the instance(s), we can come to an even more interesting situation, as shown in *Figure 7.8*. In the table, we create a simple compound metric to measure the cost-performance efficiency of a configuration by multiplying **ModelLatency** by the price per hour of the instance configuration.

Instance type	A: ModelLatency (ms)	B: Price per hour ($/hr)	C: Number of instances	Cost-performance efficiency (A*B*C)	Monthly cost ($)
a. ml.g4dn.xlarge	2.07	0.736	1	1.52	529.92
b. ml.c5.2xlarge	45.8	0.408	1	18.68	293.76
c. ml.c5.xlarge	33.8	0.204	2	13.79	293.76
d. ml.c5.xlarge	53.8	0.204	1	10.97	146.88

Figure 7.8 – Cost-performance comparisons

If we are constrained by cost, we should consider using the last configuration (row d), where the monthly cost is the lowest yet with the second-best cost-performance efficiency while sacrificing some model latency. If we need a model latency of around 40 milliseconds or lower, by paying the same monthly cost, we would get even more bang for our buck and lower latency with the third configuration (row c) than the second configuration (row b). The first configuration (row a) gives the best model latency and the best cost-performance efficiency. But it is also the most expensive option. Unless there is a strict single-digit model latency requirement, we might not want to use this option.

To reduce cost, when you complete the examples, make sure to uncomment and run the last cells in `02-tensorflow_sentiment_analysis_inference.ipynb`, `03-multimodel-endpoint.ipynb`, and `04-load_testing.ipynb` to delete the endpoints in order to stop incurring charges to your AWS account.

This discussion is based on the example we used, which assumes many factors, such as model framework, traffic pattern, and instance types. You should follow the best practices we introduced for your use case and test out more instance types and autoscaling policies to find the optimal solution for your use case. You can find the full list of instances, specifications, and prices per hour in the **real-time inference** tab at `https://aws.amazon.com/sagemaker/pricing/` to come up with your own cost-performance efficiency analysis.

There are other optimization features in SageMaker that help you reduce latency, such as Amazon Elastic Inference, SageMaker Neo, and Amazon EC2 Inf1 instances. **Elastic Inference** (`https://docs.aws.amazon.com/sagemaker/latest/dg/ei-endpoints.html`) attaches fractional GPUs to a SageMaker hosted endpoint. It increases the inference throughput and decreases the model latency for your deep learning models that can benefit from GPU acceleration. **SageMaker Neo** (`https://docs.aws.amazon.com/sagemaker/latest/dg/neo.html`) optimizes an ML model for inference in the cloud and supported devices at the edge with no loss in accuracy. SageMaker Neo speeds up prediction and reduces cost with a compiled model and optimized container in SageMaker hosted endpoint. **Amazon EC2 Inf1 instances** (`https://aws.amazon.com/ec2/instance-types/inf1/`) provide high performance and low cost in the cloud with **AWS Inferentia** chips designed and built by AWS for ML inference purposes. You can compile supported ML models using SageMaker Neo and select Inf1 instances to deploy the compiled model in a SageMaker hosted endpoint.

Summary

In this chapter, we learned how to efficiently make ML inferences in the cloud using Amazon SageMaker. We followed up with what we trained in the previous chapter—an IMDb movie review sentiment prediction—to demonstrate SageMaker's batch transform and real-time hosting. More importantly, we learned how to optimize for cost and model latency with load testing. We also learned about another great cost-saving opportunity by hosting multiple ML models in one single endpoint using SageMaker multi-model endpoints. Once you have selected the best inference option and instance types for your use case, SageMaker makes deploying your models straightforward. With these step-by-step instructions and this discussion, you will be able to translate what you've learned to your own ML use cases.

In the next chapter, we will take a different route to learn how we can use SageMaker's JumpStart and Autopilot to quick-start your ML journey. SageMaker JumpStart offers solutions to help you see how best practices and ML use cases are tackled. JumpStart model zoos collect numerous pre-trained deep learning models for natural language processing and computer vision use cases. SageMaker Autopilot is an autoML feature that crunches data and trains a performant model without you worrying about data, coding, or modeling. After we have learned the fundamentals of SageMaker—fully managed model training and model hosting—we can better understand how SageMaker JumpStart and Autopilot work.

8
Jumpstarting ML with SageMaker JumpStart and Autopilot

SageMaker JumpStart offers complete solutions for select use cases as a starter kit for the world of **machine learning (ML)** with Amazon SageMaker without any code development. SageMaker JumpStart also catalogs popular pretrained **computer vision (CV)** and **natural language processing (NLP)** models for you to easily deploy or fine-tune for your dataset. **SageMaker Autopilot** is an AutoML solution that explores your data, engineers features on your behalf, and trains an optimal model from various algorithms and hyperparameters. You don't have to write any code: Autopilot does it for you and returns notebooks to show you how it does it.

In this chapter, we will cover the following topics:

- Launching a SageMaker JumpStart solution
- Deploying and fine-tuning a model from the SageMaker JumpStart model zoo
- Creating a high-quality model with SageMaker Autopilot

Technical requirements

For this chapter, you need to have permission to use JumpStart templates. You can confirm it from your domain and user profile. The code used in this chapter can be found at `https://github.com/PacktPublishing/Getting-Started-with-Amazon-SageMaker-Studio/tree/main/chapter08`.

Launching a SageMaker JumpStart solution

SageMaker JumpStart is particularly useful if you would like to learn a set of best practices for how AWS services should be used together to create an ML solution. You can do the same, too. Let's open up the JumpStart browser. There are multiple ways to open it, as shown in *Figure 8.1*. You can open it from the SageMaker Studio Launcher on the right or from the JumpStart asset browser in the left sidebar.

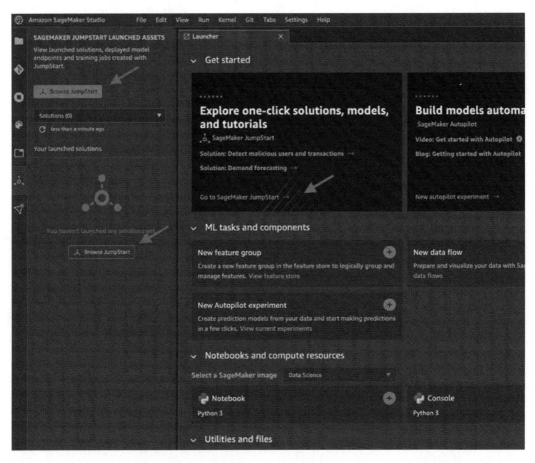

Figure 8.1 – Opening the JumpStart browser from the Launcher or the left sidebar

A new tab named **SageMaker JumpStart** will pop up in the main working area. Go to the **Solutions** section and click **View all**, as shown in *Figure 8.2*.

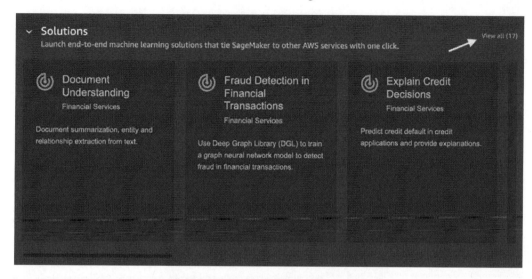

Figure 8.2 – Viewing all solutions in JumpStart

Let's next move on to the solutions catalog for industries.

Solution catalog for industries

There are more than a dozen solutions available in JumpStart as shown in *Figure 8.3*. These solutions are based on use cases spanning multiple industries, including manufacturing, retail, and finance.

Figure 8.3 – JumpStart solution catalog – Click each card to see more information

They are created by AWS developers and architects who know the given industry and use case. You can read more about each use case by clicking on the card. You will be greeted with a welcome page describing the use case, methodology, dataset, solution architecture, and any other external resources. On each solution page, you should also see a **Launch** button, which will deploy the solution and all cloud resources into your AWS account from a CloudFormation template.

Let's use the **Product Defect Detection** solution from the catalog as our example, and we will walk through the deployment and the notebooks together.

Deploying the Product Defect Detection solution

Visual inspection is widely adopted as a quality control measure in manufacturing processes. Quality control used to be a manual process where staff members would visually inspect the product either on the line or via imagery captured with cameras. However, manual inspection does not scale for the large quantities of products created in factories today. ML is a powerful tool that can identify product defects at an error rate that may, if trained properly, be even better than a human inspector. The **Product Defect Detection** SageMaker JumpStart solution is a great starting point to jump-start your CV project to detect defects in images using a state-of-the-art deep learning model. You will see how SageMaker manages training with a PyTorch script, and how model hosting is used. You will also learn how to make inferences against a hosted endpoint. The dataset is a balanced dataset across six types of surface defects and contains ground truths for both classification and drawing bounding boxes. Please follow these steps and read through the content of the notebooks:

1. From the **Solution** catalog, please select **Product Defect Detection in Images**. As shown in *Figure 8.4*, you can read about the solution on the main page. You can learn about the sample data, the algorithm, and the cloud solution architecture.

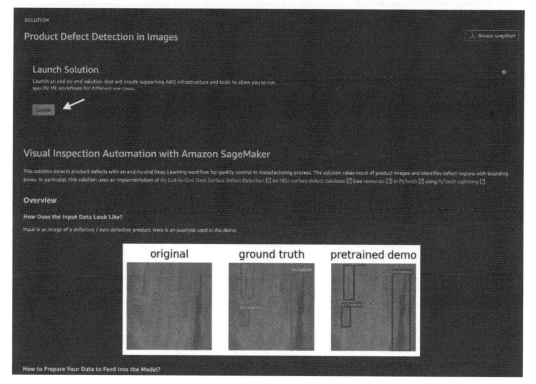

Figure 8.4 – Main page of the Product Defect Detection in Images solution

2. Hit the **Launch** button, as shown in *Figure 8.4*, to start the deployment. You should see the deployment in progress on the screen. What is happening is that we just initiated a resource deployment using **AWS CloudFormation** in the background. AWS CloudFormation is a service that helps create, provision, and manage AWS resources in an orderly fashion through a template in JSON or YAML declarative code. This deployment takes a couple of minutes.

3. Once the solution becomes **Ready**, click on **Open Notebook** in the tab to open the first notebook, 0_demo.ipynb, from the solution. This notebook is the first of four notebooks that are deployed as part of the CloudFormation setup into your home directory at S3Downloads/jumpstart-prod-dfd_xxxxxxx/notebooks/. The notebook requires the **SageMaker JumpStart PyTorch 1.0** kernel as we are going to build a PyTorch-based solution. The kernel startup might take a minute or two if this is the first time using the kernel.

4. Run all the cells in the 0_demo.ipynb notebook. This notebook downloads the NEU-DET detection dataset to the filesystem and creates a SageMaker hosted endpoint using the SageMaker SDK's sagemaker.pytorch.PyTorchModel class for a pretrained PyTorch model. At the end of the notebook, you should see a figure showing the patches detected by the pretrained model compared to the ground truth, as in *Figure 8.5*.

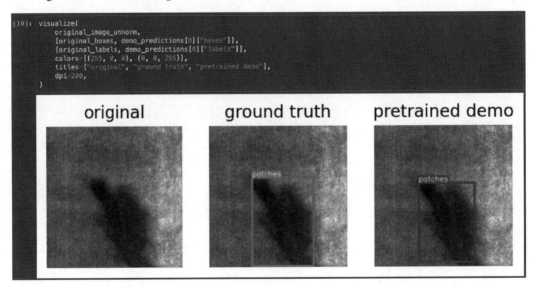

Figure 8.5 – Final output of the 0_demo.ipynb notebook, showing a steel surface example, the ground truth, and the model prediction by a pretrained model

This notebook demonstrates a key flexibility SageMaker offers, that is, you can bring a model trained from outside of SageMaker and host it in SageMaker. To create a SageMaker model from a PyTorch model, you need the model file `.pt`/`.pth` archived in a `model.tar.gz` archive and an entry point, `detector.py` script in this case, that instructs how the inference should be made. We can take a look at the `detector.py` script to learn more.

5. (Optional) Add a new cell and fill in the following commands:

```
!aws s3 cp {sources}source_dir.tar.gz .
!tar zxvf source_dir.tar.gz
```

This will get the entire code base locally. Please open the `detector.py` file and locate the part that SageMaker uses to make inferences:

```
def model_fn(model_dir):
    backbone = "resnet34"
    num_classes = 7  # including the background
    mfn = load_checkpoint(Classification(backbone, num_classes - 1).mfn, model_dir, "mfn")
    rpn = load_checkpoint(RPN(), model_dir, "rpn")
    roi = load_checkpoint(RoI(num_classes), model_dir, "roi")
    model = Detection(mfn, rpn, roi)
    model = model.eval()
    freeze(model)
    return model
```

SageMaker requires at least a `model_fn(model_dir)` function when importing a PyTorch model to instruct how the model is defined. In this example, `Detection()` class is a `GeneralizedRCNN` model defined in `S3Downloads/jumpstart-prod-dfd_xxxxxx/notebooks/sagemaker_defect_detection/models/ddn.py` with weights loaded from the provided model.

> **Note**
>
> Other inference related functions you can implement include the following:
>
> Deserializing the invoke request body into an object we can perform prediction on:
>
> ```
> input_object = input_fn(request_body, request_content_type)
> ```
>
> Performing prediction on the deserialized object with the loaded model:
>
> ```
> prediction = predict_fn(input_object, model)
> ```
>
> Serializing the prediction result into the desired response content type:
>
> ```
> output = output_fn(prediction, response_content_type)
> ```
>
> SageMaker has default implementations for these three functions if you don't override them. If you have a custom approach for making inferences, you can override these functions.

6. Proceed to the end of the notebook and click on **Click here to continue** to advance to the next notebook, `1_retrain_from_checkpoint.ipynb`.

7. Run all the cells in `1_retrain_from_checkpoint.ipynb`. This notebook fine-tunes the pretrained model from a checkpoint with the downloaded dataset for a few more epochs. The solution includes training code in `detector.py` from `osp.join(sources, "source_dir.tar.gz")`. The solution uses the SageMaker SDK's PyTorch estimator to create a training job that launches an on-demand compute resource of one `ml.g4dn.2xlarge` instance and trains it from a provided pretrained checkpoint. The training takes about 10 minutes. The following lines of code show how you can feed the training data and a pretrained checkpoint to SageMaker PyTorch estimator to perform a model fine-tuning job:

```
finetuned_model.fit(
    {
        "training": neu_det_prepared_s3,
        "pretrained_checkpoint": osp.join(s3_pretrained,
"epoch=294-loss=0.654-main_score=0.349.ckpt"),
    }
)
```

> **Note**
>
> The naming of the dictionary keys to `.fit()` call is done by design. These keys are registered as environment variables with a SM_CHANNEL_ prefix inside the training container and can be accessed in the training script. The keys need to match what is written in the `detector.py` file in order to make this `.fit()` training call work. For example, see line 310 and 349 in `detector.py`:
>
> ```
> aa("--data-path", metavar="DIR", type=str,
> default=os.environ["SM_CHANNEL_TRAINING"])
> ```
>
> ```
> aa("--resume-sagemaker-from-checkpoint", type=str,
> default=os.getenv("SM_CHANNEL_PRETRAINED_
> CHECKPOINT", None))
> ```

After the training, the model is deployed as a SageMaker hosted endpoint, as in the 0_demo.ipynb notebook. In the end, a comparison between the ground truth, the inference from the pretrained model from 0_demo.ipynb, and the inference from the fine-tuned model is visualized. We can see that the inference from the fine-tuned model has one fewer false positive, yet still isn't able to pick up a patch on the right side of the sample image. This should be considered a false negative.

8. Proceed to click on **Click here to continue** to advance to the next notebook, 2_detection_from_scratch.ipynb.

9. Run all the cells in the 2_detection_from_scratch.ipynb notebook. Instead of training from a checkpoint, we train a model from scratch with 10 epochs using the same dataset and compare the inference to that from the pretrained model. The model is significantly undertrained, as expected with the small epoch size used. You are encouraged to increase the epoch size (the EPOCHS variable) to 300 to achieve better performance. However, this will take significantly more than 10 minutes.

> **Note**
>
> We control whether we train from a checkpoint or from scratch by whether we include a `pretrained_checkpoint` key in a dictionary to `.fit()` or not.

10. Proceed to click on **Click here to continue** to advance to the next notebook, `3_classification_from_scratch.ipynb`.

In this notebook, we train a classification model using `classifier.py` for 50 epochs, instead of an object detection model from scratch, using the NEU-CLS classification dataset. A classification model is different from the previous object detection models. Image classification recognizes the types of defect in an entire image, whereas an object detection model can also localize where the defect is. Image classification is useful if you do not need to know the location of the defect, and can be used as a triage model for product defects.

Training a classification model is faster, as you can see from the job. The classification accuracy on the validation set reaches `0.99`, as shown in the cell output from the training job, which is very accurate:

```
Epoch 00016: val_acc reached 0.99219 (best 0.99219),
saving model to /opt/ml/model/epoch=16-val_loss=0.028-
val_acc=0.992.ckpt as top 1
```

11. This is the end of the solution. Please make sure to execute the last cell in each notebook to delete the models and endpoints, especially the last cell in the `0_demo.ipynb` notebook, where the deletion is commented out. Please uncomment this and execute it to delete the pretrained model and endpoint.

With this SageMaker JumpStart solution, you built and trained four deep learning models based on a PyTorch implementation of Faster RCNN to detect and classify six types of defects in steel imagery with minimal coding effort. You also hosted them as SageMaker endpoints for real-time prediction. You can expect a similar experience with other solutions in SageMaker JumpStart to learn different aspects of SageMaker features used in the context of solving common use cases.

Now, let's switch gears to the SageMaker JumpStart model zoo.

SageMaker JumpStart model zoo

There are more than 200 popular prebuilt and pretrained models in SageMaker JumpStart for you to use out of the box or continue to train for your use case. What are they good for? Training an accurate deep learning model is time consuming and complex, even with the most powerful GPU machine. It also requires large amounts of training and labeled data. Now, with these models that have been developed by the community, pretrained on large datasets, you do not have to reinvent the wheel.

Model collection

There are two groups of models: **text models** and **vision models** in SageMaker JumpStart model zoo. These models are the most popular ones among the ML community. You can quickly browse the models in SageMaker JumpStart and select the one that meets your needs. On each model page, you will see an introduction to the model, its usage, and how to prepare a dataset for fine-tuning purposes. You can deploy models into AWS as a hosted endpoint for your use case or fine-tune the model further with your own dataset.

Text models are sourced from the following three hubs: TensorFlow Hub, PyTorch Hub, and Hugging Face. Each model is specifically trained for a particular type of NLP task using a dataset such as text classification, question answering, or text generation. Notably, there are many flavors of **Bidirectional Encoder Representations from Transformers (BERT)**, **Cross-lingual Language Model (XLM)**, **ELECTRA**, and **Generative Pretrained Transformer (GPT)** up for grabs.

Vision models are sourced from TensorFlow Hub, PyTorch Hub, and Gluon CV. There are models that perform image classification, image feature vector extraction, and object detection. **Inception**, **SSD**, **ResNet**, and **Faster R-CNN** models are some of the most notable and widely used models in the field of CV.

Deploying a model

Let's find a question-answering model and see how we can deploy it to our AWS account. In the search bar, type in `question` **answering** hit **Return**, and you should see a list of models that perform such tasks returned to you, as shown in *Figure 8.6*.

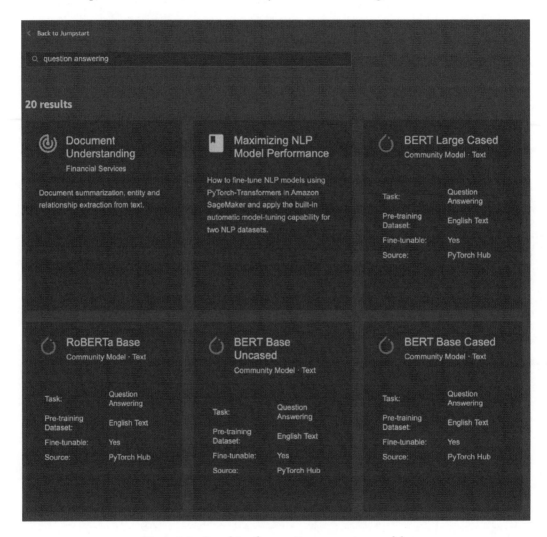

Figure 8.6 – Searching for question-answering models

Let's find and double-click **DistilRoBERTa Base** for **Question Answering** in the search results. This model is trained on `OpenWebTextCorpus` and is distilled from the RoBERTa model checkpoint. It has 6 layers, 768 hidden, 12 heads, and 82 million parameters. 82 million! It is not easy to train such a large model, for sure. Luckily with SageMaker JumpStart, we have a model that we can deploy out of the box. As shown in *Figure 8.7*, please expand the **Deployment Configuration** section, choose **Ml.M5. Xlarge** as the machine type, leave the endpoint name as default, and hit **Deploy**. Ml.M5. Xlarge is a general-purpose instance type that has 4 vCPU and 16 GB of memory, which is sufficient for this example. The deployment will take a couple of minutes.

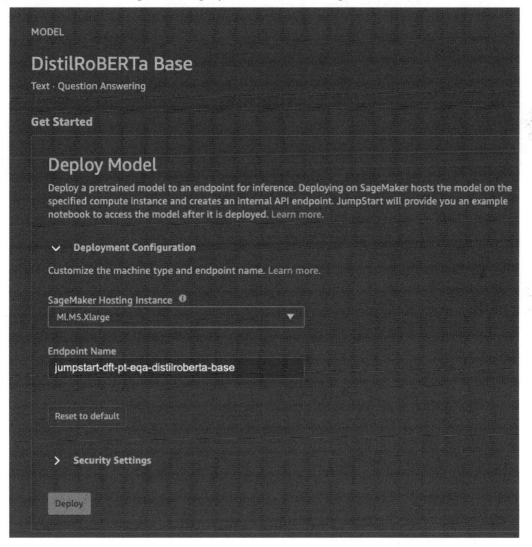

Figure 8.7 – Deploying a JumpStart DistilRoBERTa Base model

Once the model is deployed, a notebook will be provided to you to show how you can make an API call to the hosted endpoint (*Figure 8.8*). You can find a list of models in the JumpStart left sidebar.

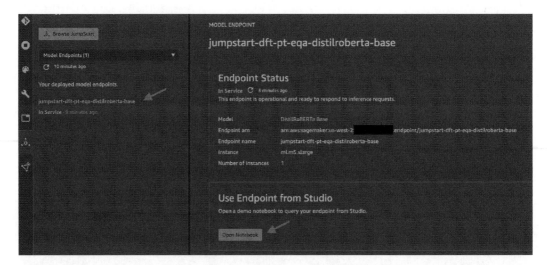

Figure 8.8 – Opening a sample inference notebook after the model is deployed

In the sample notebook, two questions from the **SQuAD v2** dataset, one of the most widely used question-answering datasets for evaluation, are provided to show how inferencing can be done. Let's also ask our model other questions based on the following passage (Can you guess where you've read it before? Yes, it's the opening statement of this chapter!):

Context:

> *SageMaker JumpStart offers complete solutions for select use cases as a starter kit to the world of machine learning (ML) with Amazon SageMaker without any code development. SageMaker JumpStart also catalogs popular pretrained computer vision (CV) and natural language processing (NLP) models for you to easily deploy or fine-tune to your dataset. SageMaker Autopilot is an AutoML solution that explores your data, engineers features on your behalf, and trains an optimal model from various algorithms and hyperparameters. You don't have to write any code: Autopilot does it for you and returns notebooks to show how it does it.*

Questions:

- *What does SageMaker JumpStart do?*
- *What is NLP?*

In the notebook, we should add the following to the second cell:

```
question_context3 = ["What does SageMaker JumpStart do?",
"SageMaker JumpStart offers complete solutions for select use
cases as a starter kit to the world of machine learning (ML)
with Amazon SageMaker without any code development. SageMaker
JumpStart also catalogs popular pretrained computer vision (CV)
and natural language processing (NLP) models for you to easily
deploy or fine-tune to your dataset. SageMaker Autopilot is an
AutoML solution that explores your data, engineers features on
your behalf and trains an optimal model from various algorithms
and hyperparameters. You don't have to write any code:
Autopilot does it for you and returns notebooks to show how it
does it."]
question_context4 = ["What is NLP?", question_context3[-1]]
```

In the third cell, append the two new question context pairs to the list in the `for` loop and execute all cells in the notebook:

```
for question_context in [question_context1, question_context2,
question_context3, question_context4]:
```

And voila! We get responses from our model that answer our questions about SageMaker JumpStart's capabilities and the full form of NLP as natural language processing.

Fine-tuning a model

It is typical to perform model fine-tuning when you take a pretrained model off the shelf to expose the model to your dataset so that it can perform better on your dataset compared to the performance without such exposure. Furthermore, model fine-tuning takes less training time and requires a smaller amount of labeled data compared to training a model from scratch. To fine-tune a pretrained model from SageMaker JumpStart, first we need to make sure that the model you would like to use supports fine-tuning. You can find this attribute in the overview cards. Secondly, you need to point a dataset to the model. Taking the DistilRoBERTa Base model as an example, SageMaker JumpStart provides the default dataset of **SQuAD-v2**, which allows you to quickly start a training job. You can also create a dataset of your own by following the instructions on the JumpStart model page. We are going to do just that.

Let's fine-tune the base DistilRoBERTa Base model with some questions and answers about Buddhism, which is one of the topics in the `SquAD-v2` dataset. Please follow these steps:

1. Open the `chapter08/1-prep_data_for_finetune.ipynb` notebook in the repository and execute all cells to download the dataset, extract the paragraphs that are related to Buddhism, and organize them as the fine-tune trainer expects. This is detailed on the description page in the **Fine-tune the Model on a New Dataset** section:

    - **Input**: A directory containing a `data.csv` file:

        - The first column of the `data.csv` should have a question.

        - The second column should have the corresponding context.

        - The third column should have the integer character starting position for the answer in the context.

        - The fourth column should have the integer character ending position for the answer in the context.

    - **Output**: A trained model that can be deployed for inference.

2. At the end of the notebook, the `data.csv` file will be uploaded to your SageMaker default bucket: `s3://sagemaker-<region>-<accountID>/chapter08/buddhism/data.csv`.

3. Once this is done, let's switch back to the model page and configure the fine-tuning job. As in *Figure 8.9*, select **Enter S3 bucket location**, paste in your CSV file URI into the box below, optionally append `-buddhism` onto the model name, leave the machine type and hyperparameters as their defaults, and hit **Train**. The default **Ml.P3.2xlarge** instance type, with one NVIDIA Tesla V100 GPU, is a great choice for fast model fine-tuning. The default hyperparameter setting performs fine-tuning with a **batch size of 4**, **learning rate of 2e-5**, and **3 epochs**. This is sufficient for us to demonstrate how the fine-tuning works. Feel free to change the values here to reflect your actual use case.

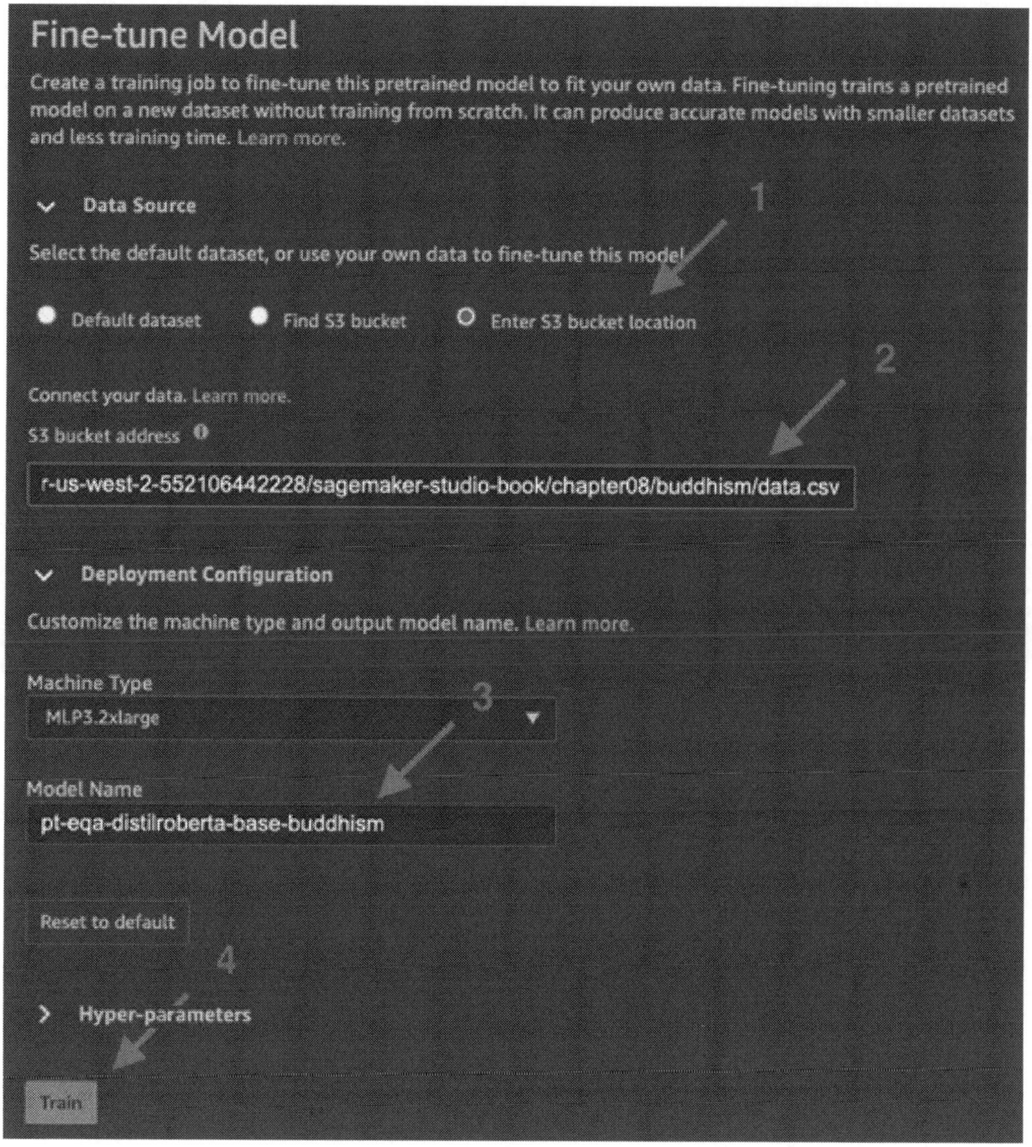

Figure 8.9 – Configuring a fine-tuning job for a custom dataset

The training job should take about 6 minutes with the **Ml.P3.2xlarge** instance.

4. Once the job completes, you can deploy the model to an endpoint with an **Ml.M5. Xlarge** instance, as shown in *Figure 8.10*. Ml.M5.Xlarge is a general-purpose CPU instance, which is a good starting point for model hosting.

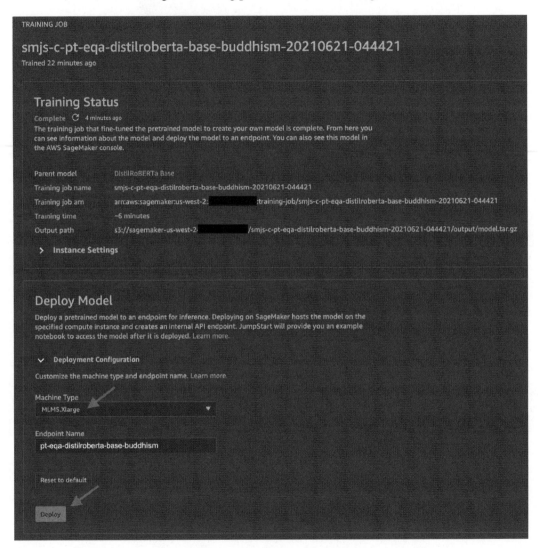

Figure 8.10 – Deploying the fine-tuned model

Of course, we now need to test how well the fine-tuned model performs on questions related to Buddha and Buddhism. Once the deployment finishes, you will be prompted with an option to open a prebuilt notebook to use the endpoint, similar to what is shown in *Figure 8.8*.

5. We can replace the question-context pair in the second cell with the following snippet from `https://www.history.com/topics/religion/buddhism`:

```
question_context1 = ["When was Buddhism founded?",
"Buddhism is a faith that was founded by Siddhartha
Gautama ("the Buddha") more than 2,500 years ago in
India. With about 470 million followers, scholars
consider Buddhism one of the major world religions. Its
practice has historically been most prominent in East and
Southeast Asia, but its influence is growing in the West.
Many Buddhist ideas and philosophies overlap with those
of other faiths."]
```

```
question_context2 = ["Where is Buddhism popular among?",
question_context1[-1]]
```

Then, execute the cells in the notebook and you will see how well our new model performs.

It's not quite what we would like the model to be. This is due to the very small epochs used and perhaps the unoptimized batch size and learning rate. As we are providing new data points for the model, the weights in the network are once again being updated and need to perform training for a sufficient number of epochs to converge on a lower loss and thus create a more accurate model. These hyperparameters often need to be tuned in order to obtain a good model even with fine-tuning. You are encouraged to further experiment with different hyperparameters to see if the model provides better responses to the questions.

We have just created three ML models, which are supposed to be complex and difficult to train, without much coding at all. Now we are going to learn how to use SageMaker Autopilot to automatically create a high-quality model without any code.

Creating a high-quality model with SageMaker Autopilot

Have you ever wanted to build an ML model without the hassle of data preprocessing, feature engineering, exploring algorithms, and optimizing the hyperparameters? Have you ever thought about how, for some use cases, you just wanted something quick to see if ML is even a possible approach for a certain business use case? Amazon SageMaker Autopilot makes it easy for you to build an ML model for tabular datasets without any code.

Wine quality prediction

To demonstrate SageMaker Autopilot, let's use a wine quality prediction use case. The wine industry has been searching for a technology that can help winemakers and the market to assess the quality of wine faster and with a better standard. Wine quality assessment and certification is a key part of the wine market in terms of production and sales and prevents the illegal adulteration of wines. Wine assessment is performed by expert oenologists based on physicochemical and sensory tests that produce features such as density, alcohol level, and pH level. However, when a human is involved, the standard can vary between oenologists or between testing trials. Having an ML approach to support oenologists in providing analytical information therefore becomes an important task in the wine industry.

We are going to train an ML model to predict wine quality based on the physicochemical sensory values for 4,898 white wines produced between 2004 and 2007 in Portugal. The dataset is available from UCI at `https://archive.ics.uci.edu/ml/datasets/Wine+Quality`.

Setting up an Autopilot job

Let's begin:

1. Please open the `chapter08/2-prep_data_for_sm_autopilot.ipynb` notebook from the repository, and execute all of the cells to download the data from the source, hold out a test set, and upload the training data to an S3 bucket. Please note the paths to the training data.

2. Next, open the Launcher and select **New Autopilot Experiment**, as in *Figure 8.11*.

Figure 8.11 – Creating a new Autopilot experiment

A new window will pop up for us to configure an Autopilot job.

3.   As shown in *Figure 8.12*, provide an **Experiment name** of your choice, such as `white-wine-predict-quality`.

Figure 8.12 – Configuring an Autopilot job

4.   As shown in *Figure 8.12*, provide the training data in the **CONNECT YOUR DATA** section, check the **Find S3 bucket** radio button, select your `sagemaker-<region>-<accountID>` from the **S3 bucket name** drop-down menu, and select the `sagemaker-studio-book/chapter08/winequality/winequality-white-train.csv` file from the **Dataset file name** drop-down menu. Set **Target** to **quality** to predict the quality of wine with the rest of attributes in the CSV file.

5.   In the lower half of the configuration page, as shown in *Figure 8.13*, provide a
     path to save the output data to, check the **Find S3 bucket** radio button, select your
     `sagemaker-<region>-<accountID>` from the **S3 bucket name** drop-down
     menu, and paste the `sagemaker-studio-book/chapter08/winequality/`
     path into the **Dataset directory name** field as the output location. This path is
     where we have the training CSV file.

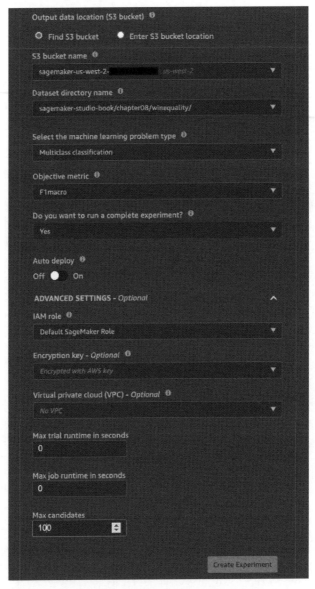

Figure 8.13 – Configuring an Autopilot job

6. As shown in *Figure 8.13*, choose **Multiclass classification** from the **Select the machine learning problem type** drop-down menu. Then choose **F1macro** from the **Objective metric** drop-down menu so that we can expect a more balanced model should the data be biased toward a certain quality rank.

7. As shown in *Figure 8.13*, choose **Yes** for **Do you want to run a complete experiment?**. Then toggle the **Auto deploy** option to **off** as we would like to walk through the evaluation process in SageMaker Studio before deploying our best model.

8. As shown in *Figure 8.13*, expand the **ADVANCED SETTINGS – Optional** section and input `100` in the **Max candidates** field. By default, Autopilot runs 250 training jobs with different preprocessing steps, training algorithms, and hyperparameters. By using a limited number of candidates, we should expect the full experiment to complete faster than with the default setting.

9. Hit **Create Experiment** to start the Autopilot job.

You will see a new window that shows the progress of the Autopilot job. Please let it crunch the numbers a bit and come back in a couple of minutes. You will see more progress and output in the progress tab, as shown in *Figure 8.14*.

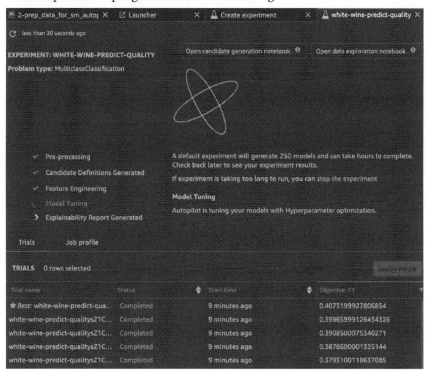

Figure 8.14   Viewing the progress of an Autopilot experiment

A lot is going on here. Let's dive in.

Understanding an Autopilot job

Amazon SageMaker Autopilot executes an end-to-end ML model-building exercise automatically. It performs **exploratory data analysis** (**EDA**), does data preprocessing, and creates feature engineering and a model-training recipe. It then executes the recipe in order to find the best model given the conditions. You can see the progress in the middle portion of *Figure 8.14*.

What makes Autopilot unique is the full visibility that it provides. Autopilot unboxes the typical AutoML black box by giving you the EDA results and the code that Autopilot runs to perform the feature engineering and ML modeling in the form of Jupyter notebooks. You can access the two notebooks by clicking the **Open data exploration notebook** button for the EDA results and the **Open candidate generation notebook** button for the recipe.

The data exploration notebook is helpful for understanding the data, the distribution, and how Autopilot builds the recipe based on the characteristics of the data. For example, Autopilot looks for missing values in the dataset, the distribution of numerical features, and the cardinality of the categorical features. This information gives data scientists a baseline understanding of the data, along with actionable insights on whether the input data contains reasonable entries or not. Should you see many features with high percentages of missing values (the **Percent of Missing Values** section), you could take the suggested actions to investigate the issue from the data creation perspective and apply some level of pre-processing to either remove the feature or apply domain-specific imputation. You may ask, "*Doesn't Autopilot apply data pre-processing and feature engineering to the data?*" Yes, it does. However, Autopilot does not have domain-specific knowledge of your data. You should expect a more generic, data science-oriented approach to the issues surfaced by Autopilot, which may not be as effective.

The candidate generation notebook prescribes a recipe for how the model should be built and trained based on the EDA of the data. The amount of code might look daunting, but if you read through it carefully, you can see, for example, what data preprocessing steps and modeling approaches Autopilot is attempting, as shown in the **Candidate Pipelines** section. The following is one example of this:

```
The SageMaker Autopilot Job has analyzed the dataset
and has generated 9 machine learning pipeline(s) that
use 3 algorithm(s).
```

Autopilot bases the pipelines on three algorithms: **XGBoost**, **linear learner**, and **multi-layer perceptron** (**MLP**). XGBoost is a popular gradient-boosted tree algorithm that combines an ensemble of weak predictors to form the final predictor in an efficient and flexible manner. XGBoost is one of SageMaker's built-in algorithms. Linear learner, also a SageMaker built-in algorithm, trains multiple linear models with different hyperparameters, and finds the best model with a distributed stochastic gradient descent optimization. MLP is a neural network-based supervised learning algorithm that can have multiple hidden layers of neurons to create a non-linear model.

You can also see the list of hyperparameters and ranges Autopilot is exploring (the **MultiAlgorithm Hyperparameter Tuning** section). Not only does Autopilot provide you visibility, but it also gives you full control of the experimentation. You can click on the **Import notebook** button the top right to get a copy of the notebook that you can actually customize and execute to obtain your next best model.

Evaluating Autopilot models

If you see that the job status in the tab, as shown in *Figure 8.14*, has changed to **Completed**, then it is time to evaluate the models Autopilot has generated. Autopilot has trained 100 models using various mixtures of feature engineering, algorithms, and hyperparameters as you can see in the list of trials. This leaderboard also shows the performance metric, the F1 score on a random validation split, used to evaluate the models. You can click on **Objective: F1** to sort the models by score.

Let's take a closer look at the best model, the one that has the highest F1 score and a star next to the trial name. Right-click on the trial and select **Open in model details** to view more information.

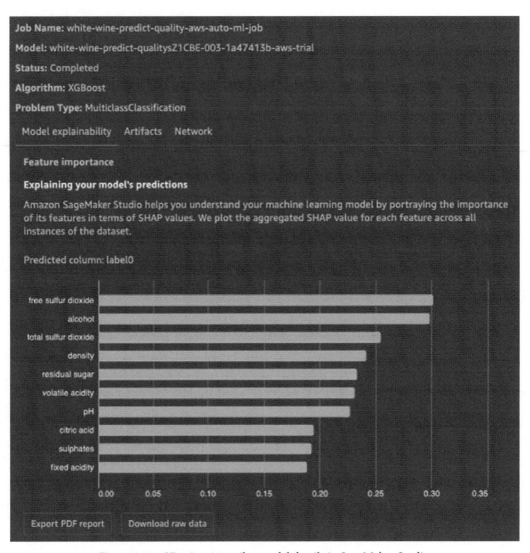

Figure 8.15 – Viewing Autopilot model details in SageMaker Studio

Autopilot reports a lot of detail on this page, as shown in *Figure 8.15*. First of all, we can see that this model is built based on the **XGBoost** algorithm. We also see a chart of feature importance that Autopilot generates for our convenience. This chart tells us how the model considers the importance, or contribution, of the input features. Autopilot computes the **SHapley Additive exPlanations (SHAP)** values using **SageMaker Clarify** for this XGBoost model and dataset. SHAP values explain how features contribute to the model forming the decision based on game theory.

> **Note**
>
> You can hover over the bars to see the actual values. SageMaker provides more detail so that you can learn more about how these SHAP values are calculated in the white papers in the **Want to learn more?** section.

Back to the chart, you can also download an automatically generated PDF report that contains this chart for review and distribution (**Export PDF report**). If you want to work with the raw data in JSON format in order to integrate the SHAP values in other applications, you can download the data (**Download raw data**). By clicking the two buttons, you will be redirected to the S3 console as shown in *Figure 8.16*. You can download the file from the S3 bucket on the console by clicking the **Download** button.

Figure 8.16 – Downloading the feature importance PDF report in the S3 console

Besides the feature importance, the model performance on the training and validation sets is also very important in understanding how the model would perform in real life. You can see the metrics captured during the training run in the **Metrics** part. In addition to the ObjectiveMetric used to rank the models on the leaderboard, we see the following metrics:

- train:f1
- train:merror
- validation:f1
- validation:merror

They are the multi-class F1macro and the multi-class error for the train and validation split of the data. As you can tell by the identical values, `ObjectiveMetric` is essentially `validation:f1`. With `train:f1` well above `validation:f1`, we may come to the conclusion that the model is overfitted to the training dataset. But why is this?

We can further verify the model performance in more detail with the test data that we held out at the beginning. Please open the `chapter08/3-evaluate_autopilot_models.ipynb` notebook from the repository and execute all cells. In this notebook, you will retrieve the top models based on the `ObjectiveMetric` from the Autopilot job, perform inference in the cloud using the **SageMaker Batch Transform** feature, and run some evaluations for each model. Feel free to change the value in `TOP_N_CANDIDATES` to a different number. You should see the F1 score computed with the macro, an unweighted mean, weighted approaches, a classification report (from a sklearn function), and a confusion matrix on the test data as the output of the last cell.

With the top model, a couple of things jump out at me here. The data is imbalanced in nature. There is a higher concentration of scores 5, 6, and 7. Few wines got a score of 3, 4, or 8. The confusion matrix also shows that wines that got a score of 3 were all incorrectly classified. Under this situation, the `f1` macro measure will be drastically lowered by incorrect classification of a minority class out of proportion. If we look at the weighted version of the `f1` score, we get a significantly higher score as the scoring weights the dominant classes more heavily:

```
Candidate name:  white-wine-predict-qualitysZ1CBE-003-1a47413b
Objective metric name:  validation:f1
Objective metric value:  0.4073199927806854
f1 = 0.51, Precision = 0.59 (macro)
f1 = 0.67, Precision = 0.68 (weighted)
```

	precision	recall	f1-score	support
3	0.00	0.00	0.00	3
4	0.70	0.39	0.50	18
5	0.63	0.67	0.65	144
6	0.67	0.77	0.72	215
7	0.76	0.57	0.65	94
8	0.78	0.44	0.56	16
accuracy			0.67	490
macro avg	0.59	0.47	0.51	490
weighted avg	0.68	0.67	0.67	490

```
[[  0   0   3   0   0   0]
 [  0   7   8   3   0   0]
```

```
[   0    2   96   45    1    0]
[   0    1   37  166   10    1]
[   0    0    8   31   54    1]
[   0    0    0    3    6    7]]
```

It is also important to measure the model's performance using the metrics that matter the most to the use case. As the author of the cited study stated about the importance of precision measure:

> *"This statistic is important in practice, since in a real deployment setting the actual values are unknown and all predictions within a given column would be treated the same."*

We should compare the precision measure used in the original research study (in *Table 3* in the study, linked in the *Further reading* section) where the individual precisions are the following:

- 4: 63.3%
- 5: 72.6%
- 6: 60.3%
- 7: 67.8%
- 8: 85.5%

when tolerance T = 0.5 for white wines. Our first Autopilot model overperforms in precision in some categories and underperforms in others.

Another strategy to find a model that serves the business problem better is to evaluate more models in addition to the best model suggested by Autopilot. We can see the evaluation for two others (or more, depending on your setting for TOP_N_CANDIDATES). We find that even though the second and third models have lower validation:f1 (macro) scores than the first model, they actually have higher F1 scores on the held-out test set. The individual precision scores for the third model are all better than the model in the original research, except for class 5, by 2.6%. What a charm! The third model in the leaderboard actually has better performance on the test data as measured by the precision metric, which makes the most sense to the use case.

After evaluation, we can deploy the optimal model into an endpoint for real-time inference. Autopilot makes it easy to deploy a model. In the leaderboard, select the line item that you would like to deploy, and click on the **Deploy model** button. A new page will pop up for you to configure the endpoint. Most options are straightforward and self-explanatory for an experienced SageMaker Studio user. Two things to note are that you can enable the data capture, which is useful if you want to set up SageMaker Model Monitor later. If you want the model to return more than just the **predicted_label**, such as the hard label of the winning class in a multiclass use case, you can choose to return the **probability** of the winning label, the **labels** of all classes, and the **probabilities** of all classes. The order of the selection will also determine the order of the output.

Summary

In this chapter, we introduced two features integrated into SageMaker Studio—JumpStart and Autopilot—with three ML use cases to demonstrate low-to-no code ML options for ML developers. We learned how to browse JumpStart solutions in the catalog and how to deploy an end-to-end CV solution from JumpStart to detect defects in products. We also deployed and fine-tuned a question-answering model using the DistilRoBERTa Base model from the JumpStart model zoo without any ML coding. With Autopilot, we built a white wine quality prediction model simply by pointing Autopilot to a dataset stored in S3 and starting an Autopilot job – no code necessary. It turned out that Autopilot even outperforms the model created by the original researchers, which may have taken months of research.

With the next chapter, we begin the next part of the book: *Production and Operation of Machine Learning with SageMaker Studio*. We will learn how we can move from prototyping to production ML training at scale with distributed training in SageMaker, how to monitor model training easily with SageMaker Debugger, how to save training cost with managed spot training..

Further reading

For more information take a look at the following resources:

- P. Cortez, A. Cerdeira, F. Almeida, T. Matos and J. Reis. *Modeling wine preferences by data mining from physicochemical properties*. In Decision Support Systems, Elsevier, 47(4):547-553, 2009. `https://bit.ly/3enCZUz`

Part 3 – The Production and Operation of Machine Learning with SageMaker Studio

In this section, you will learn how to effectively scale and operationalize the **machine learning (ML)** life cycle using SageMaker Studio so that you can reduce the amount of manual and undifferentiating work needed from a data scientist and allow them to focus on modeling.

This section comprises the following chapters:

- *Chapter 9, Training ML Models at Scale in SageMaker Studio*
- *Chapter 10, Monitoring ML Models in Production with SageMaker Model Monitoring*
- *Chapter 11, Operationalize ML Projects with SageMaker Projects, Pipelines, and Model Registry*

9
Training ML Models at Scale in SageMaker Studio

A typical ML life cycle starts with prototyping and will transition to a production scale where the data gets larger, models get more complicated, and the runtime environment gets more complex. Getting a training job done requires the right set of tools. Distributed training using multiple computers to share the load addresses situations that involve large datasets and large models. However, as complex ML training jobs use more compute resources, and more costly infrastructure (such as **Graphical Processing Units (GPUs)**), being able to effectively train a complex ML model on large data is important for a data scientist and an ML engineer. Being able to see and monitor how a training script interacts with data and compute instances is critical to optimizing the model training strategy in the training script so that it is time- and cost-effective. Speaking of cost when training at a large scale, did you know you can easily save more than 70% when training models in SageMaker? SageMaker Studio makes training ML models at scale easier and cost-effective.

In this chapter, we will be learning about the following:

- Performing distributed training in SageMaker Studio
- Monitoring model training and compute resources with SageMaker Debugger
- Managing long-running jobs with check-pointing and spot training

Technical requirements

For this chapter, you need to access the code provided at `https://github.com/PacktPublishing/Getting-Started-with-Amazon-SageMaker-Studio/tree/main/chapter09`.

Performing distributed training in SageMaker Studio

As the field of deep learning advances, ML models and training data are growing to a point that one single device is no longer sufficient for conducting effective model training. The neural networks are getting deeper and deeper, and gaining more and more parameters for training:

- **LeNet-5**, one of the first **Convolutional Neural Network** (**CNN**) models proposed in 1989 that uses 2 convolutional layers and 3 dense layers, has around 60,000 trainable parameters.

- **AlexNet**, a deeper CNN architecture with 5 layers of convolutional layers and 3 dense layers proposed in 2012, has around 62 million trainable parameters.

- **Bidirectional Transformers for Language Understanding** (**BERT**), a language representation model using a transformer proposed in 2018, has 110 million and 340 million trainable parameters in the base and large models respectively.

- **Generative Pre-trained Transformer 2** (**GPT-2**), a large transformer-based generative model proposed in 2019, has 1.5 billion trainable parameters.

- **GPT-3** is the next version, proposed in 2020, that reaches 175 billion trainable parameters.

Having more parameters to train means that there is a larger memory footprint during training. Additionally, the training data size needed to fit a complex model has also gone up significantly. For computer vision, one of the most commonly used training datasets, ImageNet, has 1.2 million images. For **Natural Language Processing** (**NLP**), GPT-3 is trained with 499 billion tokens, for example.

However, the latest and greatest GPU device would still struggle to hold up for such training requirements. The latest GPU device from NVIDIA, the A100 Tensor Core GPU available on AWS P4d.24xlarge instances, has 40 GB of GPU memory, but it would not be sufficient to hold the GPT-3 model, which has 175 billion parameters, as such a network would need *175 x 109 x 4 bytes = 700 GB* when using the *FP32* precision. Therefore, developers are going beyond single GPU device training and resorting to distributed training – that is, training using multiple GPU devices and multiple compute instances.

Let's understand why and how distributed training helps.

Understanding the concept of distributed training

In ML model training, the training data is fed into the loss optimization process in order to compute the gradients and weights for the next step. When data and parameters are much larger, as in the case of deep learning, having a full dataset that fits into the optimization becomes less feasible due to the GPU memory available on the device. It is common to use the **stochastic gradient descent optimization** approach, which estimates the gradients with a subset (**batch size**) of the full training dataset in each step, to overcome the GPU memory limitation. However, when a model or each data point is too large to have a meaningful batch size for the model training, we will not be able to converge to an optimal, accurate model in a reasonable timeframe.

Distributed training is a practice to distribute parts of the computation to multiple GPU devices and multiple compute instances (also called nodes), and synchronize the computation from all devices before proceeding to the next iteration. There are two strategies in distributed training: **data parallelism** and **model parallelism**.

Data parallelism distributes the training dataset during epochs from disk to multiple devices and instances while each device contains a portion of data and a *complete replica* of the model. Each node performs a forward and backward propagation pass using different batches of data and shares trainable weight updates with other nodes for synchronization at the end of a pass. With data parallelism, you can increase the batch size by *n*-fold, where *n* is the number of GPU devices across nodes. An appropriately large batch size allows better generalization during the estimation of gradients and also reduces the number of steps needed to run through the entire pass (**an epoch**).

> **Note**
> It has also been observed in practice that an overly large batch size will hurt the quality and generalization of a model. This is model- and dataset-dependent and requires experimentations and tuning to find out an appropriate batch size.

Data parallelism is illustrated in *Figure 9.1*:

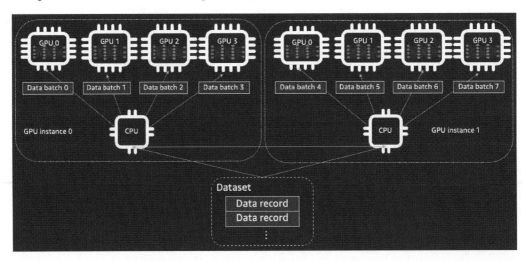

Figure 9.1 – The training data is distributed across GPU devices in data parallelism. A complete replica of the model is placed on each GPU device

Alternatively, model parallelism distributes a large model across nodes. Partitioning of a model is performed at a layers and a weights level. Each node possesses a partition of the model. Forward and backward propagations take place as a pipeline, with the data batches going through the model partitions on all nodes before the weight updates. To be more specific, each data batch is split into micro-batches and feeds into each part of the model, located on devices for forward and backward passes. With model parallelism, you can more effectively train a large model that needs a higher GPU memory footprint than a single GPU device using memory collectively from multiple GPU devices. Model parallelism is illustrated in *Figure 9.2*:

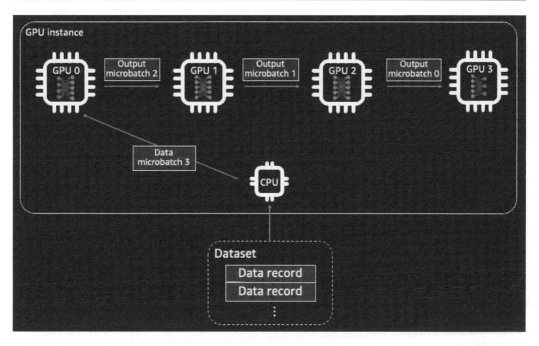

Figure 9.2 – The model is partitioned across GPU devices in model parallelism. The training data is split into micro-batches and fed into the GPUs, each of which has a part of the model as a pipeline

When should we use data parallelism or model parallelism? It depends on the data size, batch, and model sizes in training. Data parallelism is suitable for situations when a single data point is too large to have a desirable batch size during training. The immediate trade-off of having a small batch size is having a longer runtime to finish an epoch. You may want to increase the batch size so that you can complete an epoch under a reasonable timeframe. You can use data parallelism to distribute a larger batch size to multiple GPU devices. However, if your model is large and takes up most GPU memory in a single device, you will not enjoy the scale benefit of data parallelism much. This is because, in data parallelism, an ML model is fully replicated onto each of the GPU devices, leaving little space for any data. You should use model parallelism when you have a large model in relation to the GPU memory.

SageMaker makes running distributed training for large datasets and large models easy in the cloud. SageMaker's **distributed training libraries** support data parallelism and model parallelism for the two most popular deep learning frameworks, **TensorFlow** and **PyTorch**, when used in SageMaker. SageMaker's **distributed data parallel library** scales your model training with near-linear scaling efficiency, meaning that the reduction in training time in relation to the number of nodes is close to linear. SageMaker's **distributed model parallel library** automatically analyzes your neural network architecture and splits the model across GPU devices and orchestrates the pipeline execution efficiently.

In the following sections, we'll learn how we can implement data parallelism and model parallelism in SageMaker Studio for our training scripts written in TensorFlow and PyTorch.

> **Note**
> Both TensorFlow and PyTorch are supported by the two distributed training libraries. The distributed training concepts remain the same between the two deep learning frameworks. We will focus on TensorFlow for the data parallel library and PyTorch for the model parallel library.

The data parallel library with TensorFlow

SageMaker's distributed data parallel library implements simple APIs that look similar to TensorFlow's way of performing model training in a distributed fashion but conduct distributed training that is optimized with AWS's compute infrastructure. This means that you can easily adopt SageMaker's API without making sophisticated changes to your existing distributed training code written in TensorFlow. If this is your first model training with distribution, we will demonstrate the modification needed to adapt SageMaker's distributed data parallel library to your existing model training script.

Let's go to SageMaker Studio and start working with the `Getting-Started-with-Amazon-SageMaker-Studio/chapter09/01-smdp_tensorflow_sentiment_analysis.ipynb` notebook. This example is built on top of the training example we walked through in *Chapter 5, Building and Training ML Models with the SageMaker Studio IDE* (`Getting-Started-with-Amazon-SageMaker-Studio/chapter05/02-tensorflow_sentiment_ analysis.ipynb`), where we trained a deep learning model using the TensorFlow Keras API on an IMDB review dataset. Back in *Chapter 5, Building and Training ML Models with SageMaker Studio IDE*, we ran the training script on one `ml.p3.2xlarge` instance, which only has one NVIDIA Tesla V100 GPU. Now, in this chapter, we will use SageMaker's distributed data parallel library to extend the code to work with multiple GPU devices, either from an instance or from multiple instances. And remember that we can always easily specify the number of instances and the type of the instances in the `sagemaker.tensorflow.TensorFlow` estimator. Let's open the notebook and select the **Python 3 (TensorFlow 2.3 Python 3.7 CPU Optimized)** kernel and an **ml.t3.medium** instance, and run the first six cells to prepare the SageMaker session and the dataset. The cell leading with `%%writefile code/smdp_tensorflow_sentiment.py` is where modification to adopt the distributed training script will go. Follow the next steps to see the changes that need to be made to enable the distributed data parallel library:

1. First, import the TensorFlow module of the data parallel library:

    ```
    import smdistributed.dataparallel.tensorflow as sdp
    ```

2. After the library is imported, we need to initialize the SageMaker distributed data parallel library in order to use it during runtime. We can implement it right after the `import` statements or in `main` (if `__name__` == `"__main__"`):

    ```
    sdp.init()
    ```

3. Then, we discover all the GPU devices available in the compute instance fleet and configure the GPUs so that they are aware of the ranking within an instance. If an instance has eight GPU devices, each of them will get assigned a rank from zero to seven. The way to think about this is that each GPU device establishes a process to run the script and gets a unique ranking from `sdp.local_rank()`:

```
gpus = tf.config.experimental.list_physical_
devices('GPU')
if gpus:
    local_gpu = gpus[sdp.local_rank()]
    tf.config.experimental.set_visible_devices(local_gpu,
'GPU')
```

4. We also configure the GPUs to allow memory growth. This is specific to running TensorFlow with the SageMaker distributed data parallel library:

```
for gpu in gpus:
    tf.config.experimental.set_memory_growth(gpu, True)
```

The compute environment is now ready to perform distributed training.

5. We scale the learning rate by the number of devices. Because of data parallelism, we will be able to fit in a larger batch size. With a larger batch size, it is recommended to scale the learning rate proportionally:

```
args.learning_rate = args.learning_rate * sdp.size()
```

6. Previously in *Chapter 5*, *Building and Training ML Models with SageMaker Studio IDE*, we trained the model using Keras' `model.fit()` API, but we have to make some changes to the model training. SageMaker's distributed data parallel library does not yet support Keras' `.fit()` API and only works with TensorFlow core modules. To use SageMaker's distributed data parallel library, we can use the automatic differentiation (`tf.GradientTape`) and eager execution from TensorFlow 2.x. After defining the model using Keras layers in the `get_model()` function, instead of compiling it with an optimizer, we write the forward and backward pass explicitly with the `loss` function, the optimizer, and also the accuracy metrics defined explicitly:

```
model = get_model(args)
loss = tf.losses.BinaryCrossentropy(name = 'binary_
crossentropy')
acc = tf.metrics.BinaryAccuracy(name = 'accuracy')
optimizer = tf.optimizers.Adam(learning_rate = args.
```

```
      learning_rate)
    with tf.GradientTape() as tape:
        probs = model(x_train, training=True)
        loss_value = loss(y_train, probs)
        acc_value = acc(y_train, probs)
```

We then wrap `tf.GradientTape` with SMDataParallel's `DistributedGradientTape` to optimize the `AllReduce` operation during the multi-GPU training. `AllReduce` is an operation that reduces the matrixes from all distributed processes:

```
    tape = sdp.DistributedGradientTape(tape, sparse_as_dense
    = True)
```

Note that the `sparse_as_dense` argument is set to `True` because we have an embedding layer in the model that will generate a spare matrix.

7. At the start of the training, broadcast the initial model variables from the head node (`rank 0`) to all other worker nodes (`rank 1` onward). We use a `first_batch` variable to denote the start of the training epochs:

```
    if first_batch:
        sdp.broadcast_variables(model.variables, root_rank=0)
        sdp.broadcast_variables(optimizer.variables(), root_
    rank=0)
```

8. Average the loss and accuracy across devices; this process is called **all-reduce**:

```
    loss_value = sdp.oob_allreduce(loss_value)
    acc_value = sdp.oob_allreduce(acc_value)
```

9. Put these steps in a `training_step()` function to perform a forward and backward pass, decorated with `@tf.function`. Run this training step in a nested `for` loop to go over epochs and batches of training data. We need to make sure that all GPU devices are getting an equal amount of data during a pass. We do this by taking data that is divisible by the total number of GPU devices in the inner `for` loop:

```
    train_dataset.take(len(train_dataset)//sdp.size())
```

10. After the training `epoch` loop, we save the model, only using the leader device:

```
    if sdp.rank() == 0:
        model.save(os.path.join(args.model_dir, '1'))
```

11. Last but not least in the training script, we convert the training data into a `tf.data.Dataset` object and set up the batching in the `get_train_data()` function so that it will work with our eager execution implementation. Note that we need `drop_remainder` to prevent the dataset from being of an equal batch_size across devices:

```
dataset = tf.data.Dataset.from_tensor_slices((x_train, y_
    train))
dataset = dataset.batch(batch_size, drop_remainder=True)
```

12. We then move on to SageMaker's TensorFlow estimator construct. To enable the SageMaker distributed data parallel library in a training job, we need to provide a dictionary:

```
distribution = {'smdistributed': {'dataparallel':
{'enabled': True}}}
```

This is given to the estimator, as follows.

```
train_instance_type = 'ml.p3.16xlarge'
estimator = TensorFlow(source_dir='code',
        entry_point='smdp_tensorflow_sentiment.py',
        ...
        distribution=distribution)
```

Also, we need to choose a SageMaker instance from the following instance types that supports SageMaker's distributed data parallel library: **ml.p4d.24xlarge**, **ml.p3dn.24xlarge**, and **ml.p3.16xlarge**:

I.   The `ml.p4d.24xlarge` instance equips with 8 NVIDIA A100 Tensor Core GPUs, each with 40 GB of GPU memory.

II. The `ml.p3dn.24xlarge` instance comes with 8 NVIDIA Tesla V100 GPUs, each with 32 GB of GPU memory.

III. The `ml.p3.16xlarge` instance also comes with 8 NVIDIA Tesla V100 GPUs, each with 16 GB of GPU memory.

For demonstration purposes, we will choose ml.p3.16xlarge, which is the least expensive one among the three options. One single ml.p3.16xlarge is sufficient to run distributed data parallel training in SageMaker, as there will be 8 GPU devices to perform the training.

As there are more GPU devices and GPU memory to carry out the batching in an epoch, we can now increase `batch_size`. We scale `batch_size` 8 times from what we used in *Chapter 5, Building and Training ML Models with SageMaker Studio IDE* – that is, *64 x 8 = 512*.

13. With the estimator, we can proceed to call `estimator.fit()` to start the training.

To verify that the training is run with multiple GPU devices, the simplest way to tell is from the standard output. You can see a prefix of `[x, y]<stdout>: message` being added to indicate the process ranking from which the message is produced, as shown in *Figure 9.3*. We will learn more about this topic in the *Monitoring model training and compute resource with SageMaker Debugger* section:

```
[9]: # Creating a new trial for the experiment
     exp_trial = Trial.create(experiment_name=experiment_name,
                              trial_name=jobname)

     experiment_config = {'ExperimentName': experiment_name,
                          'TrialName': exp_trial.trial_name,
                          'TrialComponentDisplayName': 'Training'}

     estimator.fit(inputs=data_channels,
                   job_name=jobname,
                   experiment_config=experiment_config,
                   wait=True)

[1,6]<stdout>:sdp.size() = 8
[1,3]<stdout>:x train (25000, 400) y train (25000,)
[1,6]<stdout>:x train (25000, 400) y train (25000,)
[1,2]<stdout>:x train (25000, 400) y train (25000,)
[1,1]<stdout>:x train (25000, 400) y train (25000,)
[1,0]<stdout>:x train (25000, 400) y train (25000,)
[1,7]<stdout>:x train (25000, 400) y train (25000,)
[1,4]<stdout>:x train (25000, 400) y train (25000,)
[1,5]<stdout>:x train (25000, 400) y train (25000,)
```

Figure 9.3 – The standard output from the cell, showing messages printed from process ranks – [1,0] to [1,7]. In our example, we use one ml.p3.16xlarge instance that has eight GPU devices

Even though here I am not using PyTorch to demonstrate SageMaker's distributed data parallel library, PyTorch is indeed supported by the library under the `smdistributed.dataparallel.torch` module. This module has a set of APIs that are similar to PyTorch's native distributed data parallel library. This means that you do not require many coding changes to adopt SageMaker's distributed data parallel library for PyTorch, which is optimized for training using SageMaker's infrastructure. You can find more details on how to adopt it in your PyTorch scripts at `https://docs.aws.amazon.com/sagemaker/latest/dg/data-parallel-modify-sdp-pt.html`.

In the next section, we will run a PyTorch example and adopt model parallelism.

Model parallelism with PyTorch

Model parallelism is particularly useful when you have a large network model that does not fit into the memory of a single GPU device. SageMaker's distributed model parallel library implements two features that enable efficient training for large models so that you can easily adapt the library to your existing training scripts:

- **Automated model partitioning**, which maximizes GPU utilization, balances the memory footprint, and minimizes communication among GPU devices. In contrast, you can also manually partition the model using the library.

- **Pipeline execution**, which determines the order of computation and data movement across parts of the model that are on different GPU devices. There are two pipeline implementations: **interleaved** and **simple**. An interleaved pipeline prioritizes the backward passes whenever possible. It uses GPU memory more efficiently and minimizes the idle time of any GPU device in the fleet without waiting for the forward pass to complete to start the backward pass, as shown in *Figure 9.4*:

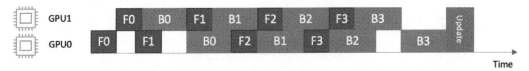

Figure 9.4 – An interleaved pipeline over two GPUs (GPU0 and GPU1). F0 represents a forward pass for the first micro-batch and B1 represents a backward pass for the second micro-batch. Backward passes are prioritized whenever possible

A simple pipeline, on the other hand, waits for the forward pass to complete before starting the backward pass, resulting in a simpler execution schedule, as shown in *Figure 9.5*:

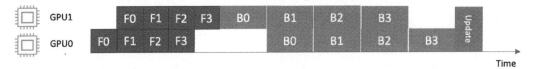

Figure 9.5 – A simple pipeline over two GPUs. Backward passes are run only after the forward passes finish

> **Note**
>
> Images in *Figure 9.4* and *9.5* are from: `https://docs.aws.amazon.`
> `com/sagemaker/latest/dg/model-parallel-core-`
> `features.html`

Let's start an example with the notebook in `chapter09/02-smmp-pytorch_mnist.`
`ipynb`, where we are going to apply SageMaker's distributed model parallel library to
train a PyTorch model to classify digit handwriting using the famous MNIST digit dataset.
Open the notebook in SageMaker Studio and use the **Python 3 (Data Science)** kernel and
an `ml.t3.medium` instance:

1. As usual, set up the SageMaker session and import the dependencies in the first cell.

2. Then, create a model training script written in PyTorch. This is a new training
   script. Essentially, it is training a convolutional neural network model on the
   MNIST handwriting digit dataset from the `torchvision` library. The model
   is defined using the `torch.nn` module. The optimizer used is the AdamW
   optimization algorithm. We implement the training epochs and batching, as it
   allows us to have the most flexibility to adopt SageMaker's distributed model
   parallel library.

3. SageMaker's distributed model parallel library for PyTorch can be imported from
   `smdistributed.modelparallel.torch`:

   ```
   import smdistributed.modelparallel.torch as smp
   ```

4. After the library is imported, initialize the SageMaker distributed model parallel
   library in order to use it during runtime. We can implement it right after the import
   statements or in `main` (if `__name__ == "__main__"`):

   ```
   smp.init()
   ```

5. We will then ping and set the GPU devices with their local ranks:

   ```
   torch.cuda.set_device(smp.local_rank())
   device = torch.device('cuda')
   ```

6. The data downloading process from `torchvision` should only take place in the leader node (`local_rank = 0`), while all the other processes (on other GPUs) should wait until the leader node completes the download:

```
if smp.local_rank() == 0:
    dataset1 = datasets.MNIST('../data', train=True,
            download=True, transform=transform)
smp.barrier() # Wait for all processes to be ready
```

7. Then, wrap the model and the optimizer with SageMaker's distributed model parallel library's implementations:

```
model = smp.DistributedModel(model)
optimizer = smp.DistributedOptimizer(optimizer)
```

Up to now, the implementation between SageMaker's distributed data parallel library and model parallel library has been quite similar. The following is where things get different for the model parallel library.

8. We create a `train_step()` for function forward and backward passes and decorate it with `@smp.step`:

```
@smp.step
def train_step(model, data, target):
    output = model(data)
    loss = F.nll_loss(output, target, reduction='mean')
    model.backward(loss)
    return output, loss
```

Create another `train()` function to implement the batching within an epoch. This is where we call `train_step()` to perform the forward and backward passes for a batch of data. Importantly, the data-related `to.(device)` calls need to be placed before `train_step()` while the typical `model.to(device)` is not required. Placing the model to a device is done automatically by the library.

Before stepping to the next batch, we need to average the loss across micro-batches with `.reduce_mean()`. Also, note that `optimizer.step()` needs to take place outside of `train_step()`:

```
def train(model, device, train_loader, optimizer, epoch):
    model.train()
    for batch_idx, (data, target) in enumerate(train_
loader):
```

```
        data, target = data.to(device), target.to(device)
        optimizer.zero_grad()
        _, loss_mb = train_step(model, data, target)
        # Average the loss across microbatches.
        loss = loss_mb.reduce_mean()
        optimizer.step()
```

9. Implement `test_step()`, decorated with `@smp.step`, and `test()` similarly for model evaluation. This allows model parallelism in model evaluation too.

10. After the epochs loop, save the model with `smp.dp_rank()==0` to avoid data racing and ensure the gathering happens properly. Note that we set `partial=True` if we want to be able to load the model later and further train it:

```
if smp.dp_rank() == 0:
    model_dict = model.local_state_dict()
    opt_dict = optimizer.local_state_dict()
    model = {'model_state_dict': model_dict, 'optimizer_
state_dict': opt_dict}
    model_output_path = f'{args.model_dir}/pt_mnist_
checkpoint.pt'
    smp.save(model, model_output_path, partial=True)
```

11. We then move on to the SageMaker PyTorch estimator construct. To enable SageMaker's distributed model parallel library in a training job, we need to provide a dictionary to configure SageMaker's distributed model parallel library and the **Message Passing Interface (MPI)**. SageMaker's distributed model parallel library uses the MPI to communicate across nodes, so it needs to be enabled. The following snippet instructs SageMaker to partition the model into two `'partitions': 2`, to optimize for speed when partitioning the model `'optimize': 'speed'`, to use a micro-batch of four `'microbatches': 4`, to employ an interleaved pipeline schedule ('pipeline': 'interleaved'), and to disable distribute data parallel `'ddp': False`. The MPI is enabled with four processes per host `'mpi':{'enabled': True, 'processes_per_host': 2}}`, which should be smaller than or equal to the number of GPU devices:

```
distribution = {'smdistributed': {
                    'modelparallel': {
                        'enabled': True,
                        'parameters': {
                            'partitions': 2,
```

```
                                    'optimize': 'speed',
                                    'microbatches': 4,
                                    'pipeline': 'interleaved',
                                    'ddp': False
                            }
                    }
            },
            'mpi': {
                    'enabled': True,
                    'processes_per_host': 2
            }
    }
```

You can find the full list of parameters for distribution at https://
sagemaker.readthedocs.io/en/stable/api/training/smd_model_
parallel_general.html#smdistributed-parameters.

12. We then apply the distribution dictionary to the PyTorch estimator and use
one ml.p3.8xlarge instance, which has four NVIDIA Tesla V100 GPUs. Unlike
SageMaker's distributed data parallel library, SageMaker's distributed model parallel
library is supported by all instances with multiple GPU devices.

13. We can then proceed to call estimator.fit() to start the training.

Adopting a TensorFlow training script with SageMaker's distributed model parallel library
employs similar concepts that we can just walk through. You can find out more about how
to use the smdistributed.modelparallel.tensorflow module at https://
docs.aws.amazon.com/sagemaker/latest/dg/model-parallel-
customize-training-script-tf.html#model-parallel-customize-
training-script-tf-23.

When training with multiple GPU devices, one of the main challenges is to understand
how expensive GPU resources are utilized. In the next section, we will discuss SageMaker
Debugger, a feature that helps us analyze the utilization of compute resources during a
SageMaker training job.

Monitoring model training and compute resources with SageMaker Debugger

Training ML models using `sagemaker.estimator.Estimator` and related classes, such as `sagemaker.pytorch.estimator.PyTorch` and `sagemaker.tensorflow.estimator.TensorFlow`, gives us the flexibility and scalability we need when developing in SageMaker Studio. However, due to the use of remote compute resources, it is rather different debugging and monitoring training jobs on a local machine or a single EC2 machine to how you would on a SageMaker Studio notebook. Being an IDE for ML, SageMaker Studio provides a comprehensive view of the managed training jobs through **SageMaker Debugger**. SageMaker Debugger helps developers monitor the compute resource utilization, detect modeling-related issues, profile deep learning operations, and identify bottlenecks during the runtime of your training jobs.

SageMaker Debugger supports TensorFlow, PyTorch, MXNet, and XGBoost. By default, SageMaker Debugger is enabled in every SageMaker estimator. It collects instance metrics such as GPU, CPU, and memory utilization every 500 milliseconds and basic tensor output such as loss and accuracy every 500 steps. The data is saved in your S3 bucket. You can inspect the monitoring results live or after the job finishes in the SageMaker Studio IDE. You can also retrieve the monitoring results from S3 into a notebook and run additional analyses and custom visualization. If the default setting is not sufficient, you can configure the SageMaker Debugger programmatically for your `Estimator` to get the level of information you need.

To get started, we can first inspect the information from the default Debugger configuration for the job we ran in `Machine-Learning-Development-with-Amazon-SageMaker-Studio/chapter09/01-smdp_tensorflow_sentiment_analysis.ipynb`:

1. Find the job name you have run. It is in the `jobname` variable, in the form of `imdb-smdp-tf-YYYY-mm-DD-HH-MM-SS`. You can also find it in the output of the last cell.

2.   Navigate to the **SageMaker Components and registries** icon on the left sidebar,
     select **Experiments and trials** from the drop-down menu, and locate the entry
     with `jobname`; double-click the entry. You will see a trial component named
     Training, as shown in *Figure 9.6*. Right-click on the entry and select **Open
     Debugger for insights**:

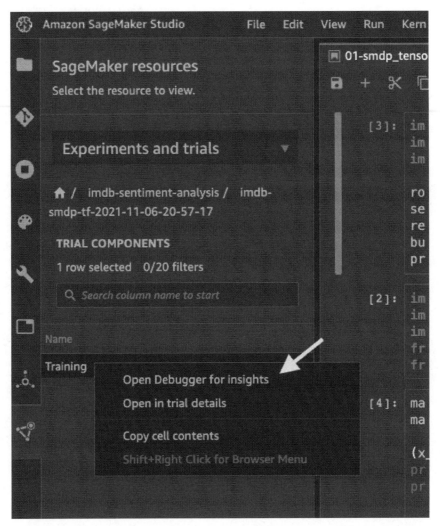

Figure 9.6 – Opening the SageMaker Debugger UI from Experiments and trials

3. A new window in the main working area will pop up. The window will become available in a couple of minutes, as SageMaker Studio is launching a dedicated instance to process and render the data in the UI. This is called the **SageMaker Debugger insights dashboard**. Once available, you can see the results in the **Overview** and **Nodes** tabs, as shown in *Figure 9.7*:

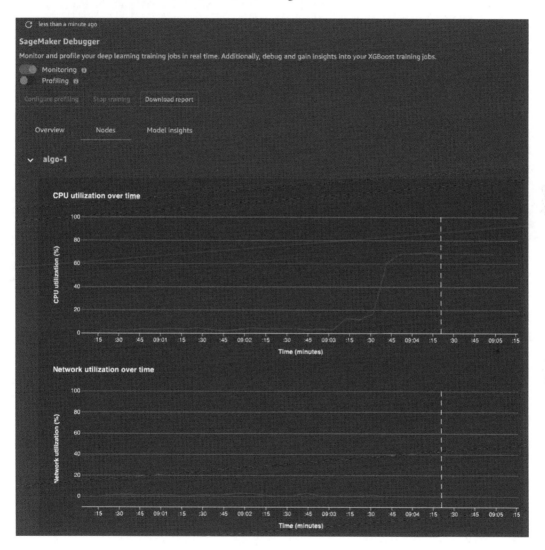

Figure 9.7 – The SageMaker Debugger insights dashboard showing the CPU and network utilization over the course of the training

In the **Nodes** tab, the mean utilization of the CPU, the network, the GPU, and the GPU memory are shown in the charts. You can narrow down the chart to a specific CPU or GPU to see whether there is any uneven utilization over the devices, as shown in *Figure 9.8*. From these charts, we can tell the following:

- The average CPU utilization peaked at around 60%, 3 minutes after the start of the job. This indicates that the training was taking place, and there was much activity on the CPU side to read in the data batches and feed into the GPU devices.

- The average GPU utilization over eight devices peaked at around 25%, also at 3 minutes after the start of the job. At the same time, there was around 5% of GPU memory used on average. This is considered low GPU utilization, potentially due to the small batch size compared to the now much larger compute capacity from an ml.p3.16xlarge instance.

- On the other hand, there was some network utilization in the first 3 minutes. This is the period when SageMaker's fully managed training downloaded the training data from the S3 bucket:

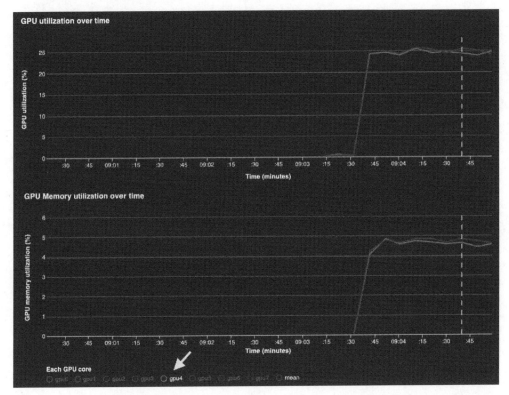

Figure 9.8 – The SageMaker Debugger insights dashboard showing the GPU utilization over the course of the training

At the bottom of the page, a heatmap of the CPU/GPU utilization in a holistic view is displayed. As an exercise, feel free to open the Debugger for the training job submitted at `Getting-Started-with-Amazon-SageMaker-Studio/ chapter06/02-tensorflow_sentiment_analysis.ipynb` and compare the difference in the CPU/GPU utilization between single-device training and distributed training.

Next, we'll move on to learn how to lower the cost of training ML models in SageMaker Studio with fully managed spot training and how to create checkpointing for long-running jobs and spot jobs.

Managing long-running jobs with checkpointing and spot training

Training ML models at scale can be costly. Even with SageMaker's pay-as-you-go pricing model on the training instances, performing long-running deep learning training and using multiple expensive instances can add up quickly. SageMaker's fully managed spot training and checkpointing features allow us to manage and resume long-running jobs easily, helping us reduce costs up to 90% on training instances over on-demand instances.

SageMaker-managed Spot training uses the concept of spot instances from Amazon EC2. EC2 spot instances let you take advantage of any unused instance capacity in an AWS Region at a much lower cost compared to regular on-demand instances. The spot instances are cheaper but can be interrupted when there is a higher demand for instances from other users on AWS. SageMaker-managed spot training manages the use of spot instances, including safe interruption and timely resumption of your training when the spot instances are available again.

Along with the spot training feature, managed checkpointing is a key to managing your long-running job. Checkpoints in ML refer to intermediate ML models saved during training. Data scientists regularly create checkpoints and keep track of the best accuracy during the epochs. They compare accuracy against the best one during progression and use the checkpoint model that has the highest accuracy, rather than the model from the last epoch.

Data scientists can also resume and continue the training from any particular checkpoint if they want to fine-tune a model. As SageMaker trains a model on remote compute instances using containers, the checkpoints are saved in a local directory in the container. SageMaker automatically uploads the checkpoints from the local bucket to your S3 bucket. You can reuse the checkpoints in another training job easily by specifying their location in S3. In the context of SageMaker-managed spot training, you do not need to worry about uploading and downloading the checkpoint files in case there is any interruption and resumption of a training job. SageMaker handles it for us.

Let's run an example to see how things work. Open `Getting-Started-with-Amazon-SageMaker-Studio/chapter09/03-spot_training_checkpointing.ipynb` using the **Python 3 (TensorFlow 2.3 Python 3.7 CPU Optimized)** kernel and an **ml.t3.medium** instance. In this notebook, we will be reusing our TensorFlow model training for the IMDB review dataset from *Chapter 5, Building and Training ML Models with SageMaker Studio IDE*, and make some changes to the code to demonstrate how you can enable the checkpointing and managed spot training using SageMaker:

1. Run the first five cells to set up the SageMaker session, and prepare the dataset. If you ran the first `chapter09/01-smdp_tensorflow_sentiment_analysis.ipynb` notebook, the dataset should be available already.

2. The cell leading with `%%writefile code/tensorflow_sentiment_with_checkpoint.py` is where we will make changes to the TensorFlow/Keras code. First of all, we are adding a new `--checkpoint_dir` argument in the `parse_args()` function to assign a default `/opt/ml/checkpoints` location set by SageMaker.

3. In `__name__ == '__main__'`, we will add a check to see whether `checkpoint_dir` exists locally in the container or not. If it does, list the directory to see whether there are any existing checkpoint files:

```
if not os.listdir(args.checkpoint_dir):
    model = get_model(args)
    initial_epoch_number = 0
else:
    model, initial_epoch_number = load_model_from_
checkpoints(args.checkpoint_dir)
```

If `checkpoint_dir` does not contain valid checkpoint files, it means that there is no prior training job and checkpoints attached to the container and that `checkpoint_dir` is newly created for brand-new model training. If it does contain files, it means that previous checkpoint files are plugged into this training job and should be used as a starting point of the training, implemented in the `load_model_from_checkpoints()` function.

4. Implement `load_model_from_checkpoints()` to list all the checkpoint files, ending with `.h5`, as this is how Keras saved the model, in a given directory and use `regex` from the `re` library to filter the epoch number in the filename. We can then identify the latest checkpoint to load and continue the training with such a model. We assume the epoch number ranges from `0` to `999` in the regular expression operation.

5. After the model is loaded, either a new one or from a checkpoint, implement a `tf.keras.callbacks.ModelCheckpoint` callback in Keras to save a model checkpoint to `args.checkpoint_dir` after every epoch.

6. When setting up the `sagemaker.tensorflow.TensorFlow` estimator, provide the following additional arguments to the estimator:

    I.   `use_spot_instances`: A Boolean to elect to use SageMaker spot instances for training.

    II. `max_wait`: A required argument when `use_spot_instances` is `True`. This is a timeout in seconds waiting for the spot training job. After this timeout, the job will be stopped.

    III. `checkpoint_s3_uri`: The S3 bucket location to save the checkpoint files persistently. If you pass an S3 bucket location that already has checkpoint models and pass a higher epoch number, the script will pick up the latest checkpoint and resume training. For example, by providing `checkpoint_s3_uri`, which has checkpoints from a previous 50-epoch run and an `epochs` hyperparameter of 60, our script will resume the training from the fiftieth checkpoint and continue for another 10 epochs.

    IV. `max_run`: The maximum runtime in seconds allowed for training. After this timeout, the job will be stopped. This value needs to be smaller than or equal to `max_wait`.

The following code snippet will construct an estimator to train a model with managed spot instances and checkpointing:

```
use_spot_instances = True
max_run = 3600
max_wait = 3600
```

```
checkpoint_suffix = str(uuid.uuid4())[:8]
checkpoint_s3_uri = f's3://{bucket}/{prefix}/checkpoint-
{checkpoint_suffix}'
estimator = TensorFlow(use_spot_instances=use_spot_
instances,
                       checkpoint_s3_uri=checkpoint_s3_
uri,
                       max_run=max_run,
                       max_wait=max_wait,
                       ...)
```

7. The rest of the steps remain the same. We specify the hyperparameters, data input, and experiment configuration before we invoke `.fit()` to start the training job.

8. Wonder how much we save by using spot instances? From **Experiments and trials** in the left sidebar, we can bring up the AWS settings details of the trial, as shown in *Figure 9.9*, and see a **70%** saving by simply using managed spot training instances:

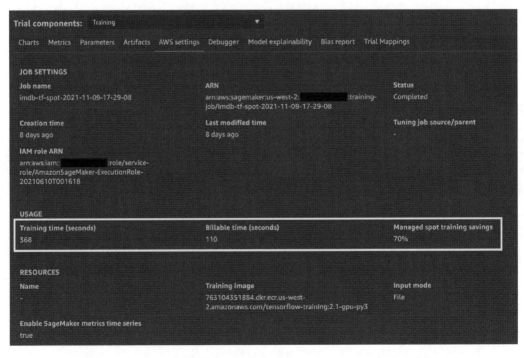

Figure 9.9 – A 70% saving using managed spot training, as seen in the trial details

A 70% saving is quite significant. This is especially beneficial to large-scale model training use cases that need expensive compute instances and have a long training time. Just four additional arguments to the estimator and some changes in the training script earn us a 70% saving.

Summary

In this chapter, we walked through how to train deep learning models using SageMaker distributed training libraries: data parallel and model parallel. We ran a TensorFlow example to show how you can modify a script to use SageMaker's distributed data parallel library with eight GPU devices, instead of one from what we learned previously. This enables us to increase the batch size and reduce the iterations needed to go over the entire dataset in an epoch, improving the model training runtime. We then showed how you can adapt SageMaker's distributed model parallel library to model training written in PyTorch. This enables us to train a much larger neural network model by partitioning the large model to all GPU devices. We further showed you how you can easily monitor the compute resource utilization in a training job using SageMaker Debugger and visualize the metrics in the SageMaker Debugger insights dashboard. Lastly, we explained how to adapt your training script to use the fully managed spot training and checkpointing to save costs when training models in SageMaker.

In the next chapter, we will be switching gear to learn how to monitor ML models in production. ML models in production taking unseen inference data may or may not produce quality predictions as expected from evaluations conducted prior to deployment. It is crucial in an ML life cycle to set up a monitoring strategy to ensure that your models are operating at a satisfactory level. SageMaker Studio has the functionality needed to help you set up model monitoring easily to monitor ML models in production. We will learn how to configure SageMaker Model Monitor and how to use it as part of our ML life cycle.

10

Monitoring ML Models in Production with SageMaker Model Monitor

Having a model put into production for inferencing isn't the end of the **machine learning** (**ML**) life cycle. It is just the beginning of an important topic: how do we make sure the model is performing as it is designed to and as expected in real life? Monitoring how the model performs in production, especially on data that the model has never seen before, is made easy with SageMaker Studio. You will learn how to set up model monitoring for models deployed in SageMaker, detect data drift and performance drift, and visualize results in SageMaker Studio, so that you can let the system detect the degradation of your ML model automatically.

In this chapter, we will be learning about the following:

- Understanding drift in ML
- Monitoring data and model performance drift in SageMaker Studio
- Reviewing model monitoring results in SageMaker Studio

Technical requirements

For this chapter, you need to access the code in `https://github.com/PacktPublishing/Getting-Started-with-Amazon-SageMaker-Studio/tree/main/chapter10`.

Understanding drift in ML

An ML model in production needs to be carefully and continuously monitored for its performance. There is no guarantee that once the model is trained and evaluated, it will be performing at the same level in production as in the testing environment. Unlike a software application, where unit tests can be implemented to test out an application in all possible edge cases, it is rather hard to monitor and detect issues of an ML model. This is because ML models use probabilistic, statistical, and fuzzy logic to infer an outcome for each incoming data point, and the testing, meaning the model evaluation, is typically done without true prior knowledge of production data. The best a data scientist can do prior to production is to create training data from a sample that closely represents the real-world data, and evaluate the model with an out-of-sample strategy in order to get an unbiased idea of how the model would perform on unseen data. While in production, the incoming data is completely unseen by the model; how to evaluate live model performance, and how to take action on that evaluation, is a critical topic for the productionization of ML models.

Model performance can be monitored with two approaches. One that is more straightforward is to capture the ground truth for the unseen data and compare the prediction against the ground truth. The second approach is to compare the statistical distribution and characteristics of inference data against the training data as a proxy to determine whether the model is behaving in an expected way.

The first approach requires ground-truth determination after the prediction event takes place so that we can directly compute the same performance metrics that data scientists would use during model evaluation. However, in some use cases, a true outcome (ground truth) may lag behind the event by a long time or may even not be available at all.

The second approach lies in the premise that an ML model learns statistically and probabilistically from the training data and would behave differently when a new dataset from a different statistical distribution is provided. A model would return gibberish when data does not come from the same statistical distribution. This is called **covariate drift**. Therefore, detecting the covariate drift in data gives a more real-time estimate of how the model is going to perform.

Amazon SageMaker Model Monitor is a feature in SageMaker that continuously monitors the quality of models hosted on SageMaker by setting up data capture, computing baseline statistics, and monitoring the drift from the traffic to your SageMaker endpoint on a schedule. SageMaker Model Monitor has four types of monitors:

- **Model quality monitor**: Monitors the performance of a model by computing the accuracy from the predictions and the actual ground-truth labels

- **Data quality monitor**: Monitors data statistical characteristics of the inference data by comparing the characteristics to that of the baseline training data

- **Model explainability monitor**: Integrates with SageMaker Clarify to compute feature attribution, using the Shapley value, over time

- **Model bias monitor**: Integrates with SageMaker Clarify to monitor predictions for data and model prediction bias

Once the model monitoring for an endpoint is set up, you can visualize the drift and any data issues over time in SageMaker Studio. Let's learn how to set up SageMaker Model Monitor in SageMaker Studio following an ML use case in this chapter. We will focus on model quality and data quality monitoring.

Monitoring data and performance drift in SageMaker Studio

In this chapter, let's consider an ML scenario: we train an ML model and host it in an endpoint. We also create artificial inference traffic to the endpoint, with random perturbation injected into each data point. This is to introduce noise, missingness, and drift to the data. We then proceed to create a data quality monitor and a model quality monitor using SageMaker Model Monitor. We use a simple ML dataset, the abalone dataset from UCI (`https://archive.ics.uci.edu/ml/datasets/abalone`), for this demonstration. Using this dataset, we train a regression model to predict the number of rings, which is proportionate to the age of abalone.

Training and hosting a model

We will follow the next steps to set up what we need prior to the model monitoring—getting data, training a model, hosting it, and creating traffic:

1. Open the notebook in `Getting-Started-with-Amazon-SageMaker-Studio/chapter10/01-train_host_predict.ipynb` with the **Python 3 (Data Science)** kernel and the **ml.t3.median** instance.

2. Run the first three cells to set up the libraries and SageMaker session.

3. Read the data from the source and perform minimal processing, namely encoding the categorical variable, `Sex`, into integers so that we can later use the XGBoost algorithm to train. Also, we change the type of the target column Rings to float so that the values from ground truth and model prediction (regression) are consistently in float for the model monitor to compute.

4. Split the data randomly into training (80%), validation (10%), and test sets (10%). Then, save the data to the local drive for model inference and upload it to S3 for model training.

5. For model training, we use `XGBoost`, a SageMaker built-in algorithm, with the `reg:squarederror` objective for regression problems:

```
image = image_uris.retrieve(region=region,
                    framework='xgboost', version='1.3-1')
xgb = sagemaker.estimator.Estimator(...)
xgb.set_hyperparameters(objective='reg:squarederror',
num_round=20)
data_channels={'train': train_input, 'validation': val_
input}
xgb.fit(inputs=data_channels, ...)
```

The training takes about 5 minutes.

6. After the model training is complete, we host the model with a SageMaker endpoint with `xgb.deploy()` just like we learned in *Chapter 7, Hosting ML Models in the Cloud: Best Practices*. However, by default, a SageMaker endpoint does not save a copy of the incoming inference data. In order to monitor the performance of the model and data drift, we need to instruct the endpoint to persist the incoming inference data. We use `sagemaker.model_monitor.DataCaptureConfig` to set up the data capture behind an endpoint for monitoring purposes:

```
data_capture_config = DataCaptureConfig(enable_
capture=True,
```

```
        sampling_percentage=100,
        destination_s3_uri=s3_capture_upload_path)
```

We specify an S3 bucket location in `destination_s3_uri`. `sampling_percentage` can be `100` (%) or lower depending on how much real-life traffic you expect. We need to make sure we capture a sample size large enough for any statistical comparison later on. If the model inference traffic is sparse, such as 100 inferences per hour, you may want to use 100% of the samples for model monitoring. If you have a high-rate-of-model-inference use case, you may be able to use a smaller percentage.

7. We can deploy the model to an endpoint with `data_capture_config`:

```
predictor = xgb.deploy(...,
                data_capture_config=data_capture_config)
```

8. Once the endpoint is ready, let's apply the regression model on the validation dataset in order to create a baseline dataset for the model quality monitoring. The baseline dataset should contain ground-truth and model prediction in two columns in a CSV file. We then upload the CSV to an S3 bucket location:

```
pred=predictor.predict(df_val[columns_no_target].values)
pred_f = [float(i) for i in pred[0]]
df_val['Prediction']=pred_f
model_quality_baseline_suffix = 'abalone/abalone_val_
model_quality_baseline.csv'
df_val[['Rings', 'Prediction']].to_csv(model_quality_
baseline_suffix, index=False)
model_quality_baseline_s3 = sagemaker.s3.S3Uploader.
upload(
        local_path=model_quality_baseline_suffix,
        desired_s3_uri=desired_s3_uri,
        sagemaker_session=sess)
```

Next, we can make some predictions on the endpoint with the test dataset.

Creating inference traffic and ground truth

To simulate real-life inference traffic, we take the test dataset and add random perturbation, such as random scaling and dropping features. We can anticipate that this simulates data drift and twists model performance. Then, we send the perturbed data to the endpoint for prediction and save the ground truth into an S3 bucket location. Please follow these steps in the same notebook:

1. Here, we have two functions to add random perturbation: add_randomness() and drop_randomly(). The former function randomly multiplies each feature value, except the Sex function, by a small factor, and randomly assigns a binary value to Sex. The latter function randomly drops a feature and fills it with NaN (not a number).

2. We also have the generate_load_and_ground_truth() function to read from each row of the test data, apply perturbation, call the endpoint for prediction, construct the ground truth in a dictionary, gt_data, and upload it to an S3 bucket as a JSON file. Notably, in order to make sure we establish correspondence between the inference data and the ground truth, we associate each pair with inference_id. This association will allow Model Monitor to merge the inference and ground truth for analysis:

```python
def generate_load_and_ground_truth():
    gt_records=[]
    for i, row in df_test.iterrows():
        suffix = uuid.uuid1().hex
        inference_id = f'{i}-{suffix}'

        gt = row['Rings']
        data = row[columns_no_target].values
        new_data = drop_random(add_randomness(data))
        new_data = convert_nparray_to_string(new_data)
        out = predictor.predict(data = new_data,
                    inference_id = inference_id)
        gt_data = {'groundTruthData': {
                        'data': str(gt),
                        'encoding': 'CSV',
                    },
                    'eventMetadata': {
                        'eventId': inference_id,
```

```
                    },
            'eventVersion': '0',
        }
    gt_records.append(gt_data)
  upload_ground_truth(gt_records, ground_truth_upload_
path, datetime.utcnow())
```

We wrap this function in a `while` loop in the `generate_load_and_ground_truth_forever()` function so that we can generate persistent traffic using a threaded process until the notebook is shut down:

```
def generate_load_and_ground_truth_forever():
    while True:
        generate_load_and_ground_truth()
from threading import Thread
thread = Thread(target=generate_load_and_ground_truth_
forever)
thread.start()
```

3. Lastly, before we set up our first model monitor, let's take a look how the inference traffic is captured:

```
capture_file = get_obj_body(capture_files[-1])
print(json.dumps(json.loads(capture_file.split('\n')
[-2]), indent=2))
{
  "captureData": {
    "endpointInput": {
      "observedContentType": "text/csv",
      "mode": "INPUT",
      "data": "1.0,0.54,0.42,0.14,0.805,0.369,0.1725,0.21
",
      "encoding": "CSV"
    },
    "endpointOutput": {
      "observedContentType": "text/csv; charset=utf-8",
      "mode": "OUTPUT",
      "data": "9.223058700561523",
      "encoding": "CSV"
    }
```

```
  },
  "eventMetadata": {
    "eventId": "a9d22bac-094a-4610-8dde-689c6aa8189b",
    "inferenceId": "846-01234f26730011ecbb8b1391
95a02686",
    "inferenceTime": "2022-01-11T17:00:39Z"
  },
  "eventVersion": "0"
}
```

Note the `captureData.endpointInput.data` function has an entry of inference data through `predictor.predict()` with the unique inference ID in `eventMetadata.inferenceId`. The output from the model endpoint is in `captureData.endpointOutput.data`.

We have done all the prep work. We can now move on to creating the model monitors in SageMaker Studio.

Creating a data quality monitor

A data quality monitor compares the statistics of the incoming inference data to that of a baseline dataset. You can set up a data quality monitor via the SageMaker Studio UI or SageMaker Python SDK. I will walk through the easy setup via the Studio UI:

1. Go to the **Endpoints** registry in the left sidebar and locate your newly hosted endpoint, as shown in *Figure 10.1*. Double-click the entry to open it in the main working area:

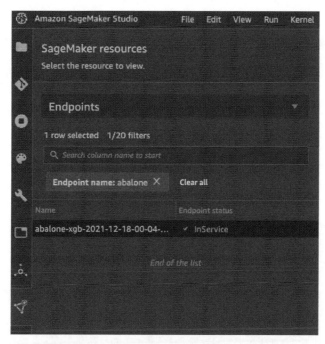

Figure 10.1 – Opening the endpoint details page

2. Click the **Data quality** tab and then **Create monitoring schedule**, as shown in *Figure 10.2*:

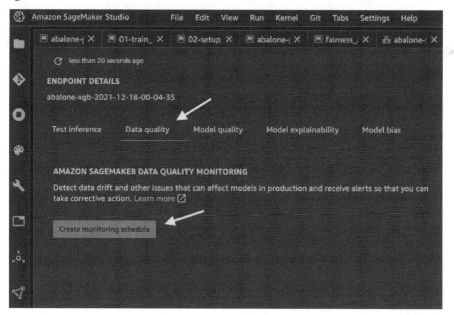

Figure 10.2 – Creating a data quality monitoring schedule on the endpoint details page

3. In the first step of the setup, as shown in *Figure 10.3*, we choose an IAM role that has access permission to read and write results to the bucket location we specify in the following pages. Let's choose **Default SageMaker Role** as it refers to the SageMaker execution role attached to the user profile. For **Schedule expression**, we can choose a **Daily** or **Hourly** schedule. Let's choose **Hourly**. For **Stopping condition (Seconds)**, we can limit the maximum runtime for the model monitoring job. We should give a number no larger than a full hour (3600 seconds) so that a monitoring job does not bleed into the next hour. Toward the bottom of the page, we leave **Enable metrics** on so that the metrics computed by the model monitor get sent to Amazon CloudWatch too. This allows us to visualize and analyze the metrics in CloudWatch. Click **Continue**:

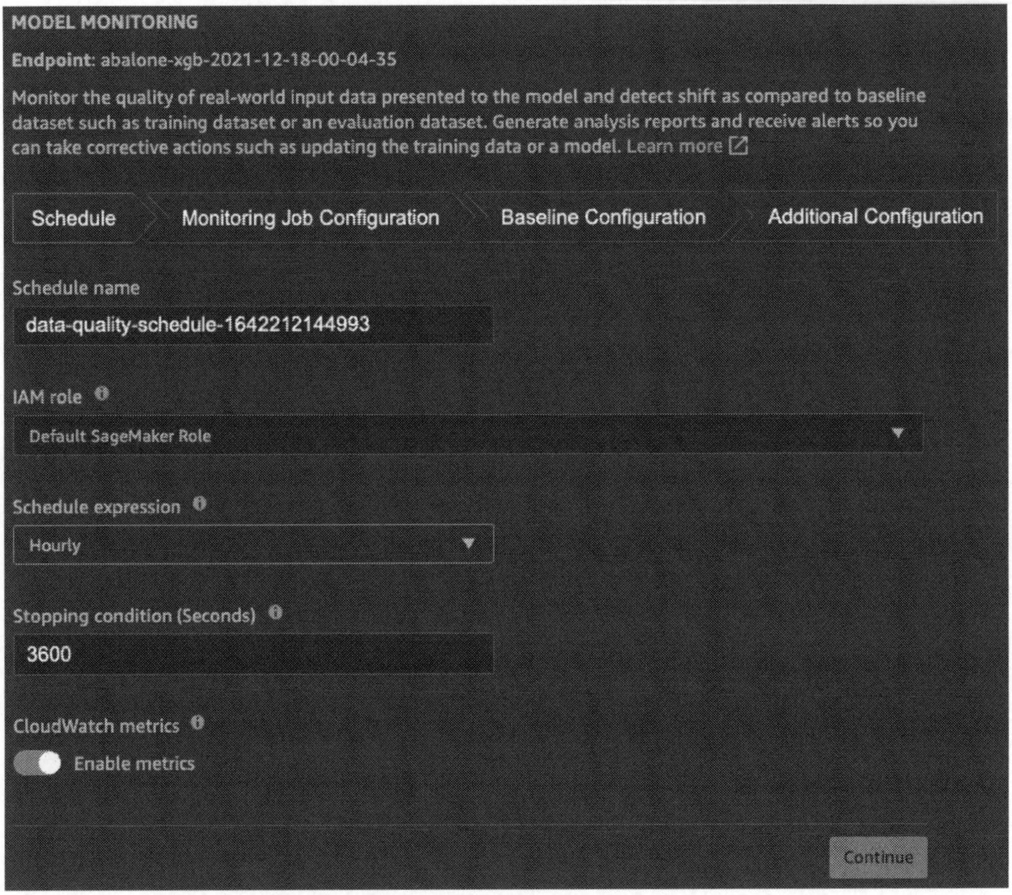

MODEL MONITORING

Endpoint: abalone-xgb-2021-12-18-00-04-35

Monitor the quality of real-world input data presented to the model and detect shift as compared to baseline dataset such as training dataset or an evaluation dataset. Generate analysis reports and receive alerts so you can take corrective actions such as updating the training data or a model. Learn more ⧉

| Schedule | Monitoring Job Configuration | Baseline Configuration | Additional Configuration |

Schedule name

data-quality-schedule-1642212144993

IAM role ❶

Default SageMaker Role ▼

Schedule expression ❶

Hourly ▼

Stopping condition (Seconds) ❶

3600

CloudWatch metrics ❶

⬤ Enable metrics

Continue

Figure 10.3 – Data quality monitor setup step 1

4. In the second step, as shown in *Figure 10.4*, we configure the infrastructure and
    output location for the hourly monitoring job. The infrastructure subject to
    configure is the SageMaker Processing job that is going to be created every hour. We
    leave the compute instance—instance type, count, and disk volume size—as default.
    We then provide an output bucket location for the monitoring result and encryption
    and networking (VPC) options:

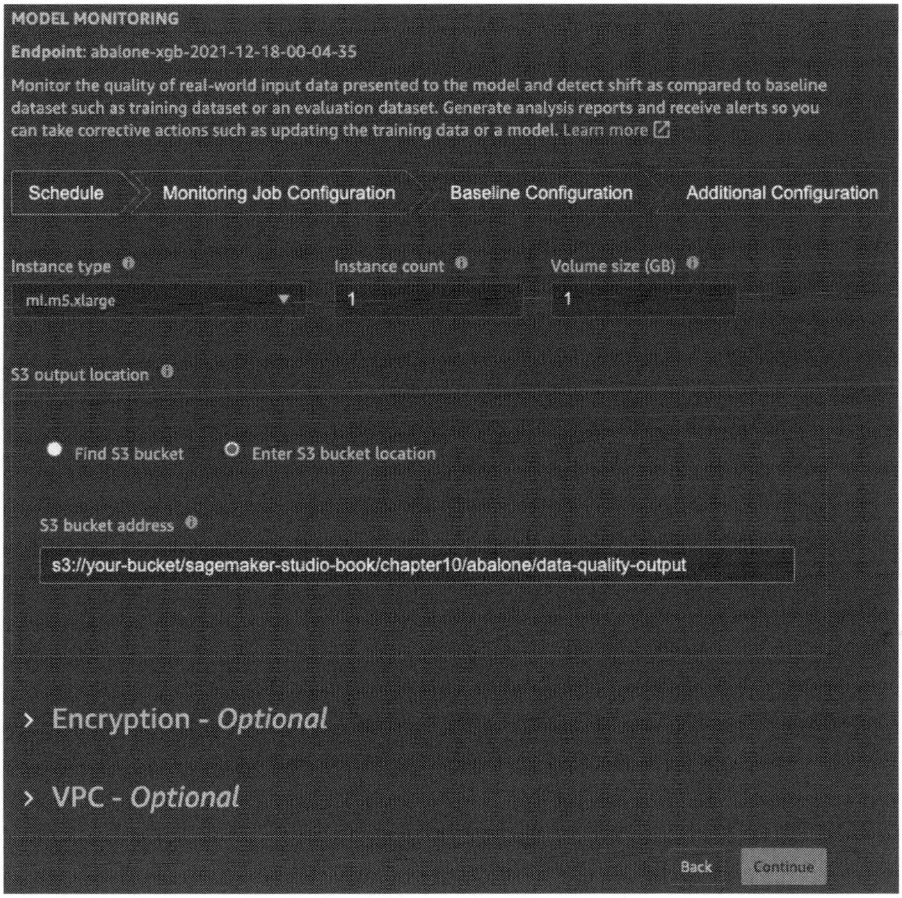

Figure 10.4 – Data quality monitor setup step 2

5. In the third step, as shown in *Figure 10.5*, we configure the baseline computation. Right after a monitor is set up, a one-time SageMaker Processing job will be launched to compute the baseline statistics. Future recurring monitoring jobs would use the baseline statistics to judge whether drift has occurred. We provide the CSV file location in an S3 bucket to the baseline dataset S3 location. We uploaded the training data to the S3 bucket and the full path is in the `train_data_s3` variable. We provide an S3 output location to the baseline S3 output location. Because our training data CSV contains a feature name in the first row, we select **CSV with header** for **Baseline dataset format**. Lastly, we configure the compute instance for the one-time SageMaker Processing job. The default configuration that uses one `ml.m5.xlarge` instance with 1 GB of baseline volume is sufficient. Click **Continue**:

Figure 10.5 – Data quality monitor setup step 3

6. In the final **Additional Configuration** page, you have an option to provide preprocessing and postprocessing scripts to the recurring monitoring job. You can customize the features and model output with your own scripts. This extension is not supported when you use a custom container for model monitoring. In our case, we use the built-in container from SageMaker. For more information about the preprocessing and postprocessing scripts, visit `https://docs.aws.amazon.com/sagemaker/latest/dg/model-monitor-pre-and-post-processing.html`.

If you go back to the **ENDPOINT DETAILS** page, under the **Data quality** tab, as shown in *Figure 10.2*, you can now see a new monitoring schedule with the **Scheduled** status. A baselining job is now being launched to compute various statistics from the baseline training dataset. After the baselining job is finished, the first hourly monitoring job will be launched as a SageMaker Processing job within 20 minutes at the top of an hour. The monitoring job computes the statistics from the inference data gathered during the hour and compares it against the baseline. We will review the monitoring result in the *Reviewing model monitoring results in SageMaker Studio* section later.

Now, let's move on to creating the model quality monitor to monitor the model performance.

Creating a model quality monitor

Creating a model quality monitor follows a similar process compared to creating a data quality monitor, with additional emphasis on handling model prediction and ground-truth labels in S3. Let's follow the next steps to set up a model quality monitor to monitor the model performance over time:

7. On the **Endpoint Details** page of the same endpoint, go to the **Model quality** tab and click **Create monitoring schedule**, as shown in *Figure 10.6*:

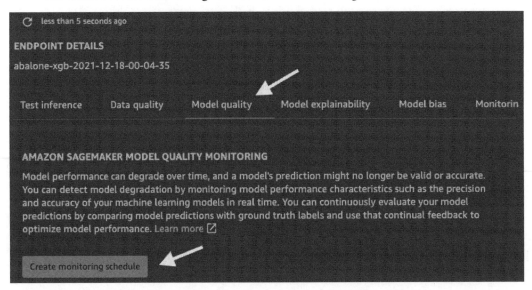

Figure 10.6 – Creating a model quality monitoring schedule on the endpoint details page

8. On the first page, **Schedule**, we choose an IAM role, scheduling frequency, and so on for the monitoring job, similar to *step 3* in the previous *Creating a data quality monitor section*.

9. On the second page, **Monitoring Job Configuration**, as shown in *Figure 10.7*, we configure the instance for the monitoring job and the input/output to a monitoring job:

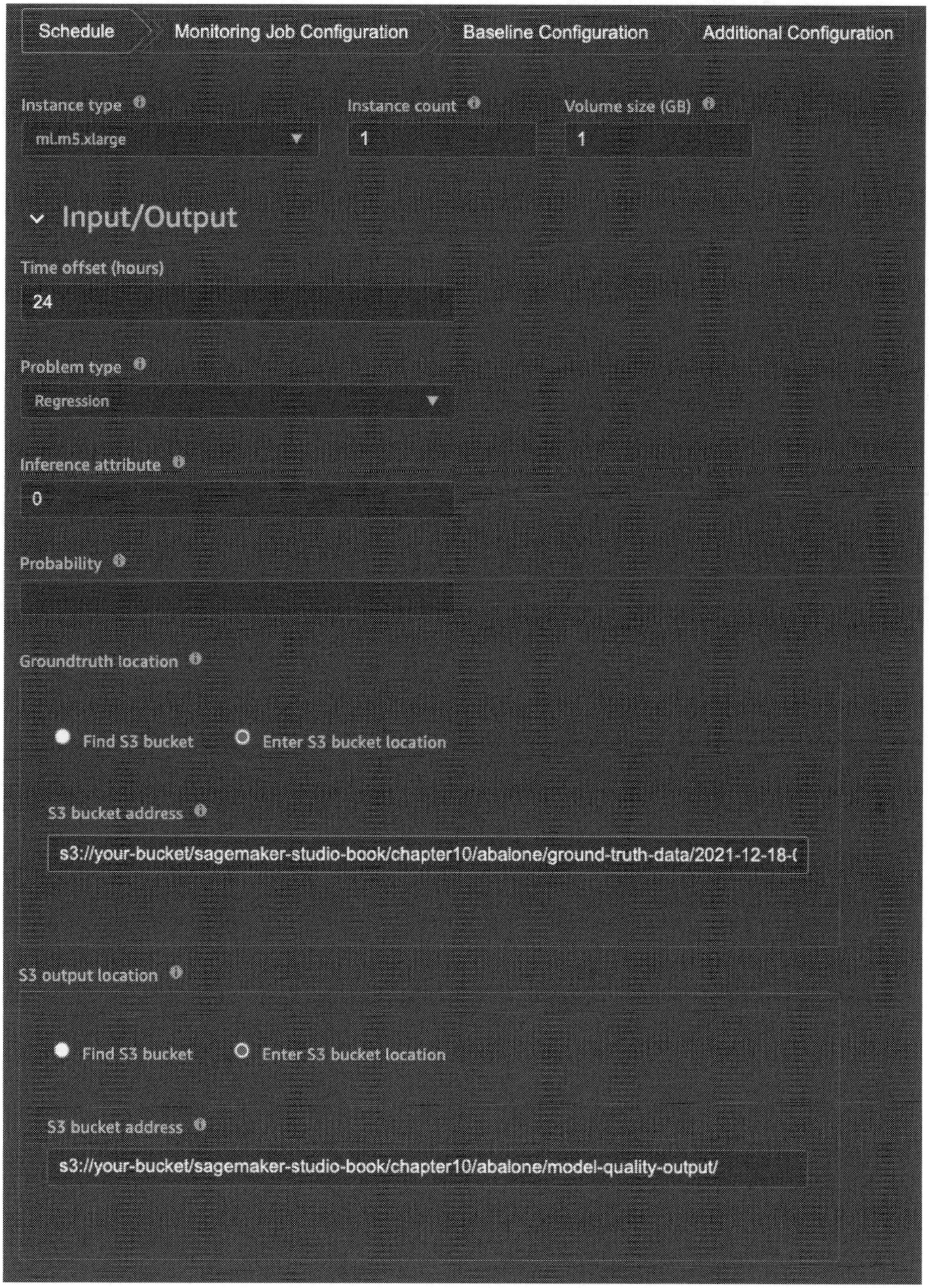

Schedule ⟩ Monitoring Job Configuration ⟩ Baseline Configuration ⟩ Additional Configuration

Instance type ⓘ
ml.m5.xlarge ▼

Instance count ⓘ
1

Volume size (GB) ⓘ
1

⌄ Input/Output

Time offset (hours)
24

Problem type ⓘ
Regression ▼

Inference attribute ⓘ
0

Probability ⓘ

Groundtruth location ⓘ

● Find S3 bucket   ○ Enter S3 bucket location

S3 bucket address ⓘ
s3://your-bucket/sagemaker-studio-book/chapter10/abalone/ground-truth-data/2021-12-18-(

S3 output location ⓘ

● Find S3 bucket   ○ Enter S3 bucket location

S3 bucket address ⓘ
s3://your-bucket/sagemaker-studio-book/chapter10/abalone/model-quality-output/

Figure 10.7 – Setting up input and output for the model quality monitor

Input refers to both model prediction from the endpoint and the ground-truth files we are uploading in the notebook. In the **Input/Output** options, **Time offset (hours)** refers to hours allowed to wait for ground-truth labels to become available in S3. We know that typically, there is a delay between the prediction event occurring and the outcome of the event becoming available. This offset addresses that delay and allows Model Monitor to look out for the corresponding ground truth for a prediction event. Because we are generating the inference data and the ground-truth label at the same time from the notebook, we can safely use the default value—24 hours. For **Problem type**, we choose **Regression** from the drop-down list as the model predicts the ring size and age of an abalone. In **Inference attribute** and **Probability**, we inform SageMaker how to interpret the model prediction from the endpoint. Depending on the output format, CSV or JSON, we would put in either the index location or JSON path, respectively. Because our model returns a regression value in CSV format and does not return a probability score, we would put 0 for **Inference attribute** to specify the first value being the model output, and leave **Probability** empty.

> **Note**
>
> If the content type for your model is JSON/JSON Lines, you would specify a JSON path in **Inference attribute** and **Probability**. For example, when a model returns `{prediction: {"predicted_label":1, "probability":0.68}}`, you would specify `"prediction. predicted_label"` in **Inference attribute** while specifying `"prediction.probability"` in **Probability**.

For **Groundtruth location**, we use the S3 location where we uploaded the ground-truth labels. It's in the `ground_truth_upload_path` variable in the notebook. For **S3 output location**, we specify an S3 bucket location for Model Monitor to save the output. Lastly, you can optionally configure the encryption and VPC for the monitoring jobs. Click **Continue** to proceed.

10. On the third page, **Baseline Configuration**, as shown in *Figure 10.8*, we specify the baseline data for the baselining. We have created baseline data from the validation set. Let's provide the S3 location of the CSV file that is saved in the `model_ quality_baseline_s3` variable in the notebook to the **Baseline dataset S3 location** field. For **Baseline S3 output location**, we provide an S3 location to save the baselining result. Choose **CSV with header** in **Baseline dataset format**. Leave the instance type and configuration as the default.

This is to configure the SageMaker Processing job for the one-time baseline computation. In the last three fields, we put the corresponding CSV header names—`Rings` for **Baseline groundtruth attribute** and `Prediction` for **Baseline inference attribute**—and leave the field empty for **Baseline probability** because, again, our model does not produce probability. Click **Continue**:

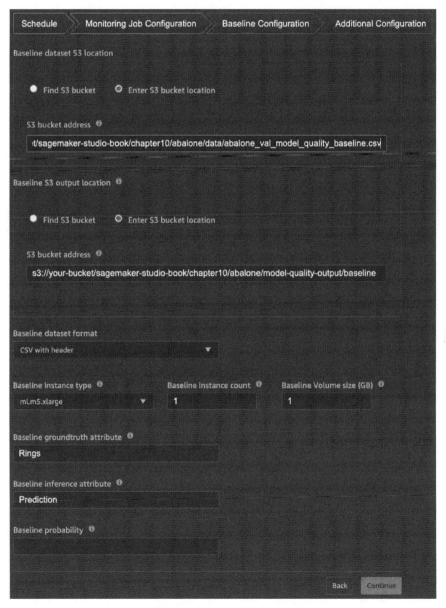

Figure 10.8 – Configuring the baseline calculation for the model quality monitor

11. In **Additional Configuration**, we can provide preprocessing and postprocessing scripts to the monitor like in the case of the data quality monitor. Let's skip this and proceed to complete the setup by clicking **Enable model monitoring**.

Now, we have created the model quality monitor. You can see the monitoring schedule is in the **Scheduled** status under the **Model quality** tab on the **ENDPOINT DETAILS**page. Similar to the data quality monitor, a baseline processing job is launched to compute the baseline model performance using the baseline dataset. An hourly monitoring job will also be launched as a SageMaker Processing job within 20 minutes at the top of an hour in order to compute the model performance metrics from the inference data gathered during the hour and compare them against the baseline. We will review the monitoring results in the next section, *Reviewing model monitoring results in SageMaker Studio*.

Reviewing model monitoring results in SageMaker Studio

SageMaker Model Monitor computes various statistics on the incoming inference data, compares them against the precomputed baseline statistics, and reports the results back to us in a specified S3 bucket, which you can visualize in SageMaker Studio.

For the data quality monitor, a SageMaker Model Monitor pre-built, default container, which is what we used, computes per-feature statistics on the baseline dataset and the inference data. The statistics include the mean, sum, standard deviation, min, and max. The data quality monitor also looks at data missingness and checks for the data type of the incoming inference data. You can find the full list at `https://docs.aws.amazon.com/sagemaker/latest/dg/model-monitor-interpreting-statistics.html`.

For the model quality monitor, SageMaker computes model performance metrics based on the ML problem type configured. For our regression example in this chapter, SageMaker's model quality monitor is computing the **mean absolute error (MAE)**, **mean squared error (MSE)**, **root mean square error (RMSE)**, and **R-squared (r2)** values. You can find the full list of computed metrics for regression, binary classification, and multiclass classification problems at `https://docs.aws.amazon.com/sagemaker/latest/dg/model-monitor-model-quality-metrics.html`.

You can see a list of the monitoring jobs launched over time in the **Monitoring job history** tab on the **ENDPOINT DETAILS** page, as shown in *Figure 10.9*:

Figure 10.9 – Viewing a list of monitoring jobs. Double-clicking a row item takes you to the detail page of a particular job

When you double-click a row item, you will be taken to the detail page of a particular monitoring job, as shown in *Figure 10.10*. Because we perturbed the data prior to sending it to the endpoint, the data contains irregularities, such as missingness. This is captured by the data quality monitor:

Monitoring Job Status

Completed With Violations

FEATURE STATISTICS

Visualize and analyze the statistics and data collected during this job run in an Amazon SageMaker notebook. Open Amazon SageMaker notebook.

View Amazon SageMaker notebook

MONITORING JOB REPORT

Amazon SageMaker Model Monitor compared this run against the baseline and detected these constraint violations.

Feature	Constraint	Violation details
Height	data type check	Data type match requirement is not met. Expected data type: Fractional, Expected match: 100.0%. Observed: Only 99.99769279195246% of data is Fractional.
VisceraWeight	completeness check	Data completeness requirement is not met. Expected: 100.0%. Observed: Only 95.07467638148177%.
ShuckedWeight	data type check	Data type match requirement is not met. Expected data type: Fractional, Expected match: 100.0%. Observed: Only 99.9983527109436% of data is Fractional.
Height	completeness check	Data completeness requirement is not met. Expected: 100.0%. Observed: Only 94.95637096572273%.
ShuckedWeight	completeness check	Data completeness requirement is not met. Expected: 100.0%. Observed: Only 94.99768396805128%.
WholeWeight	completeness check	Data completeness requirement is not met. Expected: 100.0%. Observed: Only 94.99737099076091%.
ShellWeight	data type check	Data type match requirement is not met. Expected data type: Fractional, Expected match: 100.0%. Observed: Only 99.9983535571398% of data is Fractional.
Diameter	completeness check	Data completeness requirement is not met. Expected: 100.0%. Observed: Only 95.02334810586144%.
VisceraWeight	data type check	Data type match requirement is not met. Expected data type: Fractional, Expected match: 100.0%. Observed: Only 99.99868323594767% of data is Fractional.

Figure 10.10 – Details of a data quality monitoring job and violations

We can also open a model quality monitoring job to find out whether the model performs as expected. As shown in *Figure 10.11*, we can see that violations have been raised for all the metrics computed. We know it is going to happen because this is largely due to the perturbation we introduced to the data. SageMaker Model Monitor is able to detect such problems:

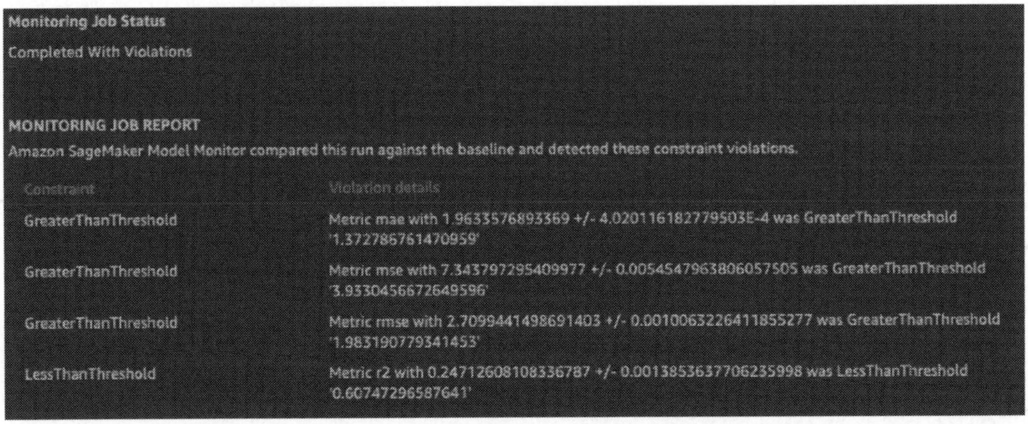

Monitoring Job Status

Completed With Violations

MONITORING JOB REPORT

Amazon SageMaker Model Monitor compared this run against the baseline and detected these constraint violations.

Constraint	Violation details
GreaterThanThreshold	Metric mae with 1.9633576893369 +/- 4.020116182779503E-4 was GreaterThanThreshold '1.372786761470959'
GreaterThanThreshold	Metric mse with 7.343797295409977 +/- 0.0054547963806057505 was GreaterThanThreshold '3.9330456672649596'
GreaterThanThreshold	Metric rmse with 2.7099441498691403 +/- 0.0010063226411855277 was GreaterThanThreshold '1.983190779341453'
LessThanThreshold	Metric r2 with 0.24712608108336787 +/- 0.0013853637706235998 was LessThanThreshold '0.60747296587641'

Figure 10.11 – Details of a model monitoring job and violations

We can also create visualizations from the monitoring jobs. Let's follow the next steps to create a chart for the data quality monitor:

1. On the **ENDPOINT DETAILS** page, go to the **Data quality** tab and click on the **Add chart** button, as shown in *Figure 10.12*:

Figure 10.12 – Adding a visualization for a data quality monitor

2. A chart properties configuration sidebar will appear on the right side, as shown in *Figure 10.13*. We can create a chart by specifying the timeline, the statistics, and the feature we would like to plot. Depending on how long you've enabled the monitor, you can choose a time span to visualize. For example, I chose **1 day**, the **Average** statistic, and **feature_baseline_drift_Length** to see the average baseline drift measure on the **Length** feature in the past day:

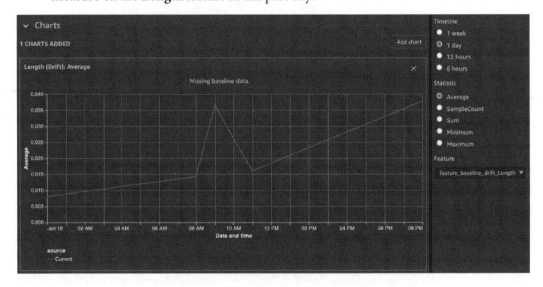

Figure 10.13 – Visualizing feature drift in SageMaker Studio

3. You can optionally add more charts by clicking the **Add chart** button.

4. Similarly, we can visualize the model performance using the **mse** metric over the last 24 hours, as shown in *Figure 10.14*:

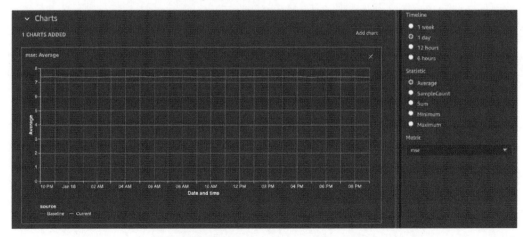

Figure 10.14 – Visualizing the mse regression metric in SageMaker Studio

> **Note**
>
> To save costs, when you complete the examples, make sure to uncomment and run the last cells in `01-train_host_predict.ipynb` to delete the monitoring schedules and the endpoint in order to stop incurring charges to your AWS account.

Summary

In this chapter, we focused on data drift and model drift in ML and how to monitor them using SageMaker Model Monitor and SageMaker Studio. We demonstrated how we set up a data quality monitor and a model quality monitor in SageMaker Studio to continuously monitor the behavior of a model and the characteristics of the incoming data, in a scenario where a regression model is deployed in a SageMaker endpoint and continuous inference traffic is hitting the endpoint. We introduced some random perturbation to the inference traffic and used SageMaker Model Monitor to detect unwanted behavior of the model and data. With this example, you can also deploy SageMaker Model Monitor to your use case and provide visibility and a guardrail to your models in production.

In the next chapter, we will be learning how to operationalize an ML project with SageMaker Projects, Pipelines, and the model registry. We will be talking about an important trend in ML right now, that is, **continuous integration/continuous delivery (CI/CD)** and **ML operations (MLOps)**. We will demonstrate how you can use SageMaker features, such as Projects, Pipelines, and the model registry, to make your ML project repeatable, reliable, and reusable, and have strong governance.

11
Operationalize ML Projects with SageMaker Projects, Pipelines, and Model Registry

Data scientists used to spend too much time and effort maintaining and manually managing ML pipelines, a process that starts with data, processing, training, and evaluation and ends with model hosting with ongoing maintenance. SageMaker Studio provides features that aim to streamline these operations with **continuous integration and continuous delivery (CI/CD)** best practices. You will learn how to implement SageMaker projects, Pipelines, and the model registry to help operationalize the ML lifecycle with CI/CD.

In this chapter, we will be learning about the following:

- Understanding ML operations and CI/CD

- Creating a SageMaker project

- Orchestrating an ML pipeline with SageMaker Pipelines

- Running CI/CD in SageMaker Studio

Technical requirements

For this chapter, you will need to ensure that the SageMaker project template permission is enabled in the Studio setting. If you have finished *Chapter 8, Jumpstarting ML with SageMaker JumpStart and Autopilot*, you should have the permissions. You can verify it in the Studio **domain** view with the following steps:

1. If either of the permissions is disabled as shown in *Figure 11.1*, you can click **Edit Settings** to change this.

Figure 11.1 – Checking and editing the SageMaker projects permissions

2. Go to **Step 2 Studio Settings** to switch on the SageMaker projects and JumpStart permissions as shown in *Figure 11.2*.

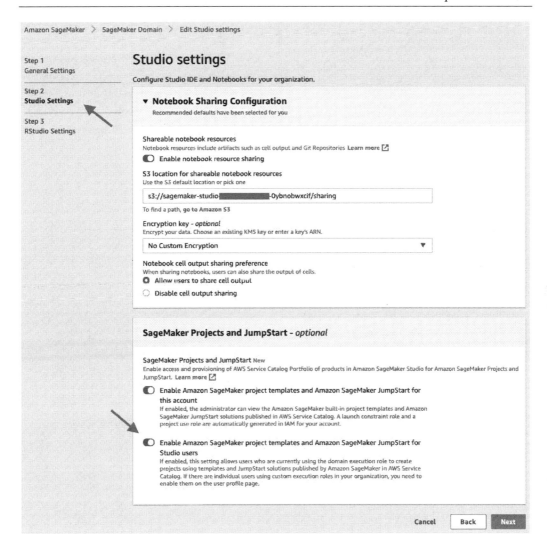

Figure 11.2 – Enabling SageMaker project templates for the account and users

3.   Then click **Next** to go to the next page and click **Submit**.

This ensures SageMaker project template permissions are enabled for you.

Understanding ML operations and CI/CD

In the ML lifecycle, there are many steps that require a skilled data scientist's hands-on interaction throughout, such as wrangling the dataset, training, and evaluating a model. These manual steps could affect an ML team's operations and speed to deploy models in production. Imagine your model training job takes a long time and finishes in the middle of the night. You either have to wait for your first data scientist to come in during the day to evaluate the model and deploy the model into production or have to employ an on-call rotation to have someone on standby at all times to monitor the model training and deployment. But neither option is ideal if you want an effective and efficient ML lifecycle.

Machine Learning Operations (**MLOps**) is critical to a team that wants to stay lean and scale well. MLOps helps you streamline and reduce manual human intervention as much as possible. It helps transform your ML lifecycle to enterprise-grade. It helps you scale and maintain the quality of your models that are put into production and it also helps you improve time to model delivery with automation.

So, what exactly is MLOps?

MLOps refers to a methodology to apply DevOps best practices to the ML lifecycle. **DevOps** stands for software **Development** (**Dev**) and IT **Operations** (**Ops**). DevOps aims to increase a team's ability to deliver applications at a high pace with high quality using a set of engineering, practices, and patterns. It also promotes a new cultural and behavioral paradigm in an organization. MLOps recommends the following practices, which are built upon DevOps best practices with some modifications tailored to the nature of ML:

- **Continuous Integration** (**CI**): In DevOps, developers constantly commit and merge their code changes into a central repository, after which tests are automatically run to validate the code. In ML, not only does the code need to be integrated and validated, but so does the training data and ML models. The training data needs to be versioned, model lineage needs to be tracked for traceability, and tests on data and models, besides the code, need to be implemented as well.

- **Continuous Delivery** (**CD**): In DevOps, this is a practice where code is built, tested, and released for production in an automatic fashion. In MLOps, similar to what was discussed about continuous integration, the operations include data and models besides the ML source code.

- **Everything as code**: In order to streamline and automate for CI and CD (CI/CD for short), everything needs to be implemented as code: the process, infrastructure, and configuration, instead of any manual setup and point-and-click process on screen. This practice also enables version control and reproducibility for your processes, infrastructures, and configurations.

- **Monitoring and logging**: This practice encourages you to log all things related to your software/ML system for visibility and auditability. You not only log the ML metrics, data lineage, data versions, and model versions, but also log the CI/CD processes, and any errors for debugging and monitoring purposes. This enables the next practice.

- **Communication and collaboration**: Because everything is code, and everything is automated and logged, you have a transparent environment that invites collaboration and communication. Instead of working in silos with a manual hand-off, which causes friction and opacity, your entire team can work more closely together on the system.

The key benefits that MLOps brings to the table are the following:

- **Faster time to market**: Because now your model deployment is automatically created and deployed as part of the CI/CD process, your model training and deployment are streamlined without any handoff or manual processes. You can expect more iterations of refinement within the same timeframe and a quicker turnaround time for a mature product.

- **Productivity**: A lot of manual processes are taken away from data scientists and ML developers so that they can focus on ML modeling where things cannot be automated.

- **Repeatability**: Also, because everything is code and is automated, your ML lifecycle can be performed by anyone at any time with exactly the same output.

- **Reliability**: With the tests and validations performed in the CI/CD process, you know that your models are high quality. You can also consistently produce high-quality models thanks to the repeatability CI/CD provides.

- **Auditability**: As code, data, and models are versioned and lineage and processes are logged, you can tell exactly how the models were trained and deployed.

- **Better quality**: Combining all the benefits above, MLOps enables us to spend more time creating better models and letting the system take care of the integration and delivery quickly, reliably, and repeatably.

You may think: *MLOps seems too perfect to be easily adopted.* Yes, you do need to incorporate additional technology into your ML lifecycle to enable the CI/CD process. And yes, you need to implement many details to enable the logging and monitoring. It is also true that to adopt the *everything as code* practice, many iterations of testing on the infrastructure code and configuration are required at the beginning. The good news is, in SageMaker Studio, adopting MLOps practices for your ML project is made easy. SageMaker Studio has templatized the CI/CD processes for numerous use cases so that you can easily pick one and adopt the MLOps best practices and technologies from the templated ML use case for your use case. The features that enable MLOps and CI/CD are **SageMaker projects**, **SageMaker Pipelines**, and **SageMaker Model Registry**.

Let's get started by creating a SageMaker project first.

Creating a SageMaker project

A **SageMaker project** enables you to automate the model building and deployment pipelines with MLOps and CI/CD from SageMaker-provided templates and your own custom templates. With a SageMaker-provided template, all the initial setup and resource provisioning is handled by SageMaker so you can quickly adopt it for your use case.

In this chapter, we will run an ML example with MLOps and CI/CD in SageMaker Studio. As we focus on MLOps and CI/CD in this chapter, we use a simple regression problem from the abalone dataset (`https://archive.ics.uci.edu/ml/datasets/abalone`) to predict the age of abalone from physical measurements. I will show you how you can create a project from SageMaker projects, and how each part of the MLOps system works. The MLOps system created from SageMaker projects enables automation of data validation, model building, model evaluation, deployment, and monitoring with a simple trigger from a code commit. This means that whenever we make any changes to the code base, the whole system will run through the complete ML lifecycle in SageMaker that we've learned about throughout this book automatically. You will see how much SageMaker has simplified MLOps for you. Let's open up SageMaker Studio and follow the steps given here:

1. On the **Launcher** page, click the *plus sign* on the **New project** card, as shown in *Figure 11.3*.

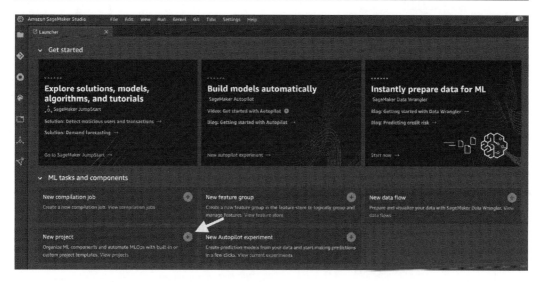

Figure 11.3 – Opening a new project in Launcher

2. There are MLOps templates for various use cases created by SageMaker (under **SageMaker templates**) for us to choose from, as shown in *Figure 11.4*. Let's select **MLOps template for model building, training, deployment and monitoring**. This template automates the entire model lifecycle, which includes model building, deployment, and monitoring workflows. Click **Select project template**.

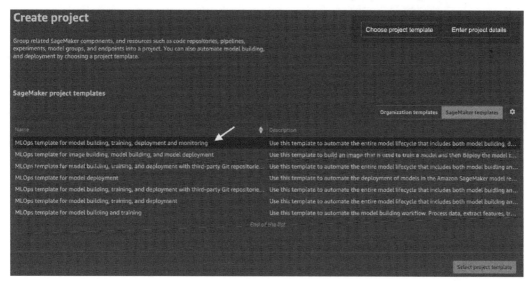

Figure 11.4 – Choosing SageMaker managed templates

> **Note**
> Templates whose names contain **with third-party Git repositories** are designed to work with your external Git repositories or CI/CD software such as **Jenkins**. You will need to provide additional information in the next step.

3. Provide a name, description, and tags for the project on the **Project details** page. Click **Create project**.

    With this project template, SageMaker Studio is now provisioning cloud resources for MLOps and deploying the sample code. Let's illustrate the MLOps architecture with the diagram shown in *Figure 11.5*:

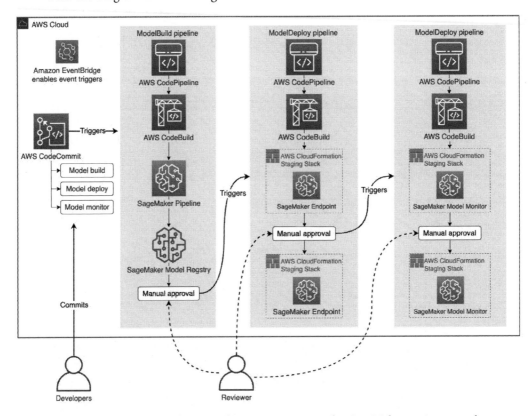

Figure 11.5 – Architecture diagram of an MLOps setup with a SageMaker projects template

The cloud resources created include the following:

- Three code repositories in **AWS CodeCommit**, a managed source control service that hosts private Git repositories. They can also be found in the AWS CodeCommit console: `https://console.aws.amazon.com/codesuite/codecommit/repositories`. Remember to switch to your own AWS Region from the URL.

- Three continuous delivery pipelines in **AWS CodePipeline**, a managed service that helps automate build, test, and release pipelines, can be found in the AWS CodePipeline console: `https://console.aws.amazon.com/codesuite/codepipeline/pipelines`. Remember to switch to your own AWS Region from the URL.

- Five event trigger rules in **Amazon EventBridge**, a managed service that makes it easier to build event-driven applications, can be found in the Amazon EventBridge console: `https://console.aws.amazon.com/events/home#/rules`. Remember to switch to your own AWS Region from the URL.

These are essentially the backbone CI/CD framework that supports MLOps in SageMaker Studio. Repositories in CodeCommit are where we store, develop, and commit our code. Every commit to a code repository in CodeCommit is going to trigger, managed by rules in EventBridge, a run of the corresponding pipeline in CodePipeline to build, test, and deploy resources.

Once the project creation is complete, you can see a portal for the project in the main working area as shown in *Figure 11.6*.

Figure 11.6 – SageMaker project detail portal

This portal contains all the important resources and information that are associated to the project—code repositories in CodeCommit, ML pipelines from SageMaker Pipelines (which we will talk about soon), experiments tracked using SageMaker Experiments, models, hosted endpoints, and other settings.

4. We can clone the repositories from CodeCommit to a local SageMaker Studio directory. As the final step before we move on to describe the ML pipeline, let's clone the `<project-name-prefix>-modelbuild` repository, which contains the ML pipeline that builds, trains, and evaluates the ML model using the abalone dataset. Click the **clone repo...** hyperlink next to the `<project-name-prefix>-modelbuild` repository as highlighted with an arrow in *Figure 11.6*.

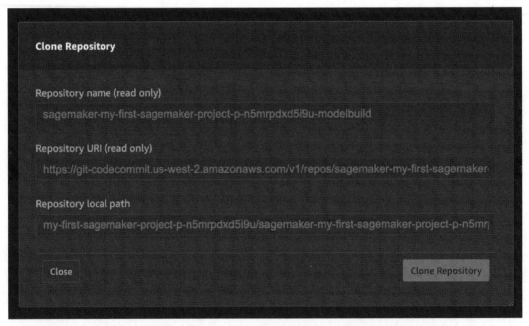

Figure 11.7 – Cloning a repository from CodeCommit to a local SageMaker Studio directory

5. In the popup shown in *Figure 11.7*, click **Clone Repository**. The repository will appear in the home directory `~/<project-name-prefix>/<project-name-prefix>-modelbuild/`.

Let's look at the ML pipeline defined in this abalone example first, before we dive into the CI/CD part.

Orchestrating an ML pipeline with SageMaker Pipelines

The template we're using contains an ML lifecycle pipeline that carries out data preprocessing, data quality checks, model training, model evaluation steps, and eventually model registration. This pipeline is a central piece of the MLOps process where the model is being created. The pipeline is defined in `<project-name-prefix>-modelbuild` using SageMaker Pipelines. **SageMaker Pipelines** is an orchestration tool for ML workflow in SageMaker. SageMaker Pipelines integrates with SageMaker Processing, training, Experiments, hosting, and the model registry. It provides reproducibility, repeatability, and tracks data/model lineage for auditability. Most importantly, you can visualize the workflow graph and runtime live in SageMaker Studio. The pipeline can be found under the **Pipelines** tab in the details portal as shown in *Figure 11.8.*

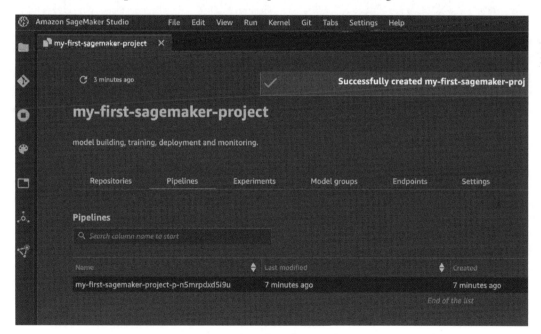

Figure 11.8 – A list of pipelines in the project

> **Note**
>
> I have used the term **pipeline** a lot in this chapter. Let's settle this once and for all. I am referring to the pipeline from SageMaker Pipelines, shown in *Figure 11.8* and *Figure 11.9*, as the **ML pipeline**. Please, do not confuse an ML pipeline with a CI/CD pipeline from AWS CodePipeline, which is briefly mentioned in the last section and will be further discussed in the *Running CI/CD in SageMaker Studio* section.

On double-clicking the pipeline, we can see the full execution graph and the live status of the pipeline, as shown in *Figure 11.9*. The corresponding pipeline code is in `~/<project-name-prefix>/<project-name-prefix>-modelbuild/pipelines/abalone/pipeline.py`.

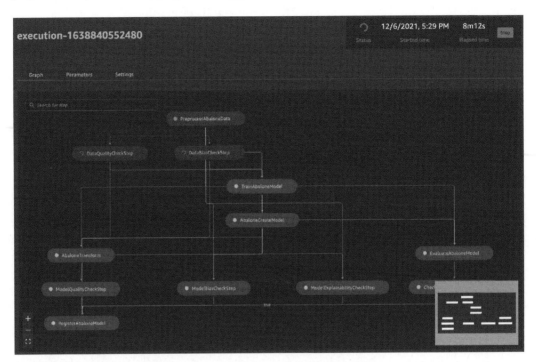

Figure 11.9 – Pipeline workflow and live status

Let's walk through the pipeline and how it is set up in the code. The pipeline contains the following steps (from top to bottom in the graph):

1. First is preprocessing the dataset with SageMaker Processing (**PreprocessAbaloneData** in *Figure 11.9*). In the pipeline code `pipeline.py` file, where we use classes and functions in the `sagemaker.workflow` module along with other `sagemaker` classes, a scikit-learn processor is defined to run a script `preprocess.py` in the same directory. Also, `ProcessingStep` is a class from the `sagemaker.workflow.steps` module:

```
# Line 209 in pipeline.py
step_process = ProcessingStep(
    name="PreprocessAbaloneData",
    processor=sklearn_processor,
    outputs=[
```

```
        ProcessingOutput(output_name="train", source="/
opt/ml/processing/train"),
        ProcessingOutput(output_name="validation",
source="/opt/ml/processing/validation"),
        ProcessingOutput(output_name="test", source="/
opt/ml/processing/test"),
    ],
    code=os.path.join(BASE_DIR, "preprocess.py"),
    job_arguments=["--input-data", input_data],
)
```

2. After the data is preprocessed, the pipeline checks against previously registered data quality and bias metrics and/or calculates the data quality and bias using SageMaker Clarify. Here, the output of the previous step `step_process.properties.ProcessingOutputConfig.Outputs["train"]` is used as the input baseline data. A `QualityCheckStep()` step object is instantiated here. This step computes the data quality statistics from the baseline training data and registers the statistics into the model registry once the model is created toward the end:

```
# Line 238
data_quality_check_config = DataQualityCheckConfig(
baseline_dataset=step_process.properties.
ProcessingOutputConfig.Outputs["train"].S3Output.S3Uri,
    dataset_format=DatasetFormat.csv(header=False,
output_columns_position="START"),
    output_s3_uri=Join(on='/', values=['s3:/', default_
bucket, base_job_prefix, ExecutionVariables.PIPELINE_
EXECUTION_ID, 'dataqualitycheckstep'])
)
data_quality_check_step = QualityCheckStep(
    name="DataQualityCheckStep",
    skip_check=skip_check_data_quality,
    register_new_baseline=register_new_baseline_data_
quality,
    quality_check_config=data_quality_check_config,
    check_job_config=check_job_config,
supplied_baseline_statistics=supplied_baseline_
statistics_data_quality,
supplied_baseline_constraints=supplied_baseline_
constraints_data_quality,
```

```
        model_package_group_name=model_package_group_name
)
```

3. At the same time, the pipeline also computes the data bias using a step instantiated from the `ClarifyCheckStep()` class:

```
data_bias_check_config = DataBiasCheckConfig(
    data_config=data_bias_data_config,
    data_bias_config=data_bias_config,
)
data_bias_check_step = ClarifyCheckStep(
    name="DataBiasCheckStep",
    clarify_check_config=data_bias_check_config,
    check_job_config=check_job_config,
    skip_check=skip_check_data_bias,
    register_new_baseline=register_new_baseline_data_
bias,
    model_package_group_name=model_package_group_name
)
```

These two checking steps are conditional based on the `skip_check` arguments. `skip_check_data_quality` and `skip_check_data_bias` are pipeline input parameters and can be configured for each run. For the first run, you may skip the checks because there are no baseline statistics to check against. `register_new_baseline` is also conditional from pipeline input parameters, but most of the time you would register new baseline statistics when you have a new dataset unless you have a specific reason not to update the statistics.

4. After the data quality and bias checks, a training job is created from a SageMaker estimator. In this example, the built-in XGBoost algorithm is used. `TrainingStep` is dependent on `DataQualityCheckStep` and `DataBiasCheckStep`, meaning that the training step waits for the two check steps to complete before starting, and takes the output from the preprocessing step, `step_process`:

```
# Line 326
step_train = TrainingStep(
    name="TrainAbaloneModel",
    depends_on=["DataQualityCheckStep",
"DataBiasCheckStep"],
```

```
        estimator=xgb_train,
    inputs={
        "train": TrainingInput(
s3_data=step_process.properties.ProcessingOutputConfig.
Outputs["train"].S3Output.S3Uri,
            content_type="text/csv",
        ),
        "validation": TrainingInput(
s3_data=step_process.properties.ProcessingOutputConfig.
Outputs["validation"].S3Output.S3Uri,
            content_type="text/csv",
        ),
    },
)
```

5. Next is to create a SageMaker Model from the training job using `CreateModelStep()`. `CreateModelInput()` takes instance types used for hosting purposes:

```
# Line 346
model = Model(
    image_uri=image_uri,
model_data=step_train.properties.ModelArtifacts.
S3ModelArtifacts,
    sagemaker_session=sagemaker_session,
    role=role,
)
inputs = CreateModelInput(
    instance_type="ml.m5.large",
    accelerator_type="ml.eia1.medium",
)
step_create_model = CreateModelStep(
    name="AbaloneCreateModel",
    model=model,
    inputs=inputs,
)
```

6. Once the SageMaker Model is created, two branches of model evaluation are performed. One is applied on a held-out test set for evaluation purposes using SageMaker Batch Transform `Transformer`:

```
# Line 364
transformer = Transformer(
    model_name=step_create_model.properties.ModelName,
    instance_type="ml.m5.xlarge",
    instance_count=1,
    accept="text/csv",
    assemble_with="Line",
    output_path=f"s3://{default_bucket}/
AbaloneTransform",
)
step_transform = TransformStep(
    name="AbaloneTransform",
    transformer=transformer,
    inputs=TransformInput(        data=step_process.
properties.ProcessingOutputConfig.Outputs["test"].
S3Output.S3Uri,
        ...)
)
```

> **Note**
> The additional arguments in the `TransformInput()` class that have been omitted here in text but are available in `pipeline.py` are to configure Batch Transform input/output and to associate the output results with the input records. For more information, see `https://docs.aws.amazon.com/sagemaker/latest/dg/batch-transform-data-processing.html`.

The output of the Batch Transform, which is the prediction, is then used to calculate model quality metrics such as mean absolute error, root mean squared error, and the r-squared value:

```
model_quality_check_config = ModelQualityCheckConfig(
    baseline_dataset=step_transform.properties.
TransformOutput.S3OutputPath,
    dataset_format=DatasetFormat.csv(header=False),
```

```
    output_s3_uri=Join(on='/', values=['s3:/', default_
bucket, base_job_prefix, ExecutionVariables.PIPELINE_
EXECUTION_ID, 'modelqualitycheckstep']),
    problem_type='Regression',
    inference_attribute='_c0',
    ground_truth_attribute='_c1'
)
model_quality_check_step = QualityCheckStep(
    name="ModelQualityCheckStep",
    skip_check=skip_check_model_quality,
    register_new_baseline=register_new_baseline_model_
quality,
    quality_check_config=model_quality_check_config,
    check_job_config=check_job_config,
supplied_baseline_statistics=supplied_baseline_
statistics_model_quality,
supplied_baseline_constraints=supplied_baseline_
constraints_model_quality,
    model_package_group_name=model_package_group_name
)
```

7. The other evaluation route EvaluateAbaloneModel and
    CheckMSEAbaloneEvalution aims to evaluate the test dataset and use the
    performance metric as a condition in the ML pipeline to only proceed to register
    the model in the model registry if the mean squared error is less than or equal
    to 6.0:

```
# Line 650
cond_lte = ConditionLessThanOrEqualTo(
    left=JsonGet(
        step=step_eval,
        property_file=evaluation_report,
        json_path="regression_metrics.mse.value"
    ),
    right=6.0,
)
step_cond = ConditionStep(
    name="CheckMSEAbaloneEvaluation",
    conditions=[cond_lte],
```

```
      if_steps=[step_register],
      else_steps=[],
)
```

8. Two other checks are applied on models too in `ModelBiasCheckStep` and `ModelExplainabilityCheckStep`. They both use SageMaker Clarify to compute model bias and model explainability:

```
# Line 450
model_bias_check_step = ClarifyCheckStep(
    name="ModelBiasCheckStep",
    clarify_check_config=model_bias_check_config,
    check_job_config=check_job_config,
    skip_check=skip_check_model_bias,
    register_new_baseline=register_new_baseline_model_
bias,
supplied_baseline_constraints=supplied_baseline_
constraints_model_bias,
    model_package_group_name=model_package_group_name
)
# Line 494
model_explainability_check_step = ClarifyCheckStep(
    name="ModelExplainabilityCheckStep",
    clarify_check_config=model_explainability_check_
config,
    check_job_config=check_job_config,
    skip_check=skip_check_model_explainability,
register_new_baseline=register_new_baseline_model_
explainability,
supplied_baseline_constraints=supplied_baseline_
constraints_model_explainability,
    model_package_group_name=model_package_group_name
)
```

9. After the checks to confirm the model's performance, the model is registered in SageMaker Model Registry along with evaluation metrics, stored in the `model_metrics` variable, captured during the process, including performance metrics on test data, data bias, and model bias:

```
# Line 635
step_register = RegisterModel(
    name="RegisterAbaloneModel",
    estimator=xgb_train,
model_data=step_train.properties.ModelArtifacts.
S3ModelArtifacts,
    content_types=["text/csv"],
    response_types=["text/csv"],
    inference_instances=["ml.t2.medium", "ml.m5.large"],
    transform_instances=["ml.m5.large"],
    model_package_group_name=model_package_group_name,
    approval_status=model_approval_status,
    model_metrics=model_metrics,
    drift_check_baselines=drift_check_baselines
)
```

10. With the steps defined, they are put into the `steps` argument in a `Pipeline` object. Parameters that are exposed to users are placed in the `parameters` argument:

```
# Line 666
pipeline = Pipeline(
    name=pipeline_name,
    parameters=[
        processing_instance_type,
        processing_instance_count,
        ...],
    steps=[step_process, data_quality_check_step,
data_bias_check_step, step_train, step_create_model,
step_transform, model_quality_check_step, model_bias_
check_step, model_explainability_check_step, step_eval,
step_cond],
    sagemaker_session=sagemaker_session,
)
```

You may wonder how SageMaker determines the order of the steps. SageMaker determines the order based on the data dependency and any explicit, custom dependency. We put the steps in a list of the `steps` argument and SageMaker takes care of the rest.

> **Note**
>
> After the project is created, the three CodePipeline pipelines are run automatically. Only the first pipeline, `<project-name-prefix>-modelbuild`, will proceed correctly. The other two pipelines, `<project-name-prefix>-modeldeploy` and `<project-name-prefix>-modelmonitor`, depend on the output of the first pipeline so they will fail in the first run. Don't worry about the failure status now.

11. At the end, a successfully executed pipeline creates and registers a model in SageMaker Model Registry. You can see the model in the model registry in the left sidebar, as shown in *Figure 11.10*. We will learn more about the model registry in later sections.

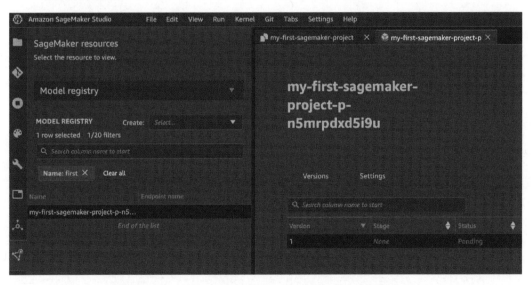

Figure 11.10 – Resulting model in SageMaker Model Registry

There are several ways to run a pipeline. One is with the CI/CD process, which is how the pipeline initially runs after deployment from the template. We will talk more about the CI/CD process in the next section, *Running CI/CD in SageMaker Studio*. The following shows how to trigger the pipeline manually:

1. You can click **Start an execution** from the SageMaker Studio UI as depicted in *Figure 11.11*.

Figure 11.11 – Starting an execution of a pipeline in the pipeline list

2. You can specify user inputs such as instance types, training data location, and other conditions for the checks, as shown in *Figure 11.12*. Click **Start** to start the workflow individually for a new dataset.

Figure 11.12 – Starting the execution of a pipeline with user inputs

3.   You can also run a pipeline using the SageMaker Python SDK. The templatized code repository `~/<project-name-prefix>/<project-name-prefix>-modelbuild/` has an example notebook, `sagemaker-pipelines-project.ipynb`, explaining the code structure in greater detail and showing how to run a pipeline programmatically. You can open the notebook, as shown in *Figure 11.13*, and run it as an alternative.

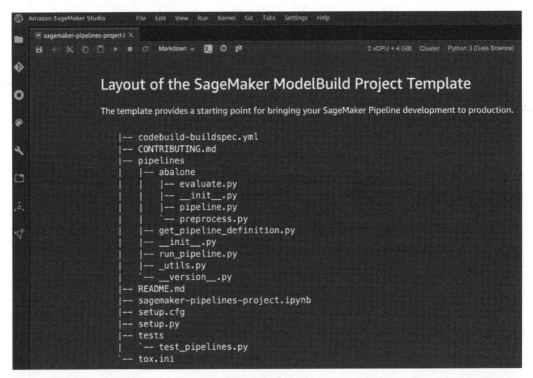

Figure 11.13 – A screenshot of the sagemaker-pipelines-project.ipynb notebook that shows you details such as code structure in the repository, and runs the pipeline programmatically

With SageMaker Pipelines, we can orchestrate steps that use SageMaker managed features to run an ML lifecycle. In the next section, let's see how the CI/CD system that the template creates uses SageMaker Pipelines for MLOps.

Running CI/CD in SageMaker Studio

The ML pipeline we've seen running previously is just one part of our CI/CD system at work. The ML pipeline is triggered by a CI/CD pipeline in AWS CodePipeline. Let's dive into the three CI/CD pipelines that the SageMaker project template sets up for us.

There are three CodePipeline pipelines:

- `<project-name-prefix>-modelbuild`: The purpose of this pipeline is to run the ML pipeline and create an ML model in SageMaker Model Registry. This CI/CD pipeline runs the ML pipeline as a build step when triggered by a commit to the repository. The ML model in the SageMaker model registry needs to be approved in order to trigger the next pipeline, `modeldeploy`.

- `<project-name-prefix>-modeldeploy`: The purpose of this pipeline is to deploy the latest approved ML model in the SageMaker model registry as a SageMaker endpoint. The build process deploys a staging endpoint first and requests manual approval before proceeding to deploy the model into production. This ensures the model and endpoint configuration are working correctly before deploying to production. Once the staging endpoint is deployed and becomes live with an `InService` status, it triggers the next pipeline, `modelmonitor`.

- `<project-name-prefix>-modelmonitor`: The purpose of this pipeline is to deploy SageMaker Model Monitor to the two SageMaker endpoints created in the `modeldeploy` pipeline. This pipeline is triggered whenever a staging endpoint goes live and asks for manual approval on the model monitoring deployment for the staging endpoint before it deploys Model Monitor to the prod endpoint.

Coming back to our previous ML pipeline execution, which is part of the `modelbuild` build process, we have a model created and registered in **the model registry**. This is the first checkpoint of the CI/CD system: *to manually verify the model performance metrics*. In order to proceed, we need to go to the model registry as shown in *Figure 11.10* to review the results.

1. From the view in *Figure 11.10*, double-click the model version entry in the model registry to see more detail about this model version, as shown in *Figure 11.14*.

Figure 11.14 – Detail page of a model version

2. We can view the model's performance in the **Model quality** tab, model explainability in the **Explainability** tab, and data bias in the **Bias report** tab. These are all relevant pieces of information to help us decide whether this is an acceptable model or not.

3. Click the **Update status** button at the top right to approve or reject this model after review. For the sake of demonstration, we approve the model to proceed with the MLOps system, as shown in *Figure 11.15*. If we reject the model, nothing happens from this point.

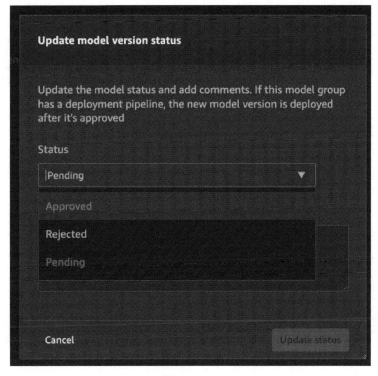

Figure 11.15 – Approve or reject a model version. You can put a comment in the box too

4. Model approval automatically triggers the execution of the modeldeploy pipeline. If you go to the CodePipeline console, you can see it in the **In progress** state, as shown in *Figure 11.16*.

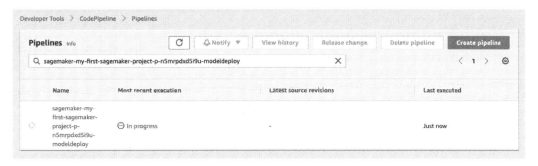

Figure 11.16 – Model approval automatically triggers the modeldeploy pipeline

5. As mentioned before, the `modeldeploy` pipeline first deploys a staging SageMaker endpoint for review. Once the endpoint is created (in 5-7 minutes), you can see a new event on the model version page, as shown in *Figure 11.17*. Click on **Endpoint: <project-name-prefix>-staging** to find out more information about the endpoint. You can test out the endpoint.

Activity	Model quality	Explainability	Bias report	Inference recommender	Load test	Settings

Event type	Event	Comment	Modified by	Last modified	Acti
ModelDeployment	Endpoint: my-first-sagemaker-project-staging	stage: staging		4 hours ago	...
Approval	Status updated to Approved		michaelhsieh	4 hours ago	...
Approval	Status updated to PendingManualApproval			6 hours ago	...

Figure 11.17 – Model version showing the latest event in the deployment of the staging endpoint

6. After confirming the endpoint's status, we can approve the staging endpoint deployment in the CodePipeline console. Click the pipeline name from *Figure 11.16*. We can see the current progress of the pipeline is pending in the **DeployStaging** stage, as shown in *Figure 11.18*. Click the **Review** button in the **ApproveDeployment** step to approve/reject the deployment.

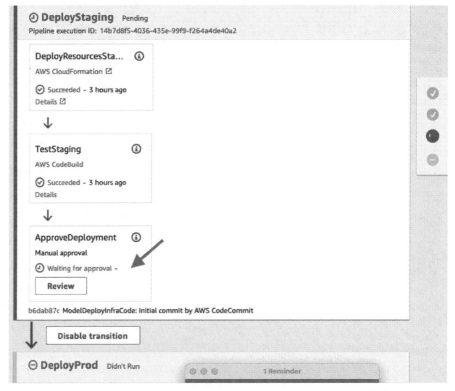

Figure 11.18 – Manual approval required by the modeldeploy pipeline

7. Approve or reject the deployment with any comments in the popup, as shown in *Figure 11.19*. As the endpoint is live and working, let's approve the staging deployment.

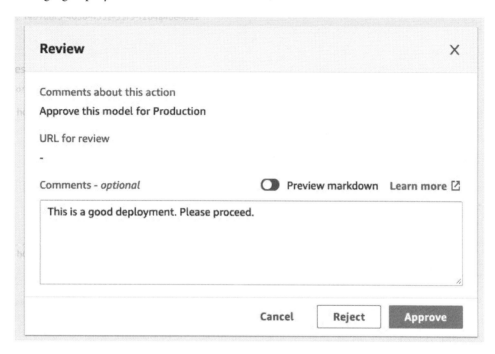

Figure 11.19 – Approve/reject a staging deployment

8. The `modeldeploy` pipeline moves on to the final stage, **DeployProd**, to deploy the model to a production endpoint. Once deployed, the pipeline is updated to the **Succeeded** status. You can see a new event on the model version page, as shown in *Figure 11.20*. Also notice **Last Stage** is now **prod**.

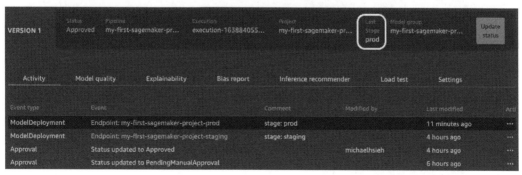

Figure 11.20 – Model version is now updated to prod

9. When we approve the staging deployment, the `modelmonitor` pipeline is triggered to deploy SageMaker Model Monitor to the staging endpoint. We can see in the CodePipeline console that the `modelmonitor` pipeline is **In progress**, as shown in *Figure 11.21*.

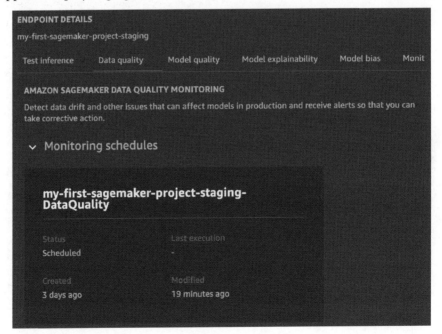

○	sagemaker-my-first-sagemaker-project-p-n5mrpdxd5i9u-modeldeploy	⊘ Succeeded	**ModelDeployInfraCode** – b6dab87c: Initial commit by AWS CodeCommit	Just now
○	sagemaker-my-first-sagemaker-project-p-n5mrpdxd5i9u-modelmonitor	⊖ In progress	**CodeCommit** – 97b3ee41: Initial commit by AWS CodeCommit	3 hours ago

Figure 11.21 – Staging endpoint deployment triggers the modelmonitor pipeline

10. The `modelmonitor` pipeline also requires manual approval in the DeployStaging stage. We should review the endpoint to see if Model Monitor is enabled. As shown in *Figure 11.22*, we can see in the **Data quality** tab that Model Monitor is indeed enabled and scheduled. We do not have a live traffic setup yet for the endpoint, and the monitoring schedule will only kick in at the top of the hour, so let's proceed and approve DeployStaging in the CodePipeline console similar to *step 6* and *step 7*.

Figure 11.22 – Reviewing the Model Monitor schedule for the staging endpoint

11. Lastly, the DeployProd stage will also deploy SageMaker Model Monitor to the prod endpoint. This marks the end of the complete MLOps and CI/CD system.

The three CI/CD pipelines in CodePipeline constitute a common MLOps system that enables continuous integration and continuous delivery of an ML model in response to any code changes to the `modelbuild` repository and to any manual ML pipeline runs. You do not have to worry about the complicated implementation as these steps take place automatically, thanks to the SageMaker projects template.

SageMaker Projects make it easy to bring a robust MLOps system to your own ML use case with the templatized code and repositories. You don't have to build a sophisticated system. You can just choose a template provided by SageMaker projects that suits your use case and follow the README files in the repositories in CodeCommit to customize the configuration and code for your own use case. For example, we can update the model training in `pipeline.py` to use a different set of hyperparameters as shown in the following code block and commit the change to the `modelbuild` repository:

```
# Line 315 in pipeline.py
xgb_train.set_hyperparameters(
    objective="reg:linear",
    num_round=70, # was 50
    max_depth=7, # was 7
    eta=0.2,
    gamma=4,
    min_child_weight=6,
    subsample=0.7,
    silent=0)
```

You can see a new execution from the `modelbuild` pipeline with the latest commit message, as shown in *Figure 11.23*.

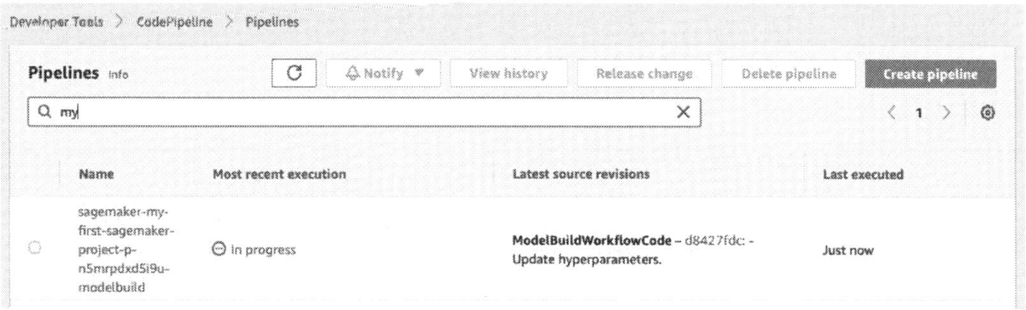

Figure 11.23 – A new modelbuild execution is triggered by a commit to the repository

The CI/CD pipelines are going to be run as we described in this chapter once again to deliver a new model/endpoint automatically (except the manual approval steps) after we update the version of the core training algorithm. You can apply this to any changes to the ML pipeline, in the `modelbuild` pipeline, or configurations in the other two CI/CD pipelines.

Summary

In this chapter, we described what MLOps is and what it does in the ML lifecycle. We discussed the benefits MLOps brings to the table. We showed you how you can easily spin up a sophisticated MLOps system powered by SageMaker projects from the SageMaker Studio IDE. We deployed a model build/deploy/monitor template from SageMaker projects and experienced what *everything as code* really means.

We made a complete run of the CI/CD process to learn how things work in this MLOps system. We learned in great detail how an ML pipeline is implemented with SageMaker Pipelines and other SageMaker managed features. We also learned how the SageMaker model registry works to version control ML models.

Furthermore, we showed how to monitor the CI/CD process and approve deployments in CodePipeline, which gives you great control over the quality of the models and deployment. With the MLOps system, you can enjoy the benefits we discussed: faster time to market, productivity, repeatability, reliability, auditability, and high-quality models.

This example also perfectly summarizes what we've learned about Amazon SageMaker Studio throughout the book. Amazon SageMaker Studio is a purpose-built ML IDE that makes building ML models with an end-to-end ML lifecycle easy with its rich user interface. With the 11 chapters, code examples, and real-world ML use cases in this book, you've learned how to use SageMaker Studio and many SageMaker features for preparing data, building, training, deploying ML models, and running an MLOps system for a production-grade ML project. You now can start building your own ML projects in Amazon SageMaker Studio.

Index

F

Faster R-CNN model 191
feature group 86
Float type 55
fractional 86
frequency distribution
   with histogram 62-64

G

Generative Pre-trained Transformer
   2 (GPT-2) 214
Generative Pre-trained Transformer
   3 (GPT-3) 214
Generative Pre-trained
   Transformer (GPT) 191

H

High-Performance Cluster (HPC) 13
high-quality model
   creating, with SageMaker Autopilot 199
histogram
   about 62
   using, in frequency distribution 62-64
Hugging Face 124
hyperparameter optimization 9
hyperparameter tuning 9

I

IAM policies 14
IAM role
   about 14
   reference link 14

IAM user
about 14
creating 15-18
image analysis 106
image classification 106
inception model 191
inference 5
integral 86
interleaved pipeline 224

J

Jenkins 270
joining tables
   overview 58, 60

K

KernelGateway app 39
kernels
   demystifying 39-42
k-means 106

L

LeNet-5 214
linear learner algorithm 205
live inference 154
load testing
   about 170
   used, for optimizing autoscale 170-178
   used, for optimizing instance
      type 170-178
locust
   about 170
   reference link 170

S

Packt.com

Subscribe to our online digital library for full access to over 7,000 books and videos, as well as industry leading tools to help you plan your personal development and advance your career. For more information, please visit our website.

Why subscribe?

- Spend less time learning and more time coding with practical eBooks and Videos from over 4,000 industry professionals

- Improve your learning with Skill Plans built especially for you

- Get a free eBook or video every month

- Fully searchable for easy access to vital information

- Copy and paste, print, and bookmark content

Did you know that Packt offers eBook versions of every book published, with PDF and ePub files available? You can upgrade to the eBook version at packt.com and as a print book customer, you are entitled to a discount on the eBook copy. Get in touch with us at customercare@packtpub.com for more details.

At www.packt.com, you can also read a collection of free technical articles, sign up for a range of free newsletters, and receive exclusive discounts and offers on Packt books and eBooks.

Other Books You May Enjoy

If you enjoyed this book, you may be interested in these other books by Packt:

Learn Amazon SageMaker – Second Edition

Julien Simon

ISBN: 978-1-80181-795-0

- Become well-versed with data annotation and preparation techniques
- Use AutoML features to build and train machine learning models with AutoPilot
- Create models using built-in algorithms and frameworks and your own code
- Train computer vision and natural language processing (NLP) models using real-world examples
- Cover training techniques for scaling, model optimization, model debugging, and cost optimization
- Automate deployment tasks in a variety of configurations using SDK and several automation tools

Machine Learning with Amazon SageMaker Cookbook

Joshua Arvin Lat

ISBN: 978-1-80056-703-0

- Train and deploy NLP, time series forecasting, and computer vision models to solve different business problems

- Push the limits of customization in SageMaker using custom container images

- Use AutoML capabilities with SageMaker Autopilot to create high-quality models

- Work with effective data analysis and preparation techniques

- Explore solutions for debugging and managing ML experiments and deployments

- Deal with bias detection and ML explainability requirements using SageMaker Clarify

- Automate intermediate and complex deployments and workflows using a variety of solutions

Amazon SageMaker Best Practices

Sireesha Muppala, Randy DeFauw, Shelbee Eigenbrode

ISBN: 978-1-80107-052-2

- Perform data bias detection with AWS Data Wrangler and SageMaker Clarify
- Speed up data processing with SageMaker Feature Store
- Overcome labeling bias with SageMaker Ground Truth
- Improve training time with the monitoring and profiling capabilities of SageMaker Debugger
- Address the challenge of model deployment automation with CI/CD using the SageMaker model registry
- Explore SageMaker Neo for model optimization
- Implement data and model quality monitoring with Amazon Model Monitor
- Improve training time and reduce costs with SageMaker data and model parallelism

Packt is searching for authors like you

If you're interested in becoming an author for Packt, please visit `authors.packtpub.com` and apply today. We have worked with thousands of developers and tech professionals, just like you, to help them share their insight with the global tech community. You can make a general application, apply for a specific hot topic that we are recruiting an author for, or submit your own idea.

Share Your Thoughts

Now you've finished *Getting Started with Amazon SageMaker Studio*, we'd love to hear your thoughts! Scan the QR code below to go straight to the Amazon review page for this book and share your feedback or leave a review on the site that you purchased it from.

https://packt.link/r/1-801-07015-6

Your review is important to us and the tech community and will help us make sure we're delivering excellent quality content.

Manufactured by Amazon.ca
Bolton, ON